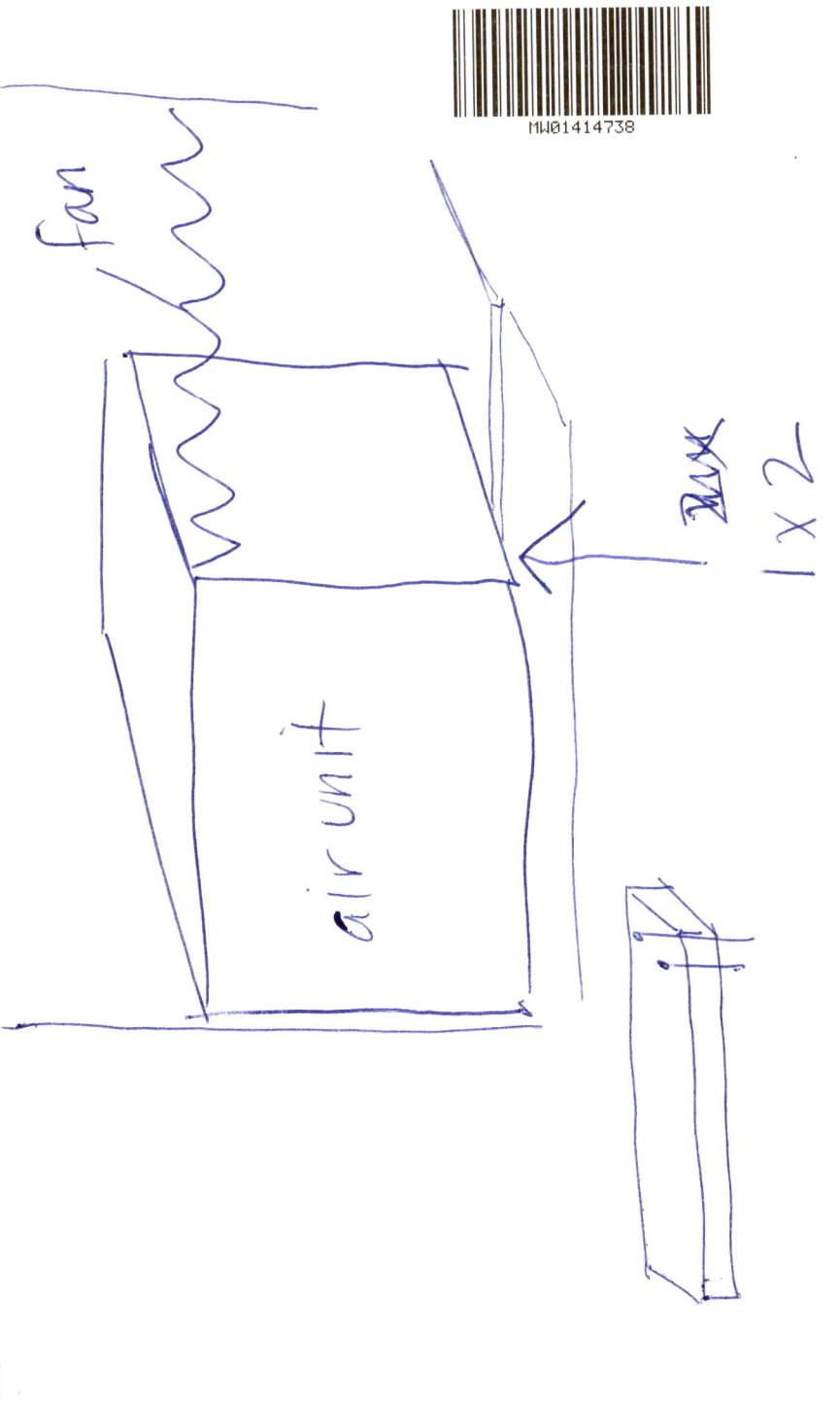

Debbie Trasto — clifine issues
December, husband died.
Call Batina Finley real. agent
↳ together meet

10/31
exchange
I need cash flow

My Life *with* Crazy

Learning to Thrive While Coping with
Mentally Ill Family Members

NAN WALKER

BALBOA.PRESS
A DIVISION OF HAY HOUSE

Copyright © 2020 Nan Walker.

All rights reserved. No part of this book may be used or reproduced by any means, graphic, electronic, or mechanical, including photocopying, recording, taping or by any information storage retrieval system without the written permission of the author except in the case of brief quotations embodied in critical articles and reviews.

Balboa Press books may be ordered through booksellers or by contacting:

Balboa Press
A Division of Hay House
1663 Liberty Drive
Bloomington, IN 47403
www.balboapress.com
844-682-1282

Because of the dynamic nature of the Internet, any web addresses or links contained in this book may have changed since publication and may no longer be valid. The views expressed in this work are solely those of the author and do not necessarily reflect the views of the publisher, and the publisher hereby disclaims any responsibility for them.

The author of this book does not dispense medical advice or prescribe the use of any technique as a form of treatment for physical, emotional, or medical problems without the advice of a physician, either directly or indirectly. The intent of the author is only to offer information of a general nature to help you in your quest for emotional and spiritual well-being. In the event you use any of the information in this book for yourself, which is your constitutional right, the author and the publisher assume no responsibility for your actions.

Any people depicted in stock imagery provided by Getty Images are models, and such images are being used for illustrative purposes only. Certain stock imagery © Getty Images.

Print information available on the last page.

ISBN: 978-1-9822-5850-4 (sc)
ISBN: 978-1-9822-5852-8 (hc)
ISBN: 978-1-9822-5851-1 (e)

Library of Congress Control Number: 2020922253

Balboa Press rev. date: 12/07/2020

Dedicated to all of us who have lost loved ones to mental illness

CONTENTS

Prologue: The Other Side of Mental Illness ix

PART 1: MY FAMILY'S STORIES

Chapter 1   Sam, My Husband 1
Chapter 2   Triage, Otherwise Known as Divorce 29
Chapter 3   Sam's Death 45
Chapter 4   Galen, early signs of trouble 55
Chapter 5   Galen and psychosis 75
Chapter 6   Galen After the Death of Sam 87
Chapter 7   Ella, my daughter 101
Chapter 8   Zach, my younger son 111

PART 2: GUNS, HIPAA, LEGAL ISSUES,
AND BEACONS OF HOPE

Chapter 9   Guns 141
Chapter 10   HIPAA, Your Child, and You 151
Chapter 11   The Legal System and Mental Illness 163
Chapter 12   Beacons of Hope 175

PART 3: OK, LET'S BE PRACTICAL AND
LOOK AT WHERE WE ARE

Chapter 13   Cleaning Up the Mess 187
Chapter 14   How About Cutting Ourselves Some Slack? 197
Chapter 15   Compassion in Compartments 211
Chapter 16   Shame 217
Chapter 17   Acceptance 231
Chapter 18   The Future for Our Loved Ones 241

PART 4: TAKING CARE OF OURSELVES

Chapter 19   Taking Care of Ourselves 251
Chapter 20   Awakening our Intuition Through Art and
              Creativity 287

Epilogue 299
Addenda: Mental Illness Statistics 303

PROLOGUE

The Other Side of Mental Illness

I) Mental illness from up close

Among all the possible miseries human beings can experience, surely being the parent, sibling, or mate of someone with mental illness or an addiction ranks high on the list. Some of us, including me, have had more than one afflicted family member. When mental illness began to appear in my family twenty-five years ago, I was completely ignorant; I had no idea what severe mental illness looked like, let alone what to do about it. I didn't know what I was dealing with or how to go about addressing the complex problems it brought about.

Mental illness in my family has been severe, and it is a horrible, often fatal disease. One must approach mental illness with open eyes and ears and all of the tools and helpers available. It rips families apart, savaging all, the "sane" along with the afflicted. We are victims of a senseless war who find ourselves strewn across a distant, foreign battlefield, and we have no choice but to pick ourselves up and go on with our lives. What we endure and the price we pay is immense, almost beyond description to those who have not experienced it themselves, and PTSD is virtually guaranteed for the whole family. Years later, we are still dealing with and processing all the collateral damage, and it never stops.

I'm going to use the phrase "serious mental illness", or SMI, at times, and mean for that acronym to cover all serious mental illnesses. I do not mean to exclude alcoholism, drug addiction, or any other addictions. They are, in fact, all mental illnesses, according to the National Institute of Mental Health:

"Serious mental illness (SMI) is defined as a mental, behavioral, or emotional disorder resulting in serious functional impairment, which substantially interferes with or limits one or more major life activities. The burden of mental illnesses is particularly concentrated among those who experience disability due to SMI."

The American Psychiatric Association calls addiction a brain disorder. The Diagnostic and Statistical Manual of Mental Disorders, 5th Edition, lists them all, including alcohol use disorder and substance use disorder.

My purpose in writing this book is not to define these terms precisely or place them in the right box, but to outline the experiences of family members who look after the afflicted, and offer some tangible suggestions on improving their lives. I'd like to make it especially clear from the outset that my intention here is not to write a "misery memoir", because nobody needs to hear anybody else complain at length. However, because what we go through is not generally known in the outside world, I hope that by recollecting all that happened in my family I can increase awareness of the difficulties and traumas of those for whom mental illness affects an immediate family member. In truth our experiences are rarely acknowledged openly and out loud by anyone, including ourselves. Though I recognize how difficult it is for most of us to openly express all that has happened within our families, I believe opening a discussion is perhaps in our best interest. In this book I am initiating the vital and difficult conversation about families and mental illness, so that others might understand just how exhausting and vexing our situation really is, and perhaps also comprehend why so few address it openly. I'm not a mental health or medical professional and I am writing about my own personal experiences, from my own point of view. But I can say, after all I have lived through, that when we look after a family member with any form of mental illness, the experience ranges from challenging to unbearable.

Many do not understand that all mental illness, including addiction and alcoholism, is an actual disease, and not some sort of moral failing or demonstration of poor character. It might be tempting to think that we can cure an addiction once the addict stops ingesting alcohol, drugs, or whatever the addictive substance, just like depressed people were once told they should just snap out of it. But let's not fool ourselves, because that's not what happens. Rates of recidivism among people who have stopped using or drinking (including people who have been through rehab) are high, and enormous numbers of them succumb to their illness. Every successful recovering addict, just like anyone else with SMI, needs a lot of ongoing support to successfully manage their disease. But this is possible, and I'll write more about addiction specifically in later chapters.

Coping with serious mental illness in a loved one has a wide spectrum of effects on family members, and they begin so subtly and arrive so silently we barely notice them. We do not remain unaffected, even if our own sanity remains intact, but begin to grow around our loved ones like an old tree might grow around a fence, a sign, or a gravestone. We've all seen such trees, or photos of them, and marveled that they still live and thrive even though they are misshapen, even though they no longer resemble their natural form because circumstances caused them to grow so irregularly. Making room in one's heart and life for other people's madness, in all its forms, causes a wound that constantly reopens, bleeds and closes again while it grows into a thickening scar. Perhaps this extra scarred, bleeding part of us offers our ill family members the room to act out and be safe within it. I don't know, but I do know that eventually you will wake up and realize you are forever changed.

A wide variety of help is available to us, and it almost doesn't need saying that help from therapists, counselors, healers, body workers, and so forth is highly recommended, as much as you can afford or have time for. But none of them, none of your healers or helpers, will understand this wounded place within you as fully as you do. That is what makes this such a lonely experience, even if you are surrounded by caring friends and have capable doctors involved. Few have any comprehension of what you are going through. Experiences you deal with daily are totally outside the frame of reference for almost everyone you know, even kind and generous friends who genuinely want to understand and help. No one can fathom the true extent of the events we experience every day and the pain we endure.

In significant ways our experience is vastly different from those dealing with other types of illness. Often in such cases one's friends and family, neighbors, and even strangers rally around the individual and the family with support, love, and compassion, offering practical help like walking the dog and bringing over casseroles. This is not the case with mental illness, which can cause even close friends to turn their backs, even those we assumed were very good friends. Many of these friends and colleagues are ill at ease with the mentally ill, and their discomfort extends to the ill person's immediate family. Social situations are awkward, and keep us home rather than out in the world, interacting with people who have no idea what to say. Understandably, they don't have a clue about your endless stream of problems, and clearly nothing for them is more of a downer than an awful situation that doesn't seem to have a solution and may end tragically. This is understandable. We get it. But you may find your growing social isolation becomes more and more pronounced, and increasingly difficult to cope with. This is the other side of mental illness, the dark side of the moon experienced by afflicted families.

To compound matters, getting a loved one into treatment is a solitary experience on its own. There is no well beaten trail, making the venture more like cutting a path through a jungle or other impenetrable undergrowth, a path-making that is also ironic because unseen others are forging the same path elsewhere in the same jungle. This book is written in part because we need to work together as we navigate through the underbrush, and investigate novel solutions that challenge current models surrounding patient admissions. And we need to be vocal about our experiences, as maybe then others will notice and hear us. And maybe, just maybe, we will change a few things, address some of the burdensome problems and stilted laws that make our lives so challenging, and improve things for everyone: the afflicted, the family members who care for them, and society at large.

If you are reading this someone in your family likely has some problems. You may have discovered their illness differs from other illnesses that have clearer treatment protocols and diagnoses. With mental illness the first (usually enormous) step is to figure out what your situation actually is, and then what to do about it, including what you will be allowed to do about it legally. The medical and therapeutic people might not agree with one another. Sadly, in fact, medical paradigms as well as legal limits may place enormous roadblocks in your path. It is not hyperbole to state, and I am quoting a mental health professional (a psychiatric nurse who cared for my older son at a mental health facility in Washington State), that the current legal framework regarding mental health treatment "is sicker than the sick people it is supposed to help". That same nurse also said to me that "the laws of Washington State firmly protect your son's right to remain crazy." Sadly, such laws are not unique to the state of Washington.

With every step forward, you will hear conflicting information, even from professionals, but one thing you're going to hear from them all is that it is really tough to compel treatment once your mentally ill loved one turns 18. If you can't persuade your loved one to get treated voluntarily, and if he or she isn't considered an immediate threat to another person or him/herself, you can find yourself in a situation where you won't be able to do a thing but sit and watch a catastrophe unfolding in front of your eyes. It is impossible to imagine anything more dreadful or heartbreaking.

But even if you have persuaded your loved one to see a clinician such as a psychiatrist or other capable professional (a huge assumption after the age of 18), your relative may not consent to receive treatment or take medication, or may not do either with regularity. Because a large number of mentally ill adults have Anosognosia, the inability to understand that they are ill, many often refuse to comply with anything their clinician suggests. I have tremendous admiration for an organization founded by Dr. E. Fuller Torrey called The Treatment Advocacy Center, or TAC. Based in Arlington, VA, they offer excellent information on their website and in their publications. According to their website, (www.treatmentadvocacycenter.org), Anosognosia is defined in this way:

> "Anosognosia, also called 'lack of insight,' is a symptom of severe mental illness experienced by some that impairs a person's ability to understand and perceive his or her illness. It is the single largest reason why people with schizophrenia or bipolar disorder refuse medications or do not seek treatment. Without awareness of the illness, refusing treatment appears rational, no matter how clear the need for treatment might be to others.
>
> Approximately 50% of individuals with schizophrenia and 40% with bipolar disorder have symptoms of anosognosia. Long recognized in stroke, Alzheimer's disease and other neurological conditions, studies of anosognosia in psychiatric disorders is producing a growing body of evidence of anatomical damage in the part of the brain involved with self-reflection. When taking medications, insight improves in some patients."

I believe that existing laws which prevent families from getting treatment for an adult family member with mental illness, however well intended, do not help the patient in any way.

II) Harry, my personal mentor

My personal mentor, in business and life, was a wonderful man named Harry. Born at the turn of the last century, Harry had a rough and tumble beginning in New York City, and did all sorts of brave and improbable things as a young man, such as a wing-walking, which is what it sounds like: standing and doing acrobatics on the wings of barnstorming airplanes in flight. I wish I knew what sorts of planes this involved or which shows they did, but I heard of this only after Harry died, so more information is lost to me.

Harry served in the Roosevelt administration for ten years as an assistant to Harry Hopkins (henceforth referred to as "Hopkins"), and at times with other New Deal luminaries - Frances Perkins, Harold Ickes, and Henry Wallace. Hopkins was one of the principal architects of FDR's New Deal and was the liaison and negotiator between FDR, Winston Churchill, and Joseph Stalin as tensions with the Axis powers intensified. Working with Eleanor Roosevelt, Hopkins organized New Deal programs, convinced that paid work was better for morale than a handout. He supervised the Federal Emergency Relief Administration, FERA, The Civil Works Administration, CWA, and the Works Progress Administration, WPA. In fact, we have many WPA projects still in use today, like LaGuardia and Midway Airports, the Hoover Dam, the Lincoln Tunnel, Camp David, and the Triborough Bridge, amongst others. The WPA also sponsored over 5000 artists per year at its peak, including Mark Rothko, Willem de Kooning, Lee Krasner, and Jackson Pollock, musicians whose ensembles gave over 100,000 performances per week, and more than 1200 theater productions that gave opportunities to many who went on to become famous, including Sidney Lumet, Orson Welles, and John Houseman. Here in New York City, there are still murals and paintings in public buildings that were products of WPA, including those in the Madison Square Post Office and the Bronx Central Post Office.

The goal of these programs was to provide paid employment

to people on relief, and they produced a total of 8.5 million jobs. As one of Roosevelt's most trusted advisors, Hopkins also served as Secretary of Commerce from 1938-1940, and was even asked to live in the White House, which he did, for several years.

My friend Harry was a Project Administrator for the WPA. If only I'd thought to ask him more regarding which Projects he oversaw when he was still alive, or what his specific duties were as an assistant to Mr. Hopkins! He also collaborated with Mrs. Eleanor Roosevelt, creating low cost housing in rural areas. Harry gave me a long article, really a small book (that he typed with two fingers), about his experiences with the New Deal; perhaps one day I'll try to find a way to publish it. It's riveting.

Harry served in the Navy during World War I (lying about his age to get in, because he was too young to serve), and joined the Army for World War II (lying about his age, again, as this time he was too old to serve). He came home from the war with nerve damage in one leg, caused by botulism-contaminated rations, and walked with a cane for the rest of his life. After the war, he ran a successful wound care and surgical supply business.

Often called the "Last New Dealer", he was involved in politics as a Democratic Party activist and fundraiser all his life, most often behind the scenes. Always ahead of his time, he strongly supported women's rights and civil rights long before it was popular to do so. I seem to remember he told me he ran unsuccessfully for a judgeship, but primarily he was a sounding board offering advice to a number of political figures. I'm not the only one who valued his insights and counsel, as phone calls from national political figures often interrupted our conversations, once even from a presidential nominee. I'm not exaggerating when I say he could solve nearly any problem with clear thinking and a fresh approach. He had the sharpest, most creative mind I ever encountered.

As an example, one of my favorite Harry ideas was his proposal for reducing the national debt. He suggested creating a small tax, perhaps a few cents on every single share of stock bought or sold, and using the proceeds for the sole purpose of paying down the debt. He pointed out that people and institutions sufficiently wealthy to trade stocks could afford such a tax, and with the enormous numbers of shares bought and sold daily, a stock tax would eventually begin to shrink our steadily growing national debt.

As Harry had been a friend of my husband Sam's father, I knew him nearly as long as I knew Sam. On our first serious date Sam took me to dinner at Harry and Eileen's house in Riverdale, and I was enchanted with Harry and his delightful wife from the beginning. I dearly loved these two remarkable people, and their influence is etched permanently into my life in many ways. Harry told me he fell in love with Eileen the instant they met, and because he was so smitten, he forgot to ask her where she lived or her full name. He was desperate to find her, so he ran through the streets of New York's fabled Lower East Side shouting her name at the top of his lungs, until someone told Eileen some guy was running around shouting her name! They were married for 62 years, and he passed away less than two years after his wife died.

After my father's death, Harry became a friend and mentor to my mother. She inherited a substantial business, along with overwhelming business issues to go along with it, for which she was not prepared. No one was better equipped to provide friendship and good advice, about business or life, than Harry. In the forthcoming chapters about my husband, who was an accomplished musician, you will read how Harry and Sam formed a Foundation that helped Sam create some very successful new cello concertos, extending and boosting his career. I am extremely grateful we had Harry with us for as long as we did, as he lived well into his 90's. I miss him still, especially hearing his colorful tales about the remarkable people he knew, his stories about Eleanor Roosevelt, Franklin Delano Roosevelt, and the presidential candidate who once interrupted our phone conversation to seek his advice.

Harry's thinking and philosophy continue to influence me, and as I've assembled this book, I've thought about something he said to me long ago:

> "There is nothing that can happen to you in business or in life that is so terrible you can't create some advantage out of it, or some immense good can't come from it."

Harry was right. He always was. We can find some advantage to what we have collectively experienced and create some good from it, too.

III) They say writing is therapy, so I wrote a whole book.

I've never written a book before, and have had some substantial doubts as to the overall wisdom of the idea, so why am I doing this? My answer is very simple. First, for my own healing, I have wanted to catalogue all that my family went through over the past twenty-five years. For much of that time I existed in survival mode, and I wanted to look at and become more fully aware of all that happened to me, and to my family. And second, I thought it might be useful for my children at some point in their lives. Third, I have hoped to initiate conversation about all the issues involved when a family member is mentally ill.

Also, I needed a book like this at many points in my life, a book addressing specific concerns in practical ways, which, if such a book existed, I was unable to find. Most of all, I needed to have a book that helped me understand that our family's experience wasn't unique: because sadly, it is not. As I'm not the only one who has needed this book or looked for a book like this, it is my heartfelt desire to share my story, as well as give others vital, practical information and the comfort of knowing you are not alone.

We might also, through this miserable journey we collectively experience, realize a profound, priceless gift that few will ever know: for we will come to a deeper understanding of ourselves, and an understanding of what it really means to be human, to be a parent, to be a spouse. If you are in our "club", don't lose heart, because you might come to the place one day where you feel blessed to have had this experience. We can learn a lot even from our most devastating experiences. And we might be able to do some good, too.

Think about how an organization like Mothers Against Drunk Drivers, MADD, came about, or others like PADD, People Against Distracted Driving, RAPP, Relatives Against Purdue Pharma, and FADD, Fathers Against Distracted Driving. Grief stricken parents had simply had enough, and determined to do something concrete about a terrible situation. Why don't we, the parents, siblings and spouses of the mentally ill, do the same? If enough of us demand some changes, maybe some things actually could change. If we work together, we just might be able to set some goals and accomplish them. After all, there are an awful lot of us.

Specifically, we could work to change certain laws that absolutely need revision. We alluded to one of them earlier: in most states, once someone reaches 18, it is very difficult, maybe even impossible, to compel that individual into treatment, or to do anything else necessitated by their condition. Due to their Anosognosia, many adults with SMI don't even understand they are sick which means they are not compliant patients. No one, and certainly not me, will argue with the concept of preserving civil liberties, but in an attempt to preserve these liberties for everyone, we've unwittingly created a situation that guarantees the civil liberties of the mentally ill include the "right to remain crazy".

The legal situation regarding treatment for serious mental illness is a morass of confusion at best, as laws vary from state to state and there are no clear guidelines for sorting through them. I do not have qualifications to explain the legal maze, or even to create a reasonable survey of the contents of mental health laws. This book has been written only to reflect on my personal experiences with SMI in my family and record how the mental health laws that currently exist have affected the members of my family. For accurate information regarding each state's laws, I would recommend consulting the Treatment Advocacy Center website (www.treatmentadvocacycenter.org), where a summary is easily found.

I can say from my experience that options for compelling treatment are difficult to come by and extremely confusing, especially because treatment can describe events that occur in a hospital setting or in a non-hospital setting, like rehab. For example, here in the prologue I discuss how tough it is to get an adult into psychiatric treatment, and in following chapters I elaborate on my experiences with hospitalizations of my oldest son, both in New York and in other states. One of his doctors at a hospital here in New York gave me a lengthy explanation of the conditions under which a New York hospital can go to court and petition for a longer stay for a psychiatric patient. In my son's case, hospitals were successful on two occasions. The doctor also said that when a state's laws are written or interpreted more liberally, as they often are on the West Coast, courts might not grant longer stays easily, believing that compelling someone who is ill to remain in the hospital against their wishes is a violation of his/her civil liberties. In this doctor's opinion, this is one of the causes of the current homeless crisis in cities such as Los Angeles, San Francisco, and Seattle, as so many people who need psychiatric treatment desperately are unable to function on their own and are living on the streets, some of them dangerously ill.

This is an excruciatingly difficult situation for families who have nowhere to turn and have no idea what to do next. But the confusion and apparent contradiction between different psych wards, different hospitals, different laws and different states is precisely the issue I wish to shine a light on.

As an aside, the story of how we got to this confusing place is not the purpose of my book, but it is without a doubt a horrifying tale. President Kennedy began a program to close the nation's mental hospitals, an initiative that began the process of taking us to where we are today. Some of our most desperate current problems, such as the nationwide shortage of mental health hospital beds, are the regrettable legacies of these failed policies from long ago. I am not saying that we should have nostalgia for the way things were then, as that situation had its own horrors. However, from where we stand today, we should be capable of finding a path to a better future for mentally ill people and their families. I will address some ideas about what might be done in this book.

I believe there is an effective way to begin to institute such changes, and that is to open up about our experiences, and to do so often and unashamedly. Only then will we discover how common all forms of mental illness really are and how connected we are to other families facing the same problems. When I speak with people about my family's journey, I regularly encounter those with a similar story or who have a close relative or friend trudging along our common path. We will make improvements only when we keep the topic of mental illness out in public where it is visible to everyone, and where we can use our intelligence and good will to find ways to work together creating better treatments and laws.

We also have to take care of ourselves, and I have some thoughts about that. All my life, in addition to my dedication to the piano and effective piano teaching and my love of "art play" inherited from my mother, I have studied Feldenkrais, Qigong, meditation, and breath work, and have given classes and worked privately with clients. My own study of these practices during the entire time I've dealt with SMI in my family has given me much strength and has been the main reason, apart from my inborn good nature and optimism, that I have come through everything as well as I have.

It is my hope that I can share what I learned in the last twenty-five years to help others survive, and perhaps thrive, during this grueling journey. To that end, in addition to the chapters at the conclusion of this book, I am creating a website that will have additional resources, to which I will add new materials regularly. I am excited to share all I know and look forward to getting some feedback about how others are doing.

When I first began writing, I tried to record all personal and family events in chronological order. I found this next to impossible, as it became very confusing to follow all the threads of the individual stories. I felt that if it was confusing to write this way, reading it would be worse, so I have chosen to speak about one member of the family at a time. Our stories all overlap, obviously, but I think this is easier to follow. I also recognize that because of the overlapping narratives, I have occasionally repeated aspects of certain events, as they did affect each individual in different ways. In the interests of privacy, I have given my entire family pen names, including myself. Quite simply, I feel all my children ought to have a choice about how much they wish to publicly reveal about their family's history and their personal stories. I am also using pen names for others in this book, including some for whom I have used only first names.

The purpose of telling my story is to share my own journey through this awful mess, a journey that isn't over yet, and may never be over. Sharing our stories is probably the most productive means to increase awareness of what families go through in these challenging circumstances, by making our experiences more familiar to the world at large.

However, I am aware that when I talk about sharing our stories or say that speaking out about mental illness is important, my thoughts about this need clarification. While I may be personally willing to be open and vocal about my problems dealing with mental illness in my family, I am well aware that this is a formidable and frightening step for most of us. I do not expect anyone to open up as fully as I've attempted to do in this book unless you decide you want to. Not only is it scary and intimidating to let others into our worlds of sorrow and pain, there is another problem we'll come across. When we are really open, there's also the possibility of being hurtfully criticized when others, so blessedly removed from our suffering and with nothing remotely as dramatic happening in their lives, comment freely on what mighta, oughta, shoulda been done by us that "would have really helped". As I've spoken with people about how to get this book published, I have been surprised that more families than you might imagine had some mental illness problem that was swept under the rug. Speaking out flies in the face of all we have all learned about saving face, not sharing our problems, pretending our families are fine, feeling ashamed of our situation, and so forth. So please do not feel I am insisting you join me in speaking out. I am happy to do all the speaking out for anyone who isn't comfortable with doing this personally.

And there's another issue, too. Especially when we wish to change something, (and can anyone think of a more daunting or creative challenge than confronting and hoping to change the myriad problems with mental health care in this country?), many people, ignorant or otherwise, will disagree, strongly and belligerently about what we are doing. People will criticize us. They will come down on us hard. It has happened to me repeatedly. Perhaps along the way I will find a few brave souls to join me, but if you aren't up to it, don't let that be a cause of beating yourself up. Anytime anyone ventures into forbidden territory there are wild Furies all around eager to shout us down. Your own life may be so complex and so hard with all you are going through that you simply can't bear to be criticized for anything. That's OK. Don't give yourself a hard time about this. (Or anything else!) My purpose here is not to make others miserable.

Also, before I start, I'd also like to say a few words about my choice of the word "crazy" in the title of the book. I've gotten a fair amount of flak for that and recognize it may not be the most politically correct way of speaking of mental illness or describing my life. But after much reflection, I've decided to keep it. None of us are trying to be hurtful when we casually say something is "crazy" in our daily lives, and most of us use the word rather frequently, even daily. After all, in the world we live in today a great many things are truly quite crazy, objectively speaking. We don't have to look very far to find examples. Please know I mean no insult to anyone, but I just couldn't think of a more apt word with which to describe twenty-five years of my life. Perhaps when you've read the book you'll see my point.

PART ONE

My Family's Stories

CHAPTER 1

Sam, My Husband

Part 1 My life with Sam

They say to begin at the beginning. But where is the beginning? The tale is so vast and complicated that I hardly know where to start. Perhaps it is simplest to begin when we first met.

He bowled me over. Literally. I met Sam when he ran around a corner at the Juilliard School of Music and plowed right into me. I had an armful of music and books and it all went flying. I went flying too. He graciously apologized and picked me and my books up off the floor, and then scurried on his way, ever and always on the run. A few days later I was seated at a school concert with a friend of his and he came over and asked for a proper introduction.

His quickness and agility were legendary, whether playing the cello, or tennis, or just moving around. He earned nicknames like "ants" because he couldn't stop squirming, and when I had to meet him somewhere in NYC, I could always see him coming when he was many blocks away. It was a cinch. Even if I couldn't see the features on his face, I'd just look for the tall person who was walking the fastest and that person would always turn out to be Sam. I didn't see this as manic or a harbinger of bipolar illness, although who knows if it maybe was.

A few days after our formal introduction we were both walking home after our classes and ran into each other. Looking back, it would seem that nothing about the two of us would ever be anything less than dramatic, and this evening certainly got us off in that direction. In retrospect, our first evening together seemed to set the tone for the events to follow in the rest of our lives together.

As we walked from the old Juilliard building near Columbia University (this was just before it moved to Lincoln Center) to our apartments on the West Side, the whole city seemed tense and about to explode. Somehow, along the way, we heard that Martin Luther King had just been shot. The atmosphere around us, the "vibe" if you will, was like nothing I had ever experienced. We walked fast, as we were uneasy, even frightened. This part of town had a few more problems back then. In that pre-cell phone era, we had no clue about the details of what was going on other than our sense of an immense dark cloud descending upon us, and something powerful playing out.

His apartment was closer to school than mine, in a building on West End Avenue that many students and musicians shared. Sam invited me for dinner, and I accepted, not only because I was eager to get off the streets. He cooked an excellent dinner – meatloaf from the recipe on the Quaker Oats box, baked potatoes served with sour cream, steamed green beans (perfectly cooked), and a fine salad made with a dressing he did himself, plus ice cream for dessert. I was impressed. He'd already figured out one of the sexiest things a guy can do for a girl is cook some delicious food for her.

Even though his apartment was in the back of the building, we continued to hear a lot of noise from the street, and it intensified. We heard angry shouting, glass breaking, and then we even got a whiff of something burning. This was pretty unusual, and increasingly frightening, so we turned on the radio to find out what was going on and learned the city was in a state of near riot. The old Juilliard building and the Upper West Side are close neighbors of Harlem, and the rioting spilled out in our direction that night. Angry mobs were setting fires to cars and breaking glass windows and looting stores, and we heard and smelled it. I was far too scared to venture out into the riot to go home, and so the story of Sam and Nan began that night. It's crazy, but I have often thought that everything we would go through during the many years of our relationship was rooted, at least in metaphor, in the events of that night.

Soon after, within months, Sam was living in LA and studying with the great cellist Gregor Piatigorsky in a special program initiated by the Los Angeles Music Center. The teachers included Piatigorsky and Jascha Heifetz, and there were only a handful of exceptionally gifted students, all on full scholarship. When the program ended (with some sort of scandal about funding as I recall), Sam wanted to continue his work with Piatigorsky, so he moved to San Francisco and started teaching at UC Berkeley and the San Francisco Conservatory, flying back and forth to LA for lessons. As I was still at Juilliard, we began a long-distance relationship; eventually, he moved back to NY, and a few years later we married.

Sam and I began our life together as a young couple deeply in love, full of laughter, and enjoying each other and our life together immensely. His mother commented once while we were visiting her that we'd kept her up late into the night because we were laughing so long and hard she couldn't sleep. She asked me what on earth was so funny that we could laugh for so long. Sam had a devilish sense of humor and when we got going, we found the ironies of life appearing all around us irresistibly funny. His sense of humor was so resounding, in fact, that he could even instinctively create zingy puns in languages he barely knew.

Once back in NY, Sam accepted a position at Mannes College of Music, now called Mannes The New School for Music, where he remained on faculty for 38 years. He also taught at Harvard as a guest lecturer, at The New England Conservatory, and at Rutgers University; he remained at each institution for a few years, flying up to Boston one day a week to teach. He was a wonderful teacher, earning the New School's Outstanding University Teacher Award in 1997. He also continued to play concerts with major orchestras (too many to list here without sounding like a publicity brochure but including the Los Angeles Philharmonic, the New York Philharmonic, St. Louis Symphony, National Symphony, Memphis Philharmonic, and many more), and give recitals in universities and concert series around the country (including the Metropolitan Museum of Art,

Carnegie Hall, the Phillips Collection, the Corcoran Gallery, Johns Hopkins University, the University of Chicago, and lots of others).

Like many free-lance musicians, we had some unusual jobs. One of our jobs involved giving concerts for children all over Los Angeles, through a special program sponsored by the LA Music Center. We played literally hundreds of them. We would travel to LA for two or three weeks at time and play as many as a dozen small concerts a day in various schools. Sam discovered he had a knack for this, and the concerts were always an adventure. It makes me sad to consider that only one of our three children ever experienced one of his kiddie concerts in a school setting, as having that experience has given our daughter a unique appreciation of her father's offbeat and extraordinary skills.

Sam had perfected the execution of all sorts of animal sounds on the cello, some created almost invisibly, which utterly intrigued small kids. Sprinkled through the little concert came a parade of creatures, among them crickets, flies, mosquitos, cows, birds, and sheep. The grand finale was always…eating the cello! No, he didn't actually eat his cello, but he'd learned to make a fingernails-on-the-black-board, seriously-disturbing, wood-crunching sound with his bow on the side of the cello. And so as he made gnawing movements with his lips, jaw, and mouth over the pegs or the scroll or the sides of the cello, to the small students it certainly seemed that he was, in fact, eating his cello!

Around the time we married, we spent five summers at the Marlboro Music Festival, where Sam, as he put it, "played" rent on the use of the Strad cello that Marlboro had loaned to him. During the first summer there, we were given a lovely cabin in the woods and I anticipated a relaxing summer. Far from it, as I quickly discovered, not for that summer or the four that followed. Though there were marvelous things about that Festival, including the high artistic level of all participants, and incredible performances, it was always an intense experience. Young players made music side by side with older seasoned ones, and though publicity materials referred to "a society of equals", Sam used to quip that some were more equal than others. For the public concerts, participants learned of their next musical assignments only a week before the concert performances, leaving little time to prepare, and the pressure on everyone was nerve wracking.

Everyone felt they had to step up to the challenge and that sometimes meant being heroic. I remember one fellow who got a bow poked in his eye just before walking out on stage. He was in great pain, but soldiered on, with tears streaming down his face, heading to the ER only after the lengthy performance finished. I honestly don't know how he did it. And Sam himself played a concert only a few hours after learning his beloved teacher Piatigorsky had died. At the other extreme, practical jokes and napkin throwing rose to high art at meal times, perhaps as ways for the musicians to let off steam. Even the greatest musicians in the Festival, including Serkin himself, delighted in balling up their paper napkins and throwing them at people. It could be quite disconcerting to try to eat lunch with napkin balls, often wet, landing in your food, your drink, or your hair.

Sam also participated in their winter tours during each season he spent at the Festival, and the ensemble from one of these tours was invited to play at the Inaugural Reception for Jimmy Carter at the White House. I was thrilled that I might get to attend such an historic event, but none of the spouses were able to get security clearances in time, so I had to hear about it from Sam. Sam even spent a few minutes speaking with President Carter and was very impressed with his warmth and humanity. After five years, Marlboro decided to sell the Strad cello bequeathed to them, adding millions of dollars to the Festival's endowment, a decision Sam understood. He went back to playing his own cello and we moved on to other summer festivals for several years, though none were as intense, or memorable, as Marlboro.

During the academic year, there was lots of teaching; while teaching was an important part of Sam's life, developing his life as a concert performer was his passion. Any musician who wants to play concerts has to spend considerable time networking, going to other people's concerts, phoning and meeting presenters, and so forth. And in those days, before email blasts, this also meant doing large mailings of promotional materials to thousands of orchestras and concert series presenters around the country. (Email blasts are a big improvement over the old system.) Sam also spent many hours attending concerts each week, or sometimes rehearsals for concerts, as it was easier to find a way to speak with people after a rehearsal.

Sometimes we'd entertain in our home, have our friends over for dinner, or have chamber music evenings (always with all the neighbors invited, so they wouldn't object to the music). And in those days, informal spontaneous evenings with friends seemed to mandate getting Chinese food from various neighborhood restaurants, which became almost a ritual. I hate to think of how many plates of cold noodles with sesame sauce we all ate.

Years went by during which we were thoroughly enjoying our lives together, and had full schedules playing concerts, teaching, and spending many happy hours with colleagues and friends. For me personally, being Sam's wife was a blast, an absolute joy and delight, and the way things always went with our lives, anything but boring. He said to me once he couldn't believe how lucky he was to have married a woman who always woke up with a smile on her face. That might have been my innate good nature peeking out, but our life together was also just that good back then.

Often, I have wondered why I didn't see what was coming, but in truth, aside from a hypersensitive artistic temperament, which seemed par for the course for such a brilliant musician, there wasn't much for me to observe at this time. Perhaps if I could go back, after all I've been through, I'd see much more, but at the time, I was totally blind.

Later than most people become parents we had three amazing children, all of them a great joy to us. Shortly before they began to arrive, we had purchased a wonderful weekend home out of the city, with a swimming lake at the bottom of our hill and skiing nearby, and all of us relished our time there.

The weeks of our lives spent in the country, both summer and winter, provided the most enjoyable and peaceful times our family ever experienced together, before Sam's illness showed up. When the kids were small, we spent most weekends and summers in the country, where we could set the kids free and they could roam all over the side of our hill without coming to harm or getting lost. The black bears would run away if you made noise, and we seemed to be at the wrong altitude for the region's poisonous snakes, (a little too low for timber rattlers and a little too high for copperheads), a true blessing given how many snakes our oldest son caught. I used to joke that the only danger for the children were the endless poison ivy rashes they got roaming through the woods.

Sam really enjoyed frolicking in the woods with the kids, chasing snakes, frogs, and especially salamanders. It was not uncommon for Sam and the kids to come home covered in so much mud and forest debris that I wouldn't even let them in the house until they rinsed off with the hose outside. One memorable evening we chased an immature Barred Owl through the woods all night. We were completely intrigued by what sort of creature would make such a weird sound, and we chased the owl for hours until we saw what it was. Afterwards, we researched what sort of bird house a Barred Owl would need, which turned out to be a very big one, and we put one up near our house, facing the direction the experts recommended. The owls never found it, or at least they never moved in, but squirrels have occupied it for years.

Unfortunately, there was a danger in the woods I never saw, as the threat of Lyme disease never crossed my mind.

After reading my tale so far, one may intuit that Sam's story does not end happily, and that Sam's long, drawn-out suffering began just a few years after we had our kids. I also think it is important to remember that our first child, Galen, was conceived in the middle of a critically-acclaimed solo engagement with the

New York Philharmonic. No question about it, Sam, at this point in his life was truly at the top of his game. How could I (or anyone else) have realized, at this moment of immense accomplishment and professional success, that these concerts with the NY Phil represented the apex, seen through the lens of many years, of Sam's professional career and capabilities?

About five years after we bought the country house, Sam began showing symptoms of mental illness. The symptoms first began to appear a couple of years after he and Galen, our oldest, started spending lots of time in the woods together. When Sam first became bipolar and began to suffer serious depression, all the psychiatrists we saw were stumped, and they all said that it was highly unusual for someone in his early 40's to develop such a serious mental illness (most such illnesses first appear, full-blown, 20 years earlier.) During my own struggles with Lyme disease, I had discussions with some of my doctors who explained that there is a possible Lyme/mental illness connection. In retrospect, it makes you wonder. About Sam, and Galen.

Sam had begun to complain of a sore knee, which again, in retrospect, is a possible red flag for Lyme. He had all kinds of knee treatments, shots, physical therapy, and eventually knee surgery. I am not sure, or maybe I've forgotten, why the doctors decided on surgery, but they told Sam they were surprised that they found nothing specific during the procedure. He also had other strange symptoms, like unusual rashes, sweats, and unexplained fevers. From the time his first symptoms began to appear through the balance of his life, when people asked him what was wrong with him, he always said there was something physically wrong with him that the blankety-blank doctors were too blankety-blank stupid to figure out. I am ashamed to admit I never believed him either and I always just rolled my eyes when he started in on this. Now, I am convinced he was absolutely right. It pays to listen to what sick people tell you.

Many physicians have seen patients whose primary symptom for Lyme is severe psychiatric illness. One of my own doctors told me about Dr. Brian Fallon at the Lyme and Tick-Borne Diseases Research Center at Columbia University Medical Center, where they are exploring the mental illness/Lyme connection as well as many aspects of Lyme disease.

When I had Lyme, one of my own physicians shared with me the case history of one of his patients, a young man about to be sent to a mental institution whose psychological issues resolved 100% with aggressive treatment for Lyme. Of course, I can't prove Sam had Lyme, now that he is gone, but the possibility exists. I also think this is possibly, in part, what ails my oldest son. Is it feasible that both of them were genetically susceptible to Lyme's psychological affects? Could be. Is it possible they both were mentally ill and they also had Lyme? Of course. It is quite possible they might have had mental illness anyway, and Lyme simply intensified problems that were already brewing. From personal experience I can say that Lyme hits you where you are weakest, wherever that might be. It's a wretched ailment. Anybody affected by serious mental illness should be checked for Lyme. The disease is at epidemic levels. The tests are dismayingly inadequate, unreliable, and often inconclusive, so stick with it and don't give up.

When Sam started to get ill, we began to search for medical help. I could write about the various mental health professionals that he saw, the medications he tried, and the alternative treatments like vitamins and breath work that his excellent team of doctors suggested and I could take up many pages doing so. But since Sam wasn't consistent with treatment, and as a result none of it had a chance to work, it would seem rather pointless. I do feel I should mention he had some superb doctors over the years and Sam's lack of compliance wasn't something they could control. Still, his unsuccessful treatments are not the subject of this book, and I have no desire to hash it all out again. And I also wouldn't want to discourage anyone reading this book from trying the medications and therapies Sam tried, just because they didn't work for him, mostly because he really didn't use them with consistency.

Part 2, Sam the cellist

Sam the cellist – wow! – he was a wonder, a marvel almost beyond description, technically and musically stunning, in touch perfectly with the finest musical instincts any human being could possibly possess, someone with unimaginable mastery. Sam's wonderful childhood teacher Margaret said he was one in a million, and he surely possessed incredible talent from a very early age. At the cello, Sam was completely in tune with all parts of himself. His body intuitively mastered the subtle movements needed to play as magnificently as he did, his mind had the agility to pick up details of composition and harmony that never occurred to the rest of us, and with his heart and feelings he was able to express a full range of the most delicate emotional subtleties. Did anyone ever hear music more accurately, pick up on its finer nuances more clearly, feel it more deeply, or express it with more of his heart and with more of himself?

He never forgot a piece of music, a gift many musicians would die for. He could remember and play anything he'd ever played, perfectly, at any time, without practice. Once, a conductor for whom Sam was auditioning asked him if he'd ever played his grandfather's cello concerto. Sam said he loved the piece and launched into a passionate performance on the spot, playing confidently and perfectly, though he hadn't touched the piece in at least a dozen years. How many of us can do that?

He could learn music faster and with less effort than anyone I ever knew. We gave our first concert together when we were both students at the Aspen Music School and Festival. I'd been invited to give a recital in a city nearby and asked Sam if he'd like to split the concert with me. Each of us would play a solo piece, and then each of us would learn a piece the other already knew. I had just played the Kodaly Cello and Piano Sonata with another cellist at the Festival so Sam agreed to learn that.

Rehearsing in the hall a couple of hours before the concert, Sam still did not know the piece. Not at all, and I mean that quite seriously. It was as though he was sight-reading it badly. At the time I was really upset, in fact absolutely ticked off, though I later learned not to be upset at anything Sam did in rehearsal, because in performance he'd always come through magnificently. But I wasn't aware of this yet. In the concert, when we began the Kodaly, I was stunned. Can you imagine my shock and surprise when it quickly became obvious Sam had not only somehow managed to learn his part in a couple of hours, without spending any time looking at the music or practicing it, he'd also somehow managed to memorize it? And he played wonderfully! Anyone who heard that concert would have thought he'd known this piece of music all his life. Who would have believed he didn't know it at all, only a few hours earlier?

In keeping with our pattern of aligning our personal lives with significant historical events, a couple of weeks later we gave another recital in a college not far from Aspen. It turned out the concert was on the day Apollo 11 first landed on the moon, so everyone wanted to watch the moon landing on TV. We wanted to do that too, but dutifully trudged off to play the concert. Sam wondered if anybody would attend, and a few people actually did. As he said later, at least we were outnumbered. I remember scrambling around after the concert to find a restaurant that had TVs on, so we could watch some of the event while we grabbed some dinner before driving back to Aspen.

Folks always said that I was so lucky being married to my chamber music partner, because we had so much opportunity to practice. Hah! Opportunity, yes, but Sam didn't need much practice, so rarely wanted to actually work on anything. Somehow, he would absorb music in the air, by osmosis, maybe, which made life tough on those of us without this knack. I learned that there was only one way I could cope - I needed to know my part so thoroughly that I could wing it no matter what the heck he threw at me, and he really did like to try crazy new things in concerts, like bizarre tempi or fingering or bowings.

In music, Sam was the perfect Zen master of effortlessly staying in the moment. Looking back over the years, the most dramatic example of this I could think of took place several years after we were married when the Juilliard Orchestra chose him as their soloist on their first international tour in South America. In Brasilia, Brazil they were playing in an unusually large concert hall, seating thousands. Just as Sam was about to begin his cadenza, all power failed in the city and the huge hall was plunged into darkness. Sam kept playing, starting his cadenza in total blackness. As the cadenza neared the end, he knew that if he stopped playing people could panic, and in such a large space, audience members might get hurt trying to leave. So very artfully he began a Bach suite, one chosen to segue harmonically from the cadenza. After a very long time, with Sam playing the whole time in darkness, the lights came back on. Even then, Sam kept on playing and gracefully transitioned back into the end of the cadenza and the rest of the concerto, which they finished. This created an absolute sensation and earned him a spot on the cover of a major South American magazine.

He had another unusual experience one afternoon playing two concerti with the New Jersey Philharmonic. He always asked to play two concerti when hired for a concerto, by the way. Most of us are happy just playing one. The first concerto required a smaller orchestra and it was played uneventfully, but the second required more wind players. The extra players had become stuck in a terrible traffic jam coming out of NY and had not shown up by the time the second concerto was to start. They had an intermission while waiting, and it went on far longer than usual. As the concert was on Super Bowl Sunday most people were anxious to get home to see the game and the audience was starting to get restless and resentful. Finally, Sam volunteered to walk out on the stage and start playing, which he proceeded to do, playing Bach and some unaccompanied modern music. And with his ever-ready sense of humor, he turned this into a comedy act, looking offstage here and there obviously enquiring about whether the players had arrived yet, shaking his head sadly or shrugging his shoulders to great effect. The audience was enthralled and it was almost a disappointment when the missing players arrived and they could finally get on with completing the concert.

I had all sorts of wild experiences myself, just because I was married to Sam. Traveling with the Stradivarius cello, on loan from the Marlboro Music Festival, was a hoot and there were always tales to tell about it. It was like lugging around the Mona Lisa. As you might imagine, that wasn't always fun, and I was glad when they decided to sell it and he had to give it back. It was a scary responsibility as the crazy thing was worth many millions of dollars, and due to insurance constraints, it could never be out of our sight or out of our immediate possession.

Think about what that meant in our lives, practically. If we were on tour and wanted to have a meal in a restaurant, we had to drag the cello in with us. More than once a receptionist would bark at us: "You can't bring that thing in here!", to which Sam would inevitably reply, very calmly: "Madame, this 'thing' is worth more than your entire restaurant and the people that loaned it to me insist it goes everywhere with me." The biggest problem with cellos is that they don't bend, or fold, and aren't soft, so they make miserable travel companions. You can't really lean against them and their awkward shape limits where you can put them in a car or train. They don't fit very well in the seats of a movie theater, or even in the back seats of many cars. I often sat in back and the cello sat in the front passenger seat, often head down, because that was the way it fit better.

We always had to purchase a seat, at a half price child's rate, on a plane for the cello. It was not allowed in baggage. Whatever any seat holder was entitled to, Sam insisted the cello get or receive – its own frequent flyer account, meals, drinks, peanuts, whatever – and he always did it with humor. Then he would eat the food provided for the cello all by himself, plus his own. As tall and skinny as he was, he was always a bottomless pit when it came to food. In fact, for years I joked that his ability to eat and eat and eat and never gain an ounce was grounds for divorce. Years ago, when we still had paper tickets, if a flight wasn't too crowded, the stewardesses sometimes gave us back the ticket for the cello, for a refund. Once, coming back from playing a concert in Honolulu on a red eye to Seattle, the exhausted stewardess got so confused that we realized later she'd given us back all our tickets, not just the one for the cello.

By the way, if we want to consider what sort of human being Sam was before he got sick, consider that when Marlboro had been bequeathed this Strad cello and wanted to find a cellist to play it, Rudolf Serkin called Gregor Piatigorsky for a recommendation, and Piatigorsky told Serkin the only cellist he'd personally trust with such a cello was Sam, due to his integrity as a human being and the meticulous care he took of his own cello. I find it comforting to have such sweet memories of the person Sam once was, when I contemplate and deal with the realities of what happened later.

I remember so many interesting and amazing people who came through our lives. In Aspen one summer long ago, the great sitar player Ravi Shankar had been given a plate of Indian food lovingly prepared by the wife of Sam's Juilliard teacher. (She was a marvelous cook and created many delicious and memorable meals for after concert gatherings.) Ravi asked if she might have a bit more cayenne pepper in the kitchen and she reappeared with a large bottle. Ravi then dumped the entire bottle on his food, mixed it in, tasted it, and pronounced it perfect. Where would I ever have seen something like that, unless I were sitting next to Sam?

One night after a summer concert at the Mann Center in Philadelphia, at Mr. Mann's penthouse apartment in the center of the city, Leonard Bernstein was at the piano playing jazz. He and Sam had become good friends when Sam had played quite a few well-received performances of his Three Meditations from Mass, which are three short pieces for cello and orchestra, similar to a cello concerto. Lennie started making bad puns and Sam matched him pun for pun. The puns got worse and worse, and soon the dueling puns with Leonard Bernstein had everyone within earshot howling with laughter.

And speaking of Lennie, we were all invited to dinner one night by a dear mutual friend. Our friend, God rest her, was truly the worst cook in the world, and she knew it and wouldn't be insulted to hear me say it, but wanted to try to give a dinner party anyway. Before long, true to form, she'd set the dinner on fire, which she couldn't put out immediately. In fact, not at all. So the kitchen began smoldering and the place filled with smoke. So, of course, a neighbor called the fire department, and when the firemen arrived the chief turned out to be a positively HUGE Bernstein fan who kept shouting over and over, in pure joy, "I can't believe I just got to save Leonard Bernstein!" Of course, we were never in any danger, only the roast or whatever she was cooking. The fireman kept telling Lennie about his Beethoven Symphony TV specials and how much he enjoyed them. Somehow, he left out praising the 7th Beethoven Symphony. After the firemen left, Lennie said "So what was wrong with the 7th? He didn't say he liked that one."

When one works in the classical music business as a musician, one is always dealing with or working around the wide differences in wealth and income that exist between the concert donors, patrons and sponsors, and the musicians themselves. It's a very odd juxtaposition to manage, as one has to comport oneself in such a fashion that the concert supporters, who are the backbone of our industry financially, feel comfortable with us. As the classical music concert business wouldn't exist without them, we were always tremendously grateful for their generous support, and their friendship.

Sometimes, though, if we succeeded well enough, wealthy people might even forget that we weren't in their financial circle, or might assume that any person as gifted as Sam would earn more money than he did. The whole situation could feel just bizarre. The level of material success Sam achieved, measured by how much money he earned, wasn't commensurate with his enormous gifts. I believe this created some deep shame and embarrassment for him, which, in my opinion, contributed heavily to his inability to survive his incipient decline.

Shame is a huge, profoundly important topic for everyone, because our society is riddled with it, but it is especially important for those of us dealing with the mentally ill. One reason we are all in the pickle we are in is because there is so much shame and embarrassment about mental illness and as a result, about what's going on in our lives. There is a chapter devoted to this topic later in this book.

We live in a society that frequently uses money as the yardstick to measure the worth of things or human beings. This is awful, yet nonetheless true. Sam and I weren't starving for sure. Both of us worked, we enjoyed our lives, and we had all we truly needed materially. But again, in our field, surrounded by extremely wealthy donors, or colleagues more financially successful than we were, economic differences did not just magically disappear. Always the proverbial elephant in the room, such profound differences can bring down anyone's sense of self-worth. Nobody ever speaks of this, by the way, which is one reason I want to write about it and bring it out in the open.

Often, young musicians would seek Sam out, wanting to discuss their futures with him. Sometimes they'd ask Sam if they should tackle a professional concert career or do something else. Sam always said that if they had to ask, they'd better do something else. He said that the only people who can survive the hurts and disappointments, and lack of financial reward, that might come from a life in the arts are people who are all-in, and willing to pay any price, just for the privilege of spending a lifetime playing the greatest music ever written. Sometimes he'd ask these young people how they thought they might feel, years later, when their friends are financially successful, with thriving businesses and fine homes, and they are still trying to figure out how to pay the rent on an apartment?

One of Sam's friends, an excellent conductor with whom Sam had worked many times, married into great wealth. The bride's sister threw a lovely gathering for them at her beautiful 5th Avenue apartment, which occupied a full floor and had a view of Central

Park. The musician friends of the groom gathered around a couple of sofas, and, as always, were discussing their latest concerts and gigs and comparing notes about where well-paying jobs were to be found. The bride herself, who was a genuinely lovely person, sat down amongst us, listened to our chatter for a few minutes, and then blithely said "earning money isn't difficult, but what's really hard is figuring out how to give it away to good causes." We just stared at her, comprehending in one peculiar moment the vast differences in our lives. Sam talked about this comment for days, ruminating over it again and again, increasingly incredulous that she could be so unaware, in spite of being such a sweet person, and in spite of her new marriage to a musician.

For me, being around wealthy donors had another challenging aspect - acquiring acceptably nice, but affordable, clothing to wear to events, especially for concerts. Our closet was very bizarre, in fact, you could have called the closet itself bipolar. We wore the usual jeans and T shirts every day, but also had lots of formal wear, with not much in between these two extremes. Sam would hit the sales at certain Madison Avenue shops, as his tall and skinny self always looked great in Italian-made clothing. I used to haunt the old Loehmann's way uptown, at the north end of the subway line, where bargain designer clothes (including gowns suitable for concerts) could be found inexpensively in their infamous Back Room. Loehmann's was always an adventure, especially elbowing your way into its large communal dressing room, where customers occasionally spotted long lost friends among the dozens of ladies trying on clothes around the room. (And all customers felt free to comment generously, and honestly, on everything everyone else was trying on!) It was a delightful and crazy place. After a bankruptcy, I believe Loehmann's still exists as an online retailer, but nothing could ever replace its colorful incarnation up at the north end of the Number 1 IRT Subway.

Early on, I learned that if a dress or gown fit and was really cheap, I should just buy it, as a use for it always seemed to materialize. One day I was up there and found a bright pink dress made out of many layers of a sheer fabric. It had all the features that are good for me: elbow length sleeves (pianists really must have sleeves!), mid-calf length (so not floor length, which would always be too long, as I'm short), a V neck (the best one on me), rhinestone buttons down the front, a silver belt, and a very full circle skirt, several layers thick. It was a dress just made for twirling around and around and around. I think it was less than twenty dollars, so I bought it, though I had no idea where I would ever wear the thing.

A few weeks later, one of Lennie's friends organized a Viennese Waltz evening in his loft apartment. The dress was perfect and a big hit. If I'd had to comb the entire city for something suitable to wear to a Viennese Waltz (I mean Viennese Waltzes had sort of gone out of style by then), I couldn't have done better, or gotten a better deal.

One evening Sam was invited to participate in a house concert, followed by dinner, at the home of Alice Tully. Yes, "that" Alice Tully, the same one who donated the funds for Alice Tully Hall, one of NY's major concert halls. She lived in one of the fancy hotels on Central Park South in a luxuriously posh, generously gilded apartment reminiscent of Versailles. There were two different dining rooms, both with long ornate tables, and each could seat at least two dozen people.

At the conclusion of the house concert, we all sat down at one of her beautiful tables, set with exquisite embroidered table linens and hand-painted china. Food came from the world class restaurant downstairs in the hotel. We got fed take out, but very fancy (and delicious) take out! And the white-coated waiters from the restaurant served.

Somebody said to me that I look very nice and they love my dress. Sam piped up and said that I bought my dress at Loehmann's. Astonishingly, every single woman around the table (except Miss Tully) said she had purchased her dress at Loehmann's! Think of it, these women were all, save the musicians, extremely wealthy New Yorkers who could afford to shop quite literally anyplace, anywhere in the world…and we all shopped at Loehmann's. I was sitting next to the wife of the President of The Metropolitan Opera and she said to me she went to Loehmann's every few months and bought several dozen dresses at a time. She said that she and her husband had to attend hundreds of events a year and there was no way she was going to pay a lot of money for dresses for each occasion. I always thought that a re-enactment of this conversation, set in a similar elegant dining room, would have made a great commercial for Loehmann's.

Sometimes our concert experiences came with bizarre circumstances. The most extreme example I can think of involved some concerts we were going to play on a cruise ship sailing between islands in the Caribbean. This sounded like a lovely way to get away from the northeastern winter and get some sunshine while earning some money, so we readily accepted this engagement and were excited about the trip. As things turned out though, the ship sailed through an awful storm on the way south, and some sort of giant rogue wave hit it, breaking off the stabilizer on the bottom of its keel and nearly capsizing the ship. The listing ship sent the grand piano, on which I was supposed to play all the concerts, crashing through a huge plate glass window in the lounge, where it eventually landed upside down in the swimming pool on the deck below! Honestly, you can't make this stuff up. Thankfully, Sam and I missed all of this, as we had arranged to meet the ship when it docked in St. Thomas. And though we may have missed the storm, I was still stuck playing concerts on the worst honky-tonk bar piano I'd ever had occasion to attempt to play, and the poor thing was barely able to stay in tune.

Bad pianos were just a part of my life, though. Instrumentalists, like cellists, have no idea how lucky they are, because they know, and have intimate familiarity with, the particular instrument they are going to play. Once, giving a fundraising concert in the home of a Los Angeles arts patron, who was also a close relative of the President of the United States at the time (which he never let you forget), I was proudly shown a lovely concert-sized Steinway. Whew, was my initial reaction, imagining I'd have a problem free night. Unfortunately, the person who dusted and kept house, no doubt convinced he or she was taking wonderful care of the piano, had consistently waxed and polished the entire piano. And I do mean waxed and polished all of it, including its keys, with some sort of super sticky furniture polishing goop. It would be hard to describe the sensation, or my surprise, when I put a finger down on a key and then found that I could barely lift it off. Now I know how flies feel on fly paper. The first piece we played began with a quick long run up the piano, and I was struggling so much, and botching it up so badly, that Sam actually turned around in his chair and just stared at me, saying with his expression "What the heck are you doing??!" I didn't know how to tell him that I was, essentially, stuck in the mud.

We had a lot of fun playing concerts and our lives were full of some unusual adventures. And Sam took great pleasure in our concert performances. But there were two issues with the concert world that Sam faced as a classical cellist that bothered him immensely, that he always had a yen to do something about. First, concert audiences were gradually getting older, and they were dwindling in numbers; it seemed as though nobody was doing much to encourage a wider attendance or to help children and young people develop an interest in classical music. Second, Sam felt a profound artistic calling to commission new compositions to increase the repertoire for the cello, as it is so much smaller compared to other instruments. Beethoven, for instance, wrote 32 piano sonatas and 5 for the cello, Bach wrote 6 suites for cello, but produced dozens of keyboard works, and others like Mozart, wrote virtually nothing for cello solo.

Sam had an idea. Our dear friend Harry helped Sam set up a Foundation to commission works celebrating important events or people in the history of the United States. Sam had long noticed that orchestras and concert presenters are always more inclined to engage a performer if there is some extra marketable publicity likely to come their way. After all, good publicity about an unusual composition on the concert program helps them sell tickets and gives people extra motivation to come to the concert. To fund this Foundation, Sam applied for grants, and he also asked wealthy acquaintances we had met through our performance careers, many of whom were delighted to help. Though he put together enough cash to pay the composers, Sam himself never took a cent, except for the artist fees from the concerts when he played some of the commissions.

Over time many works were created. To give examples of what the Foundation did, one composition celebrated Eleanor Roosevelt's Universal Declaration of Human Rights, and was premiered on the same date in the same hall in San Francisco where the Declaration was announced 50 years before. Another was about the space program, one celebrated the Peace Corps, and yet another was about Thomas Jefferson. Harry, with his New Deal background, insisted on commissioning a work about Franklin Delano Roosevelt. It turned out that the chosen composer had witnessed the funeral cortege of FDR as a small child.

Because of their connection to historical events, the commissioned compositions also provided the opportunity for local grade and high school performances and multiple workshops with students. The children's workshops involved studying the historical period of the theme of the composition, as well as giving the kids personal creative experiences – doing their own small compositions, writing a short play, or making some art. And of course, these school projects furthered the publicity around the main concerts, encouraging the students to come to the concerts with discounted or free tickets and bring their parents and siblings. Sam raised money for all these school events as well. It's tragic that Sam's deteriorating mental health didn't allow this remarkably satisfying and valuable project to continue longer than it did.

All parents end up driving their kids around a lot, and with a country house, and three kids who played various sports after school, we did our share. While Sam was running the Foundation and commissioning the new works, he had to listen to and screen music submitted to the Foundation by a lot of lesser known composers who were applying for a grant opportunity to write a composition. We're talking about dozens and dozens of recordings. As a result, we often spent the long drives listening to CDs of contemporary music. Folks might be shocked to realize that Sam's commissioning choices were heavily influenced by what the kids liked, or rather, what they could listen to without utterly melting down. In fact, I doubt there are any kids on earth who got such a steady diet of truly offbeat contemporary music. Any way you slice it, a lot of fine new compositions were contributed to the literature, with a lot of help from our kids.

Part 3, Sam and mental illness

We were all so blessed to have known Sam and to have had him as a part of our lives and our family for as long as we did, especially for the span of time before his illness took over. What a brilliant, gifted, funny, delightful guy he could be! Of course, he was also very complex, at the end of his life deeply troubled, and I'm not sure anybody, even me, ever fully understood him.

As I'm writing this book, I've thought about the first time that I knew for sure how ill he was, and knew how his illness might completely destroy him. He'd been asked to fill in for someone who had gotten sick, so had only a couple of days to prepare for the concert; it was to be held here in the city, so no travel was involved. In what was obviously an extremely manic state, when asked if he could play the concert (a private event, for an organization of musicians), he proposed a solo recital composed of half a dozen extremely difficult works. Nobody in their right mind would ever consider playing all those killer works on one concert, let alone with only two days advance notice. But I could not persuade Sam to do otherwise, and he practiced like a fiend day and night, maniacally. (Sleep goes out the window in manic states.) All of the difficult solo pieces of music that he had selected were musical works he knew and could play well, but there were too many for him to prepare with such short notice. He hadn't played any of them in a long time, had not practiced a lot recently, and it was far too big a chunk of music to chew up, re-digest, and prepare to play in such a short time, even for someone with his gifts. It was also far too much music to expect an audience to sit through and enjoy listening to in one go. But he insisted, couldn't be "talked down", and forged ahead at full speed. Paying attention to no one, he had programs printed, and then, almost predictably, began to crash the morning of the concert. With his mood and his optimism about this concert heading into blackness, he had to call the concert organizers and tell them he was too sick to play.

 Sam's life is incredibly painful to look at honestly. It really hurts. How do any of us even begin to reconcile the two sides of Sam, and his tragic end? I, least of anyone, have the answer for that. Nobody will forget that Sam succumbed to mental illness (whatever the cause), fell apart and eventually died tragically. And there are plenty of dark episodes to ponder. But to me it seems healthier to balance the yin with the yang and appreciate the very best of Sam along with the worst. There was plenty that was nothing short of incredibly marvelous. For myself, I want to remember the joy of our personal relationship, the fun and laughter, the endless terrible puns, our beautiful children and the family life we had together, the music that filled our home daily, all those glorious concerts, the chamber music, and the pleasure we had traveling and performing together. I want to remember and cherish the interesting experiences and people that came into our lives, the stunning human beings we counted as friends, all the folks that were drawn to Sam's special gifts, and the richness of our lives before his mental illness took over and stole him from us.

 I was lucky enough to have many years to enjoy life with Sam before he got sick. But all the fun didn't last and so the question becomes, how did the mental illness that destroyed Sam's life come from all of this brilliance and talent? Is it possible that they are in fact two forms of the same thing? Are they both examples of mental capabilities at the extreme, residing at the outer edges? Though it pains me immensely to say so, I don't think Sam could have had one without the other.

I don't fully understand this, and others better qualified than I have no doubt written a lot on the subject. But as Carl Jung said "A person must pay dearly for the divine gift of creative fire." What I do just begin to comprehend is that when anyone has such a huge, near magical gift, they also seem to have a capacity for equally extreme darkness and pain. And depending on how they live their life and the strength of their own inner tenacity for seeking balance and health, the danger of falling into the darkness always exists. Yin and Yang, light and shadow cohabitate in everyone. Even those of us with lesser gifts have to stay aware of this and strive for balance in our lives. Despair is possible for anyone.

Though Sam's problems were a product of illness, in my opinion he also became more vulnerable to illness because he failed to deal in healthy ways with the disappointments that fall to all of us in life. Sadly, in the classical music business, only a few artists will ever have major careers. Those that do rise to the level of a major career do so for many reasons, not all of them based on merit, and describing that is not what I want to get into now.

But the plain truth is that those few who succeed have nearly all the work, and all the others, including those who are equally gifted, scramble for the rest. I've already written about the embarrassment and shame I believe Sam felt when he didn't develop the career his extraordinary talent deserved. In addition, the reality was that Sam had some devastating disappointments and he didn't have the inner strength, perhaps due to the early stages of mental illness, or perhaps due to other factors, to let it all go and put it behind him, and find more open roads to creative expression. Perhaps becoming a great artist requires an exquisite development of sensitivity, and those capable of that sort of sensitivity might not have the capacity for business dealings. I can remember Piatigorsky telling Sam he needed to develop a "theek skeen" (in his inimitable Russian accent), and I believe in retrospect that he was alerting Sam to the type of toughness he would need in the concert business.

Sam was happiest living in the light, pleasant, joyful side of things and didn't really want to go into the depths when things were very hurtful or just plain sad. Maybe this was left over from his childhood, I don't know, and am not qualified to say. But I witnessed several incidents that he didn't have the capacity to handle with equanimity, get beyond, and let his disappointments go.

To give one example, he had spent considerable time and effort raising money to commission a new cello concerto. This was one of his first successful efforts, many years before he and Harry created the Foundation. With the grant money raised, he picked out a composer, paid him, and worked with him frequently over many hours and weeks to consolidate which of the composer's phrases and configurations of notes would work best for a cello composition. (Not every composer "gets" how to write well for the cello.) A new cello concerto began to take shape. Even though the composition wasn't finished, efforts were made to get a performance, which ultimately materialized in a major NY hall with a major orchestra, complete with a signed contract.

Then things got weird. All of a sudden Sam stopped hearing from the composer, for whom he had raised the grant money, and with whom he had worked so diligently. He ignored all of Sam's efforts at communication. When the concert was formally announced, a more famous older cellist was advertised as the soloist.

This was a crushing disappointment to Sam. He considered suing, because he did after all have a signed contract for this engagement, but then realized that if he did that he would be forever known as the cellist that sued a major orchestra and he might never get the chance to play with another one. He let it go, at least externally.

Occasionally he'd see the composer on the street in NY and as soon as the composer saw Sam he'd run to the other side of the street. How did Sam deal with this? Unfortunately, I don't think he ever did, and as far as I could tell he refused to touch the deep feelings of hurt and rejection this surely brought up.

When the concert was finally performed, the concerto got an awful review, for the cellist as well as the composition. And Sam expressed bitter delight at the composer's misfortune, saying he got what he deserved. But is bitterness expressed in this way the same thing as really being aware of all the layers of feeling something like this brought up for him? It is not the same as working through all those feelings so that he might have let the whole experience go in a healthy way. Nor is it the same as finding a way to express his disappointment clearly and directly to the composer, in a manner that would have given Sam a chance to stand up for himself, and strongly but politely have his say.

Coping with terrible disappointment requires an inner depth of character that Sam didn't ever seem to develop. Everything came so easily to him and feelings were so freely available to him in the music he played so well that he got away without having to deal with real life's various unpleasant emotions for a very long time. I don't believe he ever let himself feel disappointed or get really mad about many of the unfair aspects of his life as a professional musician, and from where I sit now, I am fairly sure being in touch with all that might have helped him. The emotions any of us refuse to feel and deal with eventually take a big toll.

Classical music is pretty tightly controlled by the concert management system. For a variety of reasons, many of them having to do with the lack of soloist opportunities for a cellist in the concert world, and the consequential reluctance of major managers to put more cellists on their rosters, Sam never had major management. This also caused a lot of hurt for him, and he never really dealt with it. To his credit, he put out a lot of his own materials, or used smaller managements, and he had a decent small career. But after many years in this business, one has to accept that the classical music field is a tightly controlled game, with great success reserved for just a few. If you are not allowed "in", whether for good reasons or less legitimate ones, then you must find other creative expressions for your gifts, if your sanity and gifts are to survive.

For years, Sam found satisfaction in the concerts he booked, in his teaching, and with the help of our old friend Harry, the establishment of the Foundation. However, as he became sicker, the organizational skill this required eluded him, and his involvement with it diminished. The lack of success was tough for Sam to take in, and with a "thicker skin" and greater depth of inner resilience, (which might not have been possible due to incipient mental illness), Sam's life might well have been quite different. But it wasn't and there is now another more relevant question, for those of us who knew him and who are still alive, for those of us in his family, and for all his students and friends. How do we go about reconciling our feelings about what we saw happening to this troubled, but marvelous man? I don't know if any of us can.

And this has the potential to create guilt in everyone who loved Sam. Some of his friends and students have spoken to me quite openly about their feelings of guilt, that they didn't do enough, that they should have gone to visit him more, that they didn't do more to help him, and so forth. It is easy to fall into the trap of thinking, oh, if only I'd done such and such, the outcome would have been different. Well I can say, for sure, because I tried it all, and then some, that he just plain wasn't going to get better.

In truth, though, there is only way he might have gotten better. I can imagine that one day we might have a legal system that would have allowed those of us that loved Sam to get him treated, in such a way that he couldn't refuse to comply or check himself out, at any number of times in the last two decades of his life. Think about how Sam might still be here functioning and making music, and be here for his kids and his students, if anyone, me or his kids or his students or his colleagues or his friends, had the power to insist he get into treatment and stay with it long enough to get better.

Toward the end of his life Sam had enrolled in a study at a NY hospital which included some new medication specifically for treatment-resistant depression in older people. Always a prolific writer, Sam kept notes during his treatment, and from reading them I can verify he knew he was getting better, and expressed hope and even optimism about getting back to teaching and playing.

But Galen threw a fit about this hospitalization, and so Sam withdrew himself from the hospital AMA (against medical advice), never took any more medication, never did any more anything, and was dead a year later. How is this anything but horribly tragic, especially because it is quite possible it could have been prevented?

CHAPTER 2

Triage, Otherwise Known as Divorce

Eventually, somewhere in the middle of Sam's repeated depressions, each one worse than the one before, and the seemingly endless traumas and dramas, it gradually began to dawn on me that Sam and I were headed towards a divorce. I never wanted to do this, and I resisted as long as possible (far too long, in retrospect). I loved the guy, and divorce was the last thing I wanted. Also, frankly, I was raised Catholic, where divorce happens but long marriages are preferred. But there was no way of avoiding the inevitable, and divorce was going to occur, in spite of everything I'd done to prevent it.

There are so many reasons two people who love each other get divorced. Sometimes there are practical considerations. Other times, what we are feeling and experiencing becomes so intensely uncomfortable and painful that divorce is the only option. For Sam and me, both were involved.

Mood disorders affect more than moods. People who are bipolar tend towards extremes of all sorts, involving sex, drinking, drugs, work, mania, or depression, and can overdo all sorts of things, big time. While some people become very promiscuous, others work incessantly, and others never sleep. Others do other needlessly excessive things, like buy too many clothes, or gamble.

One day Sam came home and joyfully announced he'd taken a $25,000 bank loan, and guess what, we didn't have to pay it back! Well, this seemed pretty irrational, and I went to the bank and asked what had happened. Sam had indeed taken out a loan for $25,000, and for one year no interest was due. But obviously we would have to repay the loan.

I don't like to carry debt. This is most likely an attitude inherited from my depression-era parents, and also probably left over from years of freelance work as teachers and musicians, with erratic incomes, and unpredictable abilities to pay back loans. Long ago, we learned to spend only the money we actually had, to pay all credit cards off immediately, in full, and to never, ever borrow money. When there are long periods where little money comes in, it keeps one sane and feeling more secure financially to owe nothing to anyone. To this day I am arguably un-American, in that while I use credit cards for most purchases, I pay all credit card balances in full every month.

I repaid the loan immediately from my savings, but this became the incident that began to wake me up. (And for what it's worth, and this is typical for a bipolar person, I don't know exactly what he did with the money.) For me, $25,000 was not a trivial sum, and I was worried about the repeat potential of this behavior. I couldn't afford to lose chunks of money in this way.

Money became a tough subject during this time and the "gift from the bank" was Exhibit A. With every additional serious depression, more income dried up, teaching stopped, arrangements weren't made for more concerts, and sometimes mistakes were made with double bookings that are very inconvenient and embarrassing to undo. Once, Sam had to tell a small orchestra he couldn't come play with them a matter of days before a concert, just from sloppy attention to booking details while in a state of depression.

Sam had some substantial assets of his own, including IRAs, a retirement account through his university, as well as inherited funds. When Sam died, six years after our divorce, my concerns about his spending were verified, and I was beyond shocked to learn he had spent his way through almost all his retirement funds, all his other savings, his inheritances, and left multiple credit card balances that totaled well into six figures. Sam also foolishly allowed our oldest son access to his bank account and credit cards, so some of this wild spending was due to our son. But again, it is really mind-boggling to realize how out of control Sam was with money.

During the divorce, I asked the court to let Sam off the hook with child support. In spite of having ample funds of his own to live on, as well as a terrific job earning a good salary, I knew he'd never pay it, and didn't want to argue about it for years. I also didn't need it, so I saw no point. But the judge said that I could not speak for my children, legally, and they absolutely deserved child support from their father, so child support was set up. Knowing Sam would not and could not ever get it together enough to pay child support, I had an idea.

Sam and I still owned the country house jointly. I did the math and calculated that his share of the value of the home was more or less equal to the remaining years of required child support and college assistance for our 3 children. As he had no interest in using the house himself, I suggested to Sam that he assign his half of the house to the three kids, in trust, which in my opinion was an easy and creative solution that worked very well, and he agreed.

Even if the loan and other financial considerations had not come into our lives, I would still have divorced Sam. Although nothing is more gut-wrenching than realizing a marriage cannot continue, being married to him was becoming just too emotionally painful. I always loved Sam dearly. Before SMI, he was an absolute delight. Across the board, we had passion, fun, laughter, and deep love. Was he perfect? No, but neither was I. Given my choice, I would happily have gone off into the sunset with him after a long life together.

It was tough to come to terms with the realization that my own hopes and dreams for my marriage, and our whole future together, all of it, was being swallowed whole by Sam's increasing illness. And talk about feeling helpless! Because in truth there was not one thing I could do to make it better, slow its course, or improve things at all, in any way.

Divorce became inevitable when I realized the amount of anger and resentment that began to accompany my life. It grew increasingly worse and remained with me all day and every day. Trying to continue would have hurt me and the kids way too much. I could not go on being so miserable, and neither could the kids. I needed to separate from Sam legally and physically.

I have thought a lot about whether I would have accumulated the same levels of intense anger and resentment if Sam had made a serious effort to try to take care of himself, or in fact made any effort at all to get better. I think not, in retrospect. I believe my emotions might have been as strong, but I think they would have been centered more around sadness and loss, and less so on anger and resentment. I also believe it might have been possible for us to have not divorced. My smoldering resentment was mostly caused by his refusal to go forward – to do anything at all, anything, in any constructive way. Had he been a better patient, and attempted to spare his wife and kids pain and suffering, I believe the experiences of our family might have been different. For whatever reason, he wouldn't, or couldn't, and didn't.

I also believe there is something in the combination of his particular brain or his DNA and the illness that produced a symptom of stubborn unwillingness to do anything constructive. This, too, was probably just part of the illness, but it became next to impossible to live with. Unfortunately, our eldest son also has this trait, which perhaps suggests a genetic component. I will devote several chapters to him, later in the book.

I realize that medication or therapy don't work consistently for everybody, or perhaps at all for some people, and I recognize that even if Sam had been a model patient, he might have continued to decline. Even so, it would have been good for me to see him try, and it would have been good for the kids. In truth, it seemed very clear to me, especially after witnessing positive changes in Sam on the occasions when he complied briefly with his doctor's advice, that giving treatment a fair shot would have been a wise and loving thing to do for himself, for me, and for the children. And it would have made the whole experience exponentially less frustrating for me.

But he wasn't doing that, at all, most likely because he was too ill to do so. I had to face the reality of our situation.

I kept trying to determine the best solution, both for the kids, and for me: whether we should live by ourselves in peace at home, or have Sam continue to live with us, keeping everyone in an emotional uproar more or less all the time? It's pretty obvious, from the outside. But at the time, it was very hard to see clearly, or clearly enough, so that I could get myself into gear, find an attorney, and begin the divorce process.

To be fair to myself, I shouldn't leave out that the disease can wax and wane on its own, and when Sam would get into one of his saner periods, he would often improve dramatically. There was always the tantalizing hope, forever dangled just out of reach, that we could put all this chaos and craziness behind us and go back to being a calmer family. Accepting that this was almost certainly never likely to happen was tough. And it took me time to get it, and accept it.

Mental illness is a topic nobody wants to address. It is so far beyond taboo that most people refuse to accept it or see that it even exists. So not only do those of us in the middle of it have to deal with something so unpleasant nobody else even wants to look at it, we also have to deal with the reality that our own pain, our own anger and resentment, and our exhaustion, is completely ignored - quite literally by everyone.

The inner journey of all this mess and horror, coupled with my ongoing love and deep respect for the wonderful man and musician I once knew, was profoundly difficult. You come to an impossible juncture and find yourself amazed that this wretched a situation could even exist, yet it does. Life can't continue along its current path, yet you must find a way to go forward. Acceptance of the dark circumstances that surround you seems daunting, yet you must accept them. Enduring is what we have to do until we can't, until we just surrender. The surrender process comes about through an honest acknowledgement of all of our feelings, which is a tough assignment, because after so many years of coping with Sam's illness, I'd disconnected from the full range of my own deepest emotions. It was either that or become a screaming wreck.

Perhaps most hurtfully, nobody ever expressed concern to me about what I was going through. Perhaps because they just didn't want to deal with it, but probably because they recognized I am strong and can function well under a lot of stress. I don't think I ever looked flat-out miserable. But that didn't mean the whole experience, A to Z, wasn't painful, embarrassing, hurtful, and exhausting. Even people you hire to help you cope with your own sanity, your own therapists and doctors, even they can find themselves lured into focusing on the ill person in your life, rather than on you and your swirling inner world.

I honestly can't remember a single time anybody asked me how I was doing or was truly interested in knowing what this experience was like for me, what I was dealing with or how I was feeling. Even family members were often unkind and unfeeling. My wonderful mother, a remarkable lady I loved dearly and regarded as my best friend, blurted out after I told her we were divorcing "But I love Sam, don't divorce him, he's so nice!" Which he was, once. But this showed how she and others did not register what the marriage was costing me, her own daughter, or her grandchildren. Sam's sister hasn't spoken to me since the divorce, nor to her niece and nephews, as (I'm guessing) she may feel I should have continued to care for him and besides, according to her, it was probably my fault he went off the rails. I could go on and on, as this sort of resentment came my way a lot.

By contrast, there were many hours of discussion with his therapists and doctors, and his friends, about what Sam was feeling, what to do about it, and how horrible it was for him. The kids were acting out, and the misery of what was going on in the family was clearly upsetting everyone. This was obvious, but the focus remained on Sam, and everything the kids and I experienced remained a taboo topic. I had poured my heart and soul into my marriage and my family, just like so many women do, and while I may have the satisfaction today of watching two of my children prosper, I also had to deal with pure tragedy in the unresolvable illness and decline of my beloved husband, and a mentally ill son who is wandering the earth, obstinately refusing help from anyone.

How do I convey the rage, the helplessness, and the confusion, never mind the physical exhaustion, brought about by the whole situation? How do I describe what it feels like to watch someone you love dearly fall apart? To watch him refuse to do a thing to stop his decline, to almost actively pursue personal destruction, and, most unbelievably, not seem to care? And how would you imagine I felt enduring this crisis, with so little acknowledgement of my turmoil from friends or family?

The loan may have awakened me, but truthfully, it was obvious for a long time something was wrong. I am a doer, I like to take care of things, so I took care of all I had to, for years. Looking back, I can't believe how much I actually managed across all those years, but there were whole long stretches of time where I subjugated my own feelings and concerns for the family good.

Though I am strong, I knew I could not continue on this path forever. Stressed to the max, I was caring for Sam, as well as three children. Add into this running a house, my own teaching career, and taking care of my aging mother, which included overseeing and paying her medical providers and caregivers. As if this weren't enough, there were huge problems with running my father's business, now ours; problems that included an ongoing five year long lawsuit with the IRS that involved long hours of work and frequent air travel to depositions and family meetings, a simultaneous legal malpractice suit involving wrong advice given to us after my father's death (this too involved five years of misery, but it came out OK, as we won), and multi-year negotiations with the EPA concerning contaminated properties that were part of the business. We didn't contaminate anything, but a dry cleaner down the street had dumped their used waste products and chemicals in back of our business for years, and we couldn't sell or do anything with our property until we cleaned it up. You don't want to know what this cost.

And though I am dedicating my writing in this chapter to Sam, the mental health problems with our oldest son began about five years after Sam began to decline, and the addiction issues with our younger son (both described later) began soon after. In addition to Sam I was also dealing with both of them in crisis. Though my daughter never went off the rails, she was a normal teenager, which meant that she, too, was pushing the limits (rightfully), and causing me a certain amount of additional stress. As I waded through all of this, it's fairly miraculous I didn't go nuts myself.

Stretched as thin as I could go, I gave Sam an ultimatum. I told him I had nursed him through all the full-blown depressions I could, and if he again stopped cooperating with his doctors and pushed me to live through another long depression, I would divorce him.

Of course, Sam never did anything by half measures, so if he was going to be self-destructive, he was going to carry it all the way, and so he went through another depression – and it was his worst ever. The depressions always occurred when he completely stopped his meds, and this time was no different. The same day I told him he had pushed me to the point I would divorce him, Sam went off to see his psychiatrist. And when he came home, he said the psychiatrist had told him the same thing, and that since he didn't follow her advice, she was no longer going to treat him. Sam shouted "Oh great. Both my wife and my shrink want a divorce, and for the same reason!"

I had an instinct that we might divorce at two points earlier in our lives. Once, right after we met, there was an incident I had forgotten completely and was astonished to remember recently. The subject of mental illness was years away, we were sitting in front of a roaring fire (Sam loved fireplaces) and I heard an inner voice say "You will love this man dearly for many years, but one day it will be completely over." Later, in his first psychiatrist's office, I heard that same inner voice again "You've got to divorce him right now, to save you and the kids much grief." This time I spoke the thought aloud to the psychiatrist who then dismissed my concerns and my feelings rather cruelly, and shamed me into staying with Sam. The psychiatrist said that if Sam had pneumonia, or any other illness, would I be thinking of divorcing him? I had an instinct that less damage might be done to everyone in the family if I divorced him right then, because on this deep inner level, I felt certain I would be forced to do so eventually. This was 11 years before I did in fact divorce him.

In its length and severity, and in his refusal to follow treatment protocols, Sam's ongoing depression most surely was quite different from having pneumonia, and the proper answer to that psychiatrist would have been to point out that the stress of dealing with one's spouse sick for a few weeks with pneumonia is not the same thing as dealing with a spouse's serious mental illness year after year, for many years. Isn't it awful when we think of the exact right thing to say, hours after we should have said it? But the psychiatrist had beaten down my inner voice, and I didn't let this helpful inner voice of truth speak to me again for a long time, or if it was speaking to me, I wasn't listening. I was just keeping my head down and forging ahead, trying to take care of everything and everyone.

But now, years later, I am beginning to consider my options carefully. Sam is totally off the rails. I am legally tied to a man who has no concept of following sensible advice about his illness, (and cannot be compelled to do so), who has no ability to manage his finances, (but I might be responsible for his debts), who is creating such financial stress that he could upend the family, and on top of it all is behaving so erratically that the whole household is continuously swirling in emotional chaos and turmoil. I am by nature a giving, loving, and caring person, but there is a point where enough is enough. And I just couldn't go through another serious depression with Sam.

Sam's deeper depressions involved months of watching him sit on the sofa for most of the hours of the day, and staying alert for signs of potential suicidal ideation. He would also spout weird viewpoints and wild theories that could have been produced by eating weird mushrooms, except that he hadn't been doing that. For example, one day right after I had taken the kids for their annual physical exams and shown him the excellent results, he asked me why we had a pediatrician who could not see that the kids were seriously ill and starving to death? Hearing him carrying on about this was awful for the kids. Sometimes, when he was in this strange state, he would send everyone really horrible gloomy emails about how his life was almost over, emails which upset the kids and me immensely. This had to end. Holding an entire family together, while doing my level best to take care of Sam, had taken too heavy a toll.

Sam was an impossible patient, profoundly non-compliant. I'd think he would have done almost anything to avoid his downward spiral, but during all the years of Sam's illness, he declined almost all of the medical advice given to him. Especially, he hated taking medications, and perhaps as a result he never stuck to their prescribed schedules.

I recognize that medication is an exceedingly complicated subject, and don't wish to be insensitive about Sam's complaints regarding the side effects, which indeed seemed considerable. This is a real dilemma, for which I surely don't have answers. I can only relay my observations of what happened to Sam - he sank into deep depressions without meds, and came out of depressions with them. I can't put it any more simply than that. Flawed as these drugs may be, his own life experience made the necessity of these meds, for him, fairly clear.

If the docs prescribed pills for Sam, he'd take them here and there if he felt like it, or take them for a while and then stop them suddenly, which for many meds was dangerous. As his doctors were creative, they recommended alternative treatments like breath work, to lessen his anxiety and help him cope with the meds. Unfortunately, he would resist all treatment options with belligerent non-compliance. If his doctors thought he should come in for therapy sessions, maybe he would – or, depending on his mood that day, maybe not. Several times he started to get really ill and, genuinely scared, went back on the meds and would come out of it. Often though, he sank into a deep, long depression.

His depressions happened very fast, and he would plummet down in a matter of hours. I was becoming really resentful about everything his carelessness ended up forcing me to go through and endure, repeatedly, and all the messy situations these depressions created in our lives. It was infuriating, and mostly it all seemed so pointless.

Love is not the question here. I loved him. I always loved him. We all loved him. But the concept of triage is unavoidable. I am not superwoman. Given my own limited resources of time and energy, and the ongoing and deepening exhaustion, I had no choice. No matter what I might do, it wasn't going to make a difference and it wasn't going to matter. I found myself forced into a truly painful decision, but one that was becoming more apparent every day, and one which I had to make, however reluctantly.

The kids had to have one functioning stable parent. Without me, they'd be lost altogether, which I did not think was fair to them in the least. I needed to choose between continuing to cope with their father, now evident as a hopeless task, and devoting myself to taking care of myself and our kids. There was still much hope for the rest of us. For Sam, his actions made his recovery virtually impossible from the first moment he got sick.

Sometimes making the decision to divorce still bothers me, even though I know I did nothing wrong and I also know I have always done all I could to love and help all members of my family. Still, sometimes I think about whether there might have been something else that could have been done for Sam, some other creative treatment I might have found, had I kept looking. And I have continued to stumble in my worst moments over my concerns that perhaps I had failed because I hadn't looked hard enough to find a way out of the mess.

I recognize this inner negative voice is not my friend, and won't help me in the least. I fully recognize that it is never anyone's job to "save" anyone else. "Saving" somebody is altogether and categorically a foolish concept, as all of us are only responsible for ourselves and have to make the best possible decisions for ourselves, and for our children if they are young. But that has never stopped me from extending a helping hand to anyone who might need it. With Sam, all he ever had to do was grab my hand, and either he chose not to, or he couldn't. It's hard to imagine anything sadder.

For me personally, divorce was only the beginning of a process of reclaiming myself and coming to terms with all I felt and had experienced. I am not an angry person by nature. My cup is half full most of the time, and I see the good in most people and situations. But after enduring life with a husband with SMI long enough, I had lost touch with parts of myself, especially the parts where the darkest, most unpleasant emotions live. I've also wondered if this might have been so because my darker emotions seemed so much less dramatic and consequential than Sam's, to such an extreme degree that mine barely registered as needing acknowledgement or attention.

I am slowly learning that all of our feelings have to be recognized and explored and allowed space in our consciousness. If they aren't, we won't understand our feelings well enough to avoid them popping up to draw our attention somewhere down the road, most likely unexpectedly, at a time we really wish they'd stay buried. As a wise man once said "The truth will set you free, but first it will make you miserable."

It takes some courage for me to admit that even though I was beyond furious about this whole situation, and felt incredible frustration that no apparent solution existed, my strong desire to have the kids in a relatively peaceful household kept me from letting these emotions fly. There were no screaming fights the kids had to hear, though of course they had to be aware on many levels of the pain Sam's condition caused me.

I am not saying that screaming at Sam would have helped. But I strongly believe that saying to all of us, out loud, in a calm voice, "I am really frustrated and really angry about what is happening and here are some things I would like to do about this" would have been a better way to handle the situation, better than remaining silent while I fumed.

I'm not proud of this. I recognize I didn't have the time, energy, or space to deal with any of this in a more open and productive way, the way I might have if I hadn't been living in survival mode and life hadn't become so complex. This cost me and the kids dearly, and I am still sorting it all out emotionally. I think the kids are too. From where I am now, I recognize this was, to put it mildly, not the most useful way to handle deeply upsetting family problems, but it was all I could do at the time, so I have to cut myself some slack. As the expression goes, "Sometimes, self-forgiveness is all we have".

Silence itself can be a form of anger, and arguably one of the least healthy. Given my own upbringing, not being allowed to express what I was feeling, my silence was understandable. Given the tensions in the house with Sam, which didn't boil over if I stayed silent, the silence was clearly the easier alternative. Mostly though, given my own lack of understanding about good boundaries at that time, such silence was all I knew.

Over time there were enough of small annoying events, as well as some bigger more serious events, that my own personal boundaries gradually began coming into focus for me, as his unpredictable behavior reached an unbearable intensity. And so, even before the divorce proceedings, I asked Sam to move out. I had a friend in my building who said she wanted to sublet her apartment for about a year. Originally, I asked her if I could rent this apartment for my mother, so she could visit more often and be close to us, and not have her stay in a hotel. But then Mom had a minor stroke and we all realized that having a little apartment in NY was never going to be in the cards for her. I asked Sam to move into this apartment.

Theoretically, this was to become a way for us to separate without a lot of angst and drama, so he moved in and I paid the rent. Of course, I was completely fooling myself if I thought I could just rearrange the jigsaw pieces of our lives and limit the emotional intensity of everything we were about to experience. I didn't look at this clearly and didn't consider that experiencing the emotional turmoil that was upon us was not only necessary but actually essential if we were going to get through this as a family. It seems you can't go around difficult experiences, you have to go straight through them.

It almost makes me cringe now to consider how I thought back then, and the sorts of over-the-top arrangements I believed were reasonable. The adjustments any of us make to living with someone so mentally ill can derange our thinking, even if we do not have a diagnosis ourselves.

Around this time Sam enrolled in a program at a major medical center, a program that included intensive treatments for personality disorder. A kind social worker he had met lobbied hard for his admission, strongly believing it could help him. He had to spend every weekday afternoon there, and the program gave the participants homework and various assignments. True to form, in the year or more he was part of this program, he did absolutely nothing: he didn't work with the materials, he didn't ever open the study guides - nothing. As one might expect from his non-participation, the program seemed to have no effect on him in any way, and eventually he stopped going.

After getting Sam moved into the other apartment in my building, I was hoping that my kids could continue to have their beloved father in their lives daily, even as sick as he was. Wrong! The whole plan was a full-on catastrophe, in every conceivable way, from the very beginning. Sam was completely unpredictable, and now in full crash mode. The apartment gradually became an absolute mess, making it impossible for the kids to hang around and visit or go over and do their homework.

Instead of lessening the family's anguish, my hoped-for solution to keep us moderately functioning as a family only increased the suffering. Also, this was my friend's apartment, for which I felt responsible, and I grew progressively angrier about the constant mess. Frustrated beyond my breaking point, I finally asked Sam to find his own apartment, which he did, about five blocks away. This turned out to be the last place he lived.

The moral of this story is never, ever attempt to convince yourself you can outrun a crisis that is upon you. *Turn and face a crisis head on. Find all the helpful friends and associates you can muster to help you get through it. Most essentially, define your boundaries clearly!* Patch-up solutions will only delay the inevitable, and possibly make the outcome even more horrible.

During the last years of Sam's life, good friends of ours tried to help Sam by calling in Adult Protective Services. APS would come to his building to try and talk to him. Typically, he would hide from them, and they didn't have hours and hours to wait around for him to show up. Many people who cared about Sam tried to do something to help, each in their own way, but he resisted everything.

When we cleaned out Sam's apartment 6 years later, after his death, I absolutely could not believe the mess. Think hoarder, and you'll have a pretty good idea. Think about every piece of trash or mail or empty bag, dirty sock, unopened bill, or pizza box simply tossed on the floor until, like some otherworldly archeological dig, the reeking, soggy pile was stacked knee high. I won't even try to describe the refrigerator or the state of the bathroom, as some things are better left unsaid. And then imagine that after Sam's death, some fool (me) with the help of dear friends and the twins, had to sort it all out and clean the place up. We had to, so we could give it back to the landlord and get out of the rest of the lease, saving my kids, Sam's heirs, a lot of money. And doing all of this was just as awful as you would imagine. But we had to gather up items like credit card statements and bills, and whatever else might be necessary to settle Sam's Estate.

I have thought about the home help I had when I was pregnant with twins. I didn't ask for it, and didn't have to pay for it, as my obstetrician and the hospital where I was to give birth provided me the service. Because my pregnancy was considered high risk, every day during the last few months a nurse came to my home, took my blood pressure, checked a contraction monitor the hospital had given me (to make sure I wasn't going into labor too soon), and in general gave me a daily mini-physical just to make sure my unborn children were OK. This was a wonderful service and I was very grateful. It was reassuring, and though I never had any big issues, it was comforting to know that any potential issue would have been found early.

Obviously, we should care about babies and children, and support their health pre- and post-birth. Perhaps, somewhere, there are similar services for mentally fragile adults, but I never encountered any. After Sam died, I found dozens of full prescription bottles (the extra-large size) stuffed full with medication, most dating from the previous year. How could anything be sadder than knowing he did nothing to help himself get better, and that nobody could compel him to do so?

As I mentioned in the previous chapter, the last time Sam was hospitalized our oldest son pushed him to check himself out AMA (against medical advice), even though he had shown signs of improvement. I've often thought about how ridiculous this situation is. Consider that Sam was so mentally ill as to warrant hospital placement in a last-ditch experimental program for long-term severe depression. Can you imagine that such a person is still considered fully legally capable of making an intelligent and sane choice about leaving treatment before it is complete? What a joke! How can this possibly work for an SMI patient? It is unbelievable to me that courts uphold this, because it is just blatantly dangerous. And in Sam's case, it was fatal.

CHAPTER 3

Sam's Death

On May 6, 2014 my cell rings. It's rather late, around 10 pm. I check caller ID. It's my oldest son. I am surprised to see his name, as he's not supposed to call me. The problems I had been having with him have intensified, and his frightening actions have led me to obtain two protective orders against him. I'll speak about this more in the chapters about Galen, but those PO's mean that he is not supposed to be in contact with me in any way. He is calling in violation of the orders.

I let the call go to voice mail, then I listen. "Mom! Dad went off the roof! We're in the ambulance on the way to St. Luke's." Which St. Luke's? There are two of them.

I wonder how hurt you can get going off a roof. Five stories, so pretty bad I would think. I would think you could probably die. One part of me wants to freak out, another part says wait until you have all the facts, another part wants to call my son back and be there with all my love for him as a comforting Mom. But it has been such an ordeal and so much trouble to get the PO's, that I feel I can't risk undoing them by calling him.

I wait. Pepper does what the sweet kitty always does. Double cat duty, purring and rubbing on my shoulder. I wait some more. And more.

The front door bell rings. Who's there? Police. I let them in. Two detectives in suits. They ask me if I'm the ex-wife of Sam. I say that I am, and ask if he is dead. Yes, one of them says. I say that I've been waiting for this visit from them for many years.

They want me to go to the hospital to help deal with my son. I'm in a state of complete shock. My heart is pounding and my thinking isn't working at all. It seems impossible to put logical thoughts together, but I need to tell them about the Protective Orders and about how I can't be with my son right now. In fact, I am so shell-shocked and mentally muddled that I can't find a copy of the PO's. I go with them to the hospital, though looking back, I can't honestly remember anything about the ride up there.

They said that I wouldn't be violating the PO's if I see Galen, because I would be in the company of two cops, which was obviously logical, but they don't insist. The cops are concerned about letting Galen leave the hospital. A counselor Galen had seen calls me because Galen has called him. I let the cops speak to the counselor, who explains a lot to the officers. I keep explaining that Galen has such extreme psychological issues and has just witnessed his father die, either accidentally or possibly/probably a suicide. Galen himself has tried to take his own life several times. I am terrified and convinced I will have to find a way to convince them to keep Galen in the hospital so he too cannot end his life, this night, as well.

So now I'm at St. Luke's, uptown. The psychiatrist is speaking with Galen. I can see them through several thick glass windows. Some of the windows are in doors that are closed and others are in the walls of rooms (enabling people to see into the rooms from the outside), which means I can see Galen and the doctor speaking, though they are several rooms away. I tell the police I need to speak with the psychiatrist about Galen. They lead me around the back way, so I don't have to go near the room Galen is in.

On the way through we pass all the folks in the ER that night, all with medical people working on them. One bed has no one near it, but has someone in it, covered with a sheet. The person under the sheet is not shaped like a normal person, with limbs and head in the usual places, but is all crumpled up. That must be Sam, I think, my dear husband, my best friend, my lover, the father of my children, a man I knew and loved dearly for so many years.

There are many different parts of me all reacting differently. One part of me wants to pull back the sheets and look at him. One part wants to shriek and cry, another to run away, but the immediately compelling situation with Galen, for whose life I must fight, pulls the strongest part of me together, and I just keep on walking. I wonder again if I should stop and ask to see Sam, and I decide against it. They don't offer, which I take to be a sign that maybe I don't want my last look at Sam to be whatever misshapen bloody mess he's in under that sheet. I get to the room where I am supposed to wait. And I wait. And wait. An hour or two.

And of course, I think about Sam, about the way he died, and I hope he didn't have to suffer too much. But he probably did suffer. It must hurt like crazy to die falling from a building and smashing your body on a concrete patio, and it must be unbelievably terrifying. The poor guy! I am so sorry for what he experienced and that his life had to end like this!

The police said he was still alive when he was put in the ambulance. It's really painful to think about his physical injuries and what must have happened to his body, with which I was so intimately involved for so many years. I'm nearly overwhelmed by the horror of how his life has ended this night, but I fight to keep it together for Galen's sake. I am very grateful that I've done a lot of breath work, because at a time like this, paying attention to your breathing is the most useful and calming thing anyone can do. I would recommend it to anyone.

Eventually, a large, utterly exhausted young German psychiatrist comes in. He has been on duty for too many hours and can barely think and stay awake. It's about 2 am. Still, he does his job, toughs it out, and asks me what diagnoses Galen has, and I tell him the question of diagnosis has never been fully resolved. The doctor wants to know where Galen can go if he leaves the hospital. He cannot come home with me; I am too afraid of him and I cannot live in terror with him in the house. He cannot go live with his siblings. They are afraid of him too. There are no other friends or relatives who will have him. The doctor says he might let him go back to Sam's apartment. I ask him if he really thinks it's a good idea to send a young man who has a suicide attempt history back to the apartment he shared with a beloved father who has just killed himself? The doctor agrees that perhaps that wouldn't be the best idea.

Emboldened with my progress, I begin to plead a case for hospitalizing Galen. I pull out every stop I can think of, telling him every crazy thing Galen has ever done, and expressing my enormous reservations about turning him loose. He says they'll keep Galen overnight. I say that isn't good enough. Living through his father's death, which has also been the death of his enabler, is going to have immeasurable repercussions. This is going to change Galen's life completely. Eventually, after several hours of back and forth, including visits by the doctor to Galen while I am in the waiting room, the doctor says he will transfer Galen to the main psychiatric unit in the other hospital, the bigger hospital, in the morning, and the doctors in that hospital will evaluate him.

I have often said, during all the times Galen refused medical and psychiatric care, that I will have to rely on assistance from the Universe's treatment team to take care of him. This team is clearly in place. The first doctor Galen sees at the main St. Luke's hospital is the same tough Russian doctor who dealt with him after his first suicide attempt two years before. She knows him well and thinks he's really ill, far sicker than when he was her patient the first time. The doctors at the hospital are concerned about releasing him, and end up keeping him there for six weeks.

The night Sam died I was at the hospital almost the entire night, and when I had done what I needed to do to secure Galen's safety, dawn was breaking. The security guards found me a taxi to take me home, which I really appreciated. It's amazing how such a simple kind gesture can be exactly what is needed at such a time. In my exhausted state, it would have been awful to deal with getting home any other way. On the way home, I asked myself what was going to be different about my life now that Sam had died. I couldn't think of a single thing that would change. He was unreachable in life, especially during the last few years, and now he would continue to be unreachable, forever. I feel more wrung-out and numb than sad.

As I arrived home early that morning, even though I'm beyond tired, and emotionally drained as well, sleep has to wait. Now that Galen was somewhere safe, there were certain practicalities to take care of. Before I did anything else, I needed to call the twins before their brother got to them, as I wanted them to hear the news of their father's death from me, and not from Galen. The twins both attended the same university in another time zone three hours behind mine, and I waited as long as I felt I could, not wanting to wake them in the middle of the night.

Is any task more awful, emotionally wrenching and painful, than having to tell children their father has fallen to his death off a roof? I called my daughter first, and while we were on the phone her twin brother called, as Galen had reached him. Telling them both first was only partly successful. They wanted to fly home immediately, but end of the term exams were upon them and I said that they should deal with their exams if they were up to it and come home when they were finished. If I hadn't known Galen would call them the instant he had access to a phone, I might even have considered waiting a few days to tell them, so they could take their exams in peace. But I knew Galen would get on the phone as soon as he could, so I had to deal with it immediately.

Within a couple of days, other practicalities also had to be dealt with, and I was willing to do the things that needed doing to spare my children further heartbreak. I knew what I needed to do. And I set about getting it done.

First of all, someone had to identify Sam's body. I didn't want to leave this task to the twins, as I wasn't at all sure how Sam would look after a long fall from a roof. Sam's death was already hard enough on them and I didn't think they needed to have a visual picture of their dead father engraved in their memory, and so I went down to the Medical Examiner's office and took care of this. I was tremendously relieved to learn that this was going to be quite different from all the scenes I had witnessed in crime dramas, or imagined in mystery books, where someone goes into the morgue and identifies a body after it is pulled out of refrigeration on a slab. Thankfully, I was only asked to look at photos on a computer screen, and I was further relieved that I was only shown Sam's face and that he looked peaceful and calm. On his face, there were only a couple of scratches, nothing too terrible. Maybe they cleaned him up before they took photos, but I was very grateful that someone took care to present him in such a peaceful way. I could tell the kids, quite truthfully, that their father looked calmer and more at peace than he ever had while he was alive.

We knew we wanted to cremate Sam and scatter his ashes later. We weren't up for having a large formal funeral at that time. I was a bit horrified to learn that you can't just order up a cremation through the medical examiner's office, as you are required by law to use a funeral home, even in a situation like ours. We didn't want to have a funeral, and just wanted to scatter his ashes in some lovely spot.

However, even if you have no desire or need to spend money on any funeral related expenses, fees set by law will ensure it will end up costing a lot just for the simplest cremation. If Sam had known about this he would have had a lot to say and I finally understood why Sam's father had made his own arrangements in advance, at a cut-rate funeral parlor in the poorest neighborhood in San Francisco, selecting a cardboard coffin for the cremation. We were aghast and horrified at the time, but since everything was arranged and paid for in advance, the decisions were out of our hands.

But since we obviously needed to use a funeral home, a friend recommended a relatively inexpensive funeral parlor way downtown, in Chinatown. When I looked online for directions about getting to the funeral parlor, it seemed complex. I don't know the Chinatown area at all and don't have friends who live there. The walk from the train was quite far, and you had to connect with buses with routes I didn't know and none of it seemed simple. I didn't even know the names of the local bus stops, so in the end I decided to make my life easy and take a cab. Driving around the island on the highways seemed like an obvious solution. On a Saturday morning, it should have taken maybe 30 minutes at most.

I called a car service. When the car arrived, it was the tallest SUV I'd ever seen and in the process of trying to get in my foot slipped, nearly wrenching my back. Great start to the adventure, I thought. I gave the guy the address on Madison Street, said it was all the way downtown, by 1 Police Plaza and the Brooklyn Bridge, and I thought we should take the highway, either the West Side Highway, or cross town and take the FDR. He says, gruffly, we are not taking any highways because there is too much traffic on Saturdays.

Well, he's driving, so we settled on a fee and off we went. He crosses Central Park and starts heading down 5th Avenue. After a while the traffic is so bad he gets off and meanders down 3rd, and tries Lexington next. It is going from bad to worse. We are virtually at a standstill much of the time. We end up on Madison Avenue somewhere in the 40s and it suddenly dawns on me that he never heard me say we were going to Madison Street, not Madison Avenue, which I had said very clearly.

I point this out, reminding him that I said we had to go to lower Manhattan by the police headquarters, near the Brooklyn Bridge. Now he begins to wander all over town. We said hello to Galen's old dorm, and my daughter's old dorm at NYU, to Galen's college, to the pediatric dentist's office, to one of Galen's therapist's office, to a variety of stores, including the now shuttered Pearl Paint. Every single turn he made was the wrong decision. His judgment was always wrong. Unbelievably, he decided to turn south on 5th Avenue around 20th Street. I almost said, wait, we're going to run right into Washington Square Park, but at that point I realized this dude was channeling Sam and I should just sit back and enjoy the ride. If my kids had been with me, or anyone else who knew Sam well, we would have laughed so hard we wouldn't have been able to stop. I was almost hysterical all by myself.

Sam actually was better than this at directions (he would never have turned south on 5th Avenue at 20th), but he would go to ridiculous extremes while driving to avoid waiting in traffic. A Swedish au pair had a virtually uncontrollable fit of laughter one summer night as we got off highway 80 just before the George Washington Bridge and wandered all over northern New Jersey looking for a traffic-less way of getting to the Bridge. It took far longer than just waiting would have. Also, just like Sam, this guy was getting madder and madder by the moment, and was positively fuming by the time we got where we were going.

All the way down to Canal Street, every turn that would have put us in the right direction was not accessible, and finally, steaming with rage, he just crosses Canal all the way over to the West Side Highway, pointing out as we arrived that he was right - there was a lot of traffic. The "traffic" turned out to be a simple red light, and after the light changed we moved effortlessly along. Did he say "I was wrong?" Of course not! (I never heard that out of Sam either regarding his driving misadventures.) Nor did I say I was right, remembering that it is better to be kind than right. He did tell me at one point that I should have taken the subway - in other words, it was all my fault. I got a wonderful view of the harbor, which I enjoyed immensely, and five minutes later we were at the funeral home. It took an hour and a half total, for what would otherwise – on a Saturday morning – have been a 30-minute trip.

The adventure of Sam-channeling wasn't quite finished. The funeral home was its own version of Sam's apartment: dirty, musty, tired, and smelly. However, at least there weren't any pizza boxes lying around or any piles of trash stacked up a couple of feet high. The "chapel" had a huge statue of Our Lady with Baby Jesus that was chipped and cracked, and seriously needed dusting and painting. There were creepy old cracked burgundy/brown (Sam's favorite sweater color) leather chairs for the family of the deceased, and for the rest of the expected crowd, a flea market assortment of awful folding and metal convention-type chairs, none inviting or even very clean. At least the bathroom was clean, if smelly.

I arranged for the cremation, and not wishing for a repeat of my earlier travel experience, I asked the funeral parlor people for exact public transportation directions and took the bus home.

We decided to have a private ceremony scattering Sam's ashes. But first we had to decide where to go. I had some ideas that because he had fallen to his death from the roof of his building, it might be appropriate to scatter them at the top of a waterfall. The twins and I headed over to a large river near our country home, and began to look for a spot. My younger son was convinced he had located the top of a big waterfall on his phone, so he began to drive there. The road seemed unused and got rougher and rougher, with weeds starting to grow in it. Soon we came to an end altogether where a large fallen tree blocked the way. As we turned around though, we realized there was a very beautiful small lake, a pond really, next to the road, and so we parked and walked over to it. Turns out, this was the biggest, best frog pond ever! It was quite literally stuffed full of all sorts of bullfrogs, green frogs, every kind of frog, tadpoles, and probably all sorts of wildlife that was less forthcoming about making its presence known. We realized that if we scattered Sam's ashes there, he could go on chasing frogs eternally. My son took note of the exact location on his phone, longitude and latitude, so we could find it when we want to go back to pay our respects in the future. We've talked about finding the pond again many times, but so far, we've never been back. It's all just so painful, and nobody wants to revisit any of it yet. We will one day. It is a lovely, peaceful little pond. Sam would have loved it.

A few months later, some of Sam's students wanted to present a Memorial Concert celebrating his life, and made all the arrangements, for which I am profoundly grateful. At the time, pre-occupied with problems with my oldest son Galen, I didn't have it in me to pull this off. The school where Sam taught had strict rules forbidding the use of the concert hall for memorial concerts for deceased faculty members, which rather horrified me ("we have a lot of older faculty and if we allowed everyone who dies to have a memorial here we'd be having them all the time"), but all students were allowed one recital in the concert hall per year, so one of Sam's old students booked the hall for his own recital and then graciously used the evening for his teacher's Memorial. That student's parents provided exceptionally delicious refreshments, a touching and lovely gesture, much appreciated by all of us, and especially by me.

Sam's students created a wonderful evening. I am very grateful to every single one of them. It was a beautiful Memorial, with live performances of Sam's friends and students interspersed with recordings of Sam and reminiscences of friends and family. There was a video of Sam playing his last recital at the school, in the same hall, so he was visually a part of it all too.

Not surprisingly, the turnout wasn't huge, maybe fifty people, and my daughter remarked that if her father hadn't been so mentally ill for so long and if he hadn't died the way he did there would have been hundreds of people there. No doubt she was right.

CHAPTER 4

Galen, early signs of trouble

I've heard people say that the strongest love on earth is a mother's love for her first child. I'm not sure I agree, because I certainly loved my other children just as much, and my husband, and other people too. But there is no question that I fell helplessly, hopelessly in love with Galen from the minute he was born. In every way, he was an absolute joy.

Looking back, I realize there were signs of difficulty on the horizon even before Galen was born. He was incredibly active in utero, literally making the keys go down when I would play the piano. Watching him move around in my stomach was something to behold. Some bipolar experts describe this extreme pre-birth activity as the first indication of the disease. As a first-time mom, I had no idea this much wiggling around was unusual. Later, pregnant with twins, I was shocked to realize that the two of them together did not kick even half as much as Galen did all by himself.

He also refused to be born, and I was finally induced as I went into the 43rd week. Having grown to nearly 10 lbs., he was too big to push out (believe me, I tried) and so he was born by C-section. Even at birth, he was exhibiting the trait that has caused him and the rest of us so much trouble - refusing to do what he needed to do, when he needed to do it!

As a baby and as a toddler he was very active, and impossible to soothe or quiet down. I got breast infections because he would get distracted when breast feeding and relentlessly squirm after whatever had snagged his attention, forgetting to detach. Ouch!! He skipped crawling, mostly, (which I later learned in my Feldenkrais studies is not beneficial for a child's developing brain) and he got up and ran, fast, as soon as he could, tearing around the house or playground at an unbelievable speed. Later, timed at school, he ran a 7-minute mile at the age of 7! Of course, this reckless careening around meant he crashed into things or people a lot, and trips to the pediatrician to assess the seriousness of the latest bruise or "eggie" on his head were routine. He also spoke very early, beginning at nine months, and developed a huge vocabulary very quickly. He would speak so fast that he slurred his words and his pediatrician suggested speech therapy. We pursued this for several years, but I don't believe it helped much.

In spite of his intensity and the challenges of being a mother to such an energetic child, he was the most beautiful and amazing little guy, a joy to be around from morning until night. No mother ever loved a child more than I loved that little fellow. His sheer joy at being alive, his passion for all the animals around him, and his immense curiosity were just awesome. We devised a way to explore the park outside our door that wouldn't utterly exhaust me. I'd push the stroller, loaded up with drinks and snacks, and he would run constantly, but only go as far as I could still see him, then circle on back and do it all over again. His energy was unbelievable.

Galen loved birds. He discovered that if he piled birdseed on his head and arms, and stood very still, birds would land on him to get the seeds. That way, he could watch them up close. Life with him was fun and a constant thrill and we sang and danced and ran our way through our days. He loved any adventure we could come up with, and NYC is a huge playground with so many things to explore. We practically lived at the American Museum of Natural History, and he learned his first letters by tracing with his fingers the raised wooden letters that spelled the animal's names in the galleries. I even pulled my best-ever con, convincing him that FAO Schwartz, the over-the-top toy store on 5th Avenue was a "toy museum", where we could play with everything all day long, but that nothing was for sale. As a snowy day activity, a trip there couldn't be beat! If there was an unusual bug or bird or cloud or plant nearby, he would spot it. Through his eyes I saw things I would never have noticed on my own. Who wouldn't enjoy having a child like that?

He loved noisy fire engines and ambulances, calling them wee-ohs, from the sound they make. Once, at a carnival, the firemen were offering kids short rides, and Galen climbed on board and asked if he could pull the cord for the horn. They agreed, and must have regretted this immensely, because he wouldn't stop from the moment they left until they returned. You could hear it blocks away.

With his boundless energy, he climbed everything in sight, including onto the roof of our country house and the tops of big trees, as well as all the playground equipment, including the parts that kids weren't supposed to climb. He ended up in the ER a couple of times with a split open chin or other big cut from falling from one of his adventurous climbs. It's amazing he never broke any bones.

He did break his clothes, though. Parents usually get clothing for their small kids a size or two bigger so that they can wear them for a longer period of time. For Galen this strategy was useless. He could go through the knees of any pants in a matter of days, or a week or two at most, creating an ongoing need for patches I sometimes layered five or six thick. Shoes never lasted more than a couple of months as he would quite literally wear them out to the point they would begin to fall apart. Around the age of three he decided he didn't like shoes at all, and refused to wear them. There was no way I could let him careen around the parks in NYC without shoes (too much broken glass and too many other unsavory items he might have stepped on), so we had a standoff about going to the park that went on for weeks. He'd want to go out, and I'd say he had to put his shoes on, and he'd refuse, and we'd go around and around. Sometimes I'd strap him in the stroller and walk to the park, dangling the shoes in front of him. Eventually he got tired of this particular game and put his shoes on.

But then, after all the fun, after all the non-stop singing and dancing and climbing and running around, it was time to begin school, and this became a bit of a problem.

Nursery school was a disaster. He began at a small program for a few hours a week at a local school a block from our apartment, but he would not or could not follow simple instructions such as sit on his blanket at nap time. (Forget sleeping, that was never going to happen.) Eventually he refused to go. And when he refuses to do something, there is no force on earth than can make him do it. This was a harbinger of things to come, but of course, I didn't know it at the time. I went with the flow and took him to another program on the other side of town, where children attended with their mothers, the kids running around and playing on the basketball court, and the mothers chatting in the kitchen. He was very happy there and I took him faithfully for a couple of years. Eventually, when they were old enough, the twins joined us. We all enjoyed it immensely.

He began regular school at a public school in a pre-k half-day program. He was a handful, and we were not confident that he would do well in kindergarten at the same school, due to the huge increase in class size (from 15 kids in pre-K to more than 30 in K). I felt that in a large classroom he'd get into trouble constantly, surely with regular trips to the principal's office. We began to consider other options. I even considered home schooling him, but I thought that would just avoid facing the very things he found so difficult about being in school, so decided against it.

About this time, my father died. He left more money than any of us expected, but in addition to being pleasantly surprised, we quickly realized he had not prepared any of us for managing his numerous businesses or even minimally educated us about a variety of ongoing associated problems. Our lack of knowledge and preparation created a long complex family situation, stretched out over more than ten years, a whole separate story on its own. As busy as I was with my family and career, I plunged into helping my mother, to whom most of the burden fell. Without going into endless detail, especially about the two lawsuits that came about in the middle of it all, this went on for many years until it was all resolved. We came out fine. Nevertheless, I'm not going to deny the whole experience was expensive, complicated, and aggravating, and one more source of stress to contend with.

To digress for a moment, I'd like to point out that our family's experience with these estate issues is yet another example of how money does not automatically buy you happiness. One might expect that additional revenue will reduce your life's angst and stresses, and I am not saying that finding your bank account bigger than it had ever been, by far, isn't a boon, or that I was not immensely grateful for it. But it isn't that simple. Managing a sudden influx of income, as well as a number of commercial real estate properties, some with major contamination issues, has quite a few of its own time-consuming problems. Especially when the inheritance itself, and how to manage it, deal with it, and divide it becomes a source of contention within the family.

In addition to the money I had inherited myself, my kind and generous mother set up some trusts for my kids. So we now had enough money to send Galen to a private school, with smaller classes where he'd get more individual attention. In spite of all the extra work that was involved with my father's estate, and the emotional misery I experienced from watching my family fight over it (and witnessing my mother's sorrow about all the infighting), I cannot overstate the difference this extra money made in our lives. I honestly don't know what I would have done to take care of my family without it, as I fought my way through the many crises that occurred in the years to follow. And though I always worked, with Sam falling apart and eventually not working at all, I don't know how we would have made it had the inheritances not materialized. Whatever you want to say about dealing with difficult family situations, including mental health care, the plain truth is that it all can be very expensive. It's already hard enough to raise a child like Galen, or cope with a mentally ill spouse, but not having enough money to get through life's basics or pay for doctors and treatments would have made things impossibly difficult. I will be eternally grateful to my father for making astute real estate and stock market investments all his life, as well as for the savings he so relentlessly socked away. And my mother was a marvel. She could legitimately, legally, have kept for herself all the money and property my father left to her, but she chose to share her unexpected bounty with her whole family. Just when my family needed it most, she gave me and my kids much-appreciated financial stability.

Of course, no 5-year-old has any comprehension of how exhausted the hours spent on the telephone, discussing complex estate situations, made his mother. And it was actually rather refreshing for me that during all of this, Galen maintained his intense passion and love of the natural world, especially birds, until he became (without exaggeration) an expert on birds found in the northeast, with a special fascination for hawks and owls. He also read voraciously about the birds he saw in the wild and at the Central Park Zoo birdhouse, and he loved the bird exhibits at the Museum of Natural History, especially the ones with hawks and other raptors. The whole family got involved in going on nature walks and bird-watching outings every week, which were wonderful and healthy activities for all of us. For his 6th birthday party, I arranged for a Central Park Ranger to take him and his classmates on a nature walk in Central Park, followed by cake served in the Ranger's Headquarters. Afterwards, the Head Ranger told me he didn't have a single Ranger on his staff who could match Galen's knowledge of Central Park's birds and wildlife.

If they lived on our country property, no creatures were safe from being picked up by Galen. At one time he had about seventy creatures in different aquaria in his room, including frogs, snakes, and salamanders. He even wore one of his snakes, Ribbon (a garter snake) around his neck like a necklace. Among my proudest maternal accomplishments was giving Ribbon a series of antibiotic shots in an unsuccessful attempt to try to save his life when he developed sepsis following a break in his tail. That was an adventure.

Galen stood side by side with the professional bird watchers at Hawk Mountain in Pennsylvania, where migratory birds are tracked and counted, and those professionals had nothing but respect for his keen visual ability to accurately spot migrating birds, usually before they did. On one nature walk with a naturalist friend who had just written the "definitive" book on local wildlife, our friend described a certain salamander that he expected to reside in the area, though he had never found one. Galen said he found them all the time, walked over to some rocks, overturned a few, and produced four of them. Another bird expert we befriended had been involved with an effort to catalogue all the covered bridges in the Northeast, and he made a pronouncement that there were no covered bridges near our country house. Galen said there was one over a certain hill where he had gone to look for frogs, and though the covered bridge wasn't visible from any modern roads, there it was, just where Galen said it was. In fact, there were two!

We added birdhouses around our property, and worked to meet all the criteria to have our property declared an official National Wildlife Refuge. This meant we had to have the required documented amounts of groundcover, fallen trees, birdhouses, bushes and plants for attracting butterflies and bees, and so forth. When they sent us a lovely wooden plaque to display, Galen did so with great pride. He learned birdcalls, and astonishingly, learned to call down and "converse" with the barred owl that he hoped would live in the house we had put up. And what would he ask for as gifts for his birthday? Owl pellets, so that he could dissect them and see what little creatures the owl had eaten. In general, life at our Pennsylvania house was a gift for this child, except possibly for the endless poison ivy rashes acquired from crawling around looking for frogs. And, as I said before, the immense problem of Lyme disease, which I am convinced he picked up during his jaunts through the woods.

These were magical years, with much joy and pleasure along with the hard work of parenting a child with so much intensity and so much drive. Life with him wasn't easy, or relaxing, but it was a lot of fun. Just being in nature with him was eye-opening, as he saw so many things that most of us would never notice. Being his mom was a genuine gift and I enjoyed it immensely. I am very grateful he was my son.

Some doctors suggest that anyone who can present with an interest so deeply at such a young age might have signs of Asperger's syndrome, a neurological condition, which is considered a high-functioning type of autism. Here's a description of the condition found in Psychology Today at www.psychologytoday.com/us/basics/aspergers-symdrome:

> "..people with Asperger's have difficulties in social functioning and experience various communication problems. They often lack the ability to understand nonverbal signals and are poor at deciphering body language. They might fail to develop peer relationships and may be singled out by other kids as "weird" or strange. Because they lack the ability to understand the perspective of others, they often do not return social feelings or share in the happiness or distress of others. People with Asperger's often function best with rigid routines and rituals. <u>They are often intensely preoccupied with a narrow area of interest, sometimes to the point of obsessiveness.</u> And like those with full-blown autism, they engage in repetitive behaviors like finger twisting and even self-injurious practices."

I'm not convinced it is a good use of anyone's time to go into a long discussion of Galen's endless problems with school, so I'll mention only a few of the most relevant details. It is a very unhappy saga in a way, because he was clearly so smart and yet so incapable of adapting to any one school for more than 4 or 5 years. I am told this is typical of children with psychiatric issues, but even if that is true, Sam and I took a lot of flak for moving him around to different schools every few years. All I can say in retrospect is that we made the best decisions we could at the time. As I look back over those decisions, I can't figure out anything else that we might have done differently or might have done better.

But still, the bottom line is that this delightful, intelligent, and personable child attended 5 different schools from K through high school, not counting pre-K. Except for his high school, none of them seemed to know what to do with him, or how to deal with some of his learning issues along with the hints of psychiatric problems yet to come. I don't blame them at all. I didn't know what to do either, so I just kept flailing along, supporting him the best I could, and recognizing that it would be a dead end to let him continue in a school situation which was obviously not working for him.

The whole school journey was also emotionally wrenching for me as his mother. I always loved school. The terrific schools Galen attended were schools I'd have been overjoyed and thrilled to have attended myself, especially when I compared them to my years in a strict, all-girls parochial school. Perhaps in rebellion to the nun's rules, I was attracted to the idea of sending my kids to progressive schools. The problem is, this didn't take into consideration that the issues with Galen were about mental health. As I wasn't aware of this or educated to look for it, mental health never factored in the decisions. At the progressive school he attended for K, with its enormous emphasis on art, music, play, and creativity, he loved school passionately, and thrived, and he could hardly wait to get there in the morning. Until he didn't.

The school had two buildings. One housed the lower grades, the other grades 2 and up. Unfortunately, the second building was designed with open classrooms, where all children were able to hear and see each other. For a kid like Galen with possible ADD-related issues, this was a disaster, and after a few months there he became school phobic, refusing to go anymore, and getting a migraine or throwing up if we tried to get him to school.

After months of therapy appointments and consultations with professionals, the decision was made to give Galen his wish, so frequently and vehemently expressed, of going back to his beloved first grade teacher at the other building. At least he was back in school. Galen, however, has never forgiven his parents for making this decision, because it made him perpetually a year older than all his other classmates, which made him feel awkward and different for the rest of his education. To this day he says we should have "made" him go to school with his original grade. Right. Just like I should "make" him get some psychiatric treatment now. When Galen resists, and says "no", no one can budge him.

At this point, both Sam and I were beginning to recognize we had a big problem with our oldest, and a lifetime of angst, concern and confusion began. It's hard to describe what it feels like when the scales begin to fall from your eyes and you begin to see that all the brilliance and promise of one of your children might be compromised, due to a problem you don't really understand. Even at this time, there were a lot of sleepless nights, a lot of worry, and an ongoing state of confusion. If I had imagined even a few of the events that would eventually actually happen, I would probably have flipped out myself.

Sam knew someone with strong connections to a school for boys, who put in a good word in our favor. Galen went there for a second try at 2nd grade. In a school filled with many rambunctious boys, with plenty of gym time, he thrived and did very well. He won some prizes (the Public Speaking Award and the Good Citizenship Prize) and loved it there wholeheartedly. He couldn't wait to leave home for school every morning. Being in a school for boys was great for Galen, and he was very happy there.

Until he wasn't.

Everything changed in 4th grade. Suddenly, there was a big cutback in gym and recess time. Galen developed severe migraine headaches with an alarming frequency, even several times per week, and they were severe enough to require medication. Galen's migraine headaches were not minor affairs, but truly debilitating events that completely flattened him, involving days of vomiting, seeing auras (blue and purple circles and orange and red triangles, so he said), physical pain and malaise. Even when they went away, he would not feel well for days. It is interesting that as he has become more mentally ill, he claims he has fewer migraines.

As it was obvious Galen was a very physical and energetic kid who could do well in school only if he could burn off steam running around in recess or playing sports, we began a search for a school with more gym and outdoor time, and we found just such a school in the Bronx. This school also had an outstanding music and art program, and during his years there, Galen took full advantage of the program. In addition to continuing piano and cello lessons, he studied guitar, eventually attaining some level of musicianship with the instrument, and formed a band with friends. By 8th grade he was also playing the cello in the school orchestra. He played sports in all seasons, lacrosse being his favorite.

Galen thrived at this school for 4 years, until the school geared up its academic expectations and homework loads, to prepare students for high school. It is worth noting that in 6th grade Galen had the highest marks in the entire grade in math, which makes his unhappy future with algebra all the more peculiar.

Once again, he thrived in this school, and was very happy there. Until he wasn't.

In 7th and 8th grades, the school insisted he take advanced science classes, which they felt he could handle given his intelligence and his passionate interest in nature and science. However, they were classes for which he did not have the necessary organizational skills. At a back to school night at this school, parents were invited to attend mini classes with all their child's teachers. After several dozen parents had sat through the science teacher's mini class, we all commented afterwards that the little class she'd given us was far too technically advanced for us. Not only did we fail to comprehend a single thing she said, but as one father put it, the only words she uttered that he knew he understood for sure were "and" and "the". This science teacher's advanced students, including middle schoolers, had participated in creating research papers under her guidance that had actually been published. Unfortunately, this kind of pressure under a driven teacher, who oriented her class towards the very disciplined, wasn't going to work for Galen.

To top it all off, he ended up failing algebra in 8th grade which was the kiss of death for his emotional well-being. And, as if all this weren't enough for an anxious and troubled young man, there was yet another looming problem. Galen had been placed in a Study Skills class in 7th grade, after an educational/psychological evaluation diagnosed him with Executive Dysfunction Learning Disability, but this class was scheduled in the time slot allotted for a language class, so studying a language was delayed for a couple of years.

And thus, after failing algebra, he was going to have to repeat it in classes with much younger students, and due to his placement in Study Skills and delaying the study of a language, he would also wind up in a beginning language class with much younger kids. He was mortified, as he was already a year older than his classmates.

As if all that weren't enough, he would not have the assistance and support of the learning specialists in Study Skills any longer. At this particular school, they didn't make learning support available after middle school, a potential disaster for Galen once high school began. During 8th grade, I supplemented his schoolwork with tutors to help him, but even that didn't seem to be enough to pull him through, as he fell further and further behind. For the first time, out of desperation and with great reluctance on my part (and Galen's) he tried ADD meds, Adderall as I remember, which was an awful experience. He told me that the only good thing about those meds was that now he could listen to the teacher at the same time he watched the birds outside the window.

The psychiatrist he was seeing began to suspect he was bipolar in addition to having ADD, and wanted to try new meds. This doctor told us that one of the diagnostic tools for bipolar illness is the effectiveness of ADD medication: Does it work, or makes everything worse? For Galen, it made everything worse.

At the end of 8th grade, Galen got some new bipolar medication, but it had some serious potential side effects associated with it. I was told to watch carefully for itching and rashes, as this might indicate the beginning of a dangerous reaction. Wouldn't you know that Galen came home one day itching furiously. I followed my instructions and took him immediately to his pediatrician. When the doctor diagnosed a common childhood problem - head lice - I started laughing and practically jumped for joy. The doctor said he'd never had a mother react in that way, as though a diagnosis of head lice was good news! But in Galen's case, in spite of all the laundry and extra work in ridding a household of lice, it was wonderful news.

During the summer between 8th and 9th grades, Galen fell apart completely. We tried extra therapy, some tutoring (to prepare him or the algebra he had to face again), and made sure he got plenty of time to blow off steam running around outside.

The first day of high school came, and he put his foot down and refused to go. The school didn't know what do, and they weren't interested in dealing with the problem; when I asked to withdraw him, they refunded his entire tuition overnight, without question.

Now we had to figure out what to do about school, after the school year had begun. A friend of mine, an educational consultant, came up with a wonderful idea to request a teacher from the NYC Board of Education who would educate him at home until treatment for his psychological issues might settle him down and we found another school. We did a considerable amount of running around and finally we had a teacher lined up and ready to come to our home to teach Galen by the beginning of December.

Meanwhile, Galen began spending more and more time in his room, like the Japanese Hikikomori - young men who never leave their rooms.

*"A **hikikomori** is defined by the Health, Labor and Welfare Ministry of Japan as someone who has remained isolated at home for at least six consecutive months without going to school*

or work, and rarely interacts with people from outside their own immediate family." **Hikikomori** *— Japan's missing million*

Galen remained in his room, all day and all night, except to use the bathroom or grab something from the fridge.

At the point he refused to come out of his room to see the special teacher the school board provided or meet with anyone else, including his doctors, we knew we had to take some form of action.

I have to be honest here. I said "we" had to take some action, but in truth Sam was getting sicker and sicker, and waffling about making any decisions at all, especially the sorts of decisions we faced here. Sam never could set and keep clear boundaries, due both to Galen's argumentative personality, as well as his own declining state. Mentally ill and confused himself, he just didn't have the ability to take any necessary steps forward, for his own sake or Galen's.

I decided to send Galen to a wilderness program upstate, selected because my friend Jane had just sent her daughter there under similar circumstances. I felt confident about the program because Jane had spent hours telling me how much it helped her daughter. She assuaged my fears by telling me in great detail what went on in this program, and how much her daughter improved after leaving it. Galen was there for about two and a half months. I believe he resents me for sending him there to this day, mostly because I hired professional transporters to get him up there. But in retrospect, I felt I had no choice, as he could not go on living in his room, refusing to ever leave, refusing all help.

After the wilderness program, I once again had to decide what to do about school. It was clear he needed a specialized school, one that dealt with learning issues and addressed emotional problems. None of us, neither Sam, myself, nor our friends, knew of such a school in New York City, primarily because the ones that might have worked had no real sports or outdoor activities. We considered moving to the suburbs for public schools, but again, such schools are not generally equipped to deal with a kid like Galen. I recognized

I was going to have to send him to a therapeutic boarding school. I hired an educational consultant, as I had no clue which schools to look at or even what they were, and after Sam and I drove all over New England in the middle of a winter blizzard looking at a few schools (with the twins, who insisted on being part of selecting a school for their brother), we picked one as a family (minus Galen, who was still in the wilderness program), with the rest of us all agreeing. It turned out that, again, we were following the lead of my friend Jane who had also sent her daughter to the same school after the wilderness program.

The school also had a terrific guitar program with several stellar instructors, and with Galen's natural abilities and talent, the potential benefits to him were obvious. Indeed, his musicianship and guitar skills grew tremendously. The kids gave concerts from time to time and Sam and I would drive up to hear them. I'd glance away from the performers on stage, looking around the room, trying to soak up everything that I could about the experience Galen was having in this school, and then I'd hear a few bars of some truly outstanding guitar playing coming from the stage. And when I glanced back over to the stage to see who the superb player was, it was always Galen. In many good ways, along with the not-so-good ones, he is truly his father's son.

There were some good things about the school, but there were also some strange things: such as, the fact that they didn't require kids to go to class. This was unacceptable to me. (Somehow, they didn't explain that on the tour.) And the school itself was in financial trouble (which we were also not told). I decided to take Galen out of the school six months after he got there, so he could begin the fall term at a new school, and the school closed a few months later.

I needed to find yet another school. Eventually I picked a school in Connecticut, in part because the school had the best high school bird-banding program in the US and we hoped it may re-ignite Galen's interest in birds. (It didn't, and he refused to participate.) They also had a great music program, which he did join to some extent. I should point out that when this school accepted him, they did so on two conditions: that he would see a local therapist on a weekly basis and that he would continue taking medication prescribed by his psychiatrist. Many of the students at this school took medication, and they'd all line up in the morning to get what they needed from the nurse's office. This was possible, obviously, because they were all under 18, and many, like Galen, were there on the condition they take their medication and get some therapy.

A New York attorney also helped me get some funding from the NYC Board of Education, funding they cancelled when Galen refused to attend his special Study Skills classes. He needed the classes, but true to form, simply refused to go. When the funding was cancelled, he said he wished he had known that this would happen if he refused to attend the classes. Still, at a school specifically geared to deal with learning differences, even without Study Skills, he did very well.

In fact, Galen thrived at this school, where he won a special prize at graduation as the senior "who has made the most progress in all areas of life at the school." He was very active in a number of sports, in all seasons, but his favorite was lacrosse and he served as co-captain of the lacrosse team. He made good use of the gym and the weight room every single day and when he left the school he was very physically fit, in truly excellent condition. He was an RA in the dorms, and was described to me as the "go-to" RA when there was any problem at all, but especially when boys were on the verge of a fight, as he could break up disagreements skillfully. He always said he wanted to become a lawyer, and it was apparent he had great skills at getting people on the same page. He graduated with a 3.2 GPA.

To me, his high school years are a perfect example of how well Galen can do when his life is supported with therapy and medication. It is a great pity he doesn't see this himself. It is more than a pity. It is tragic.

During these high school years, I began to feel that all the difficulties with Galen might gradually diminish. I had lived on pins and needles for years, scared witless that this amazing son would never be able to pull himself together and arrive at a level of maturity allowing him to function in the world. During his time at the Connecticut school, I could allow myself to have real hope for his future. Considering what was to come, and the issues I soon had to face with Sam, it was lovely to have this little break.

He won scholarships to several colleges and picked a small college upstate. He also received several offers of full, 4-year ROTC scholarships. ROTC was his idea, and he had actively sought and applied for it, but ultimately decided against it. In particular, he liked a program in Maryland and we spent a weekend there so he could explore whether he wanted to accept their offer. I think he knew ROTC was not for him, because the military is not going to be a happy place for someone who doesn't want to follow rules or do what he is told to do.

Galen lasted one year at the college upstate. Now that he was over 18 and had attained legal age, nobody could insist he take medication or see therapists. And that's just what happened, as he stopped taking meds and stopped going to therapists, though occasionally he would drive up to Connecticut to see his old high school therapist. His grades tanked. He dropped lacrosse and stopped playing sports. One of his teachers took him under his wing and basically tutored him through the entire year. In the end, though, he decided he wanted to transfer to the university in New York City where his father taught. I agreed, but on the condition that he live in the dorm and not expect to live at home.

Galen agreed to this. Because his father was on the faculty and had taught there so long, Galen could attend tuition free. Sadly, a year later, Sam quit working altogether, and so Galen was no longer eligible for free tuition as a child of a faculty member.

When Galen first returned to NY he held various part time jobs - as a bar back, as a lifeguard (he'd gotten certified at the first college), and as a busboy in restaurants. However, as he got sicker, he was no longer capable of working or holding down a job. Every boss wants to be in charge, reasonably so, and more and more frequently Galen couldn't endure following instructions or doing what he was asked. The excellent lifeguard job, at a basement pool in an upscale condo, went up in smoke because Galen didn't like the shift hours they gave him. As the newest hire, he was asked to take the hours nobody else really wanted, which were very early in the morning (5-8 am, as I recall), and this meant Galen was often alone at the pool waiting for pre-work swimmers to show up. Being alone at this pool at such early hours made him very anxious, and he hated it, so he quit. The bus boy job meant taking endless orders from the staff, because once again, he was the low man on the totem pole. He found this intolerable, would fly into a rage, and quit before they fired him.

Now back in NY, it was evident that he would need tutoring help to get through his course work. His executive dysfunction learning disability was getting in the way of his studies. He worked with a marvelous therapist he knew since high school and a learning specialist she recommended. He also used several really great tutors and sometimes even one of my friends. Still, it was evident that without therapy and meds, he was getting sicker and sicker.

At one point, he began to think he'd be happier going to school out west. I thought the idea was nuts, but it is my practice to let my kids take their ideas and run with them. I decided to let him go look at several universities. He actually got himself admitted to several of them, but balked at transferring when he realized that the course demands were more rigorous than those at his university here in NYC. He also did something else on that trip that boggled my mind.

One of the universities asked him if he was up to date on his vaccinations. Unbelievably, he told them he'd never had any vaccinations. His pediatrician taught in one of the city's medical schools, so as anyone might imagine, he had received the full complement of standard vaccines. Instead of calling the doctor's office to inquire about his vaccination history, or calling me, Galen allowed the health services office at this university to give him all, yes, ALL, the vaccines, all over again, all at once. He was very sick for several days.

It's hard to remember when it began to dawn on me the desperation of this young man's illness. I admit I couldn't understand why he stopped taking care of himself in practical ways. Given how things were going, I knew he should have some therapeutic help, and was willing to provide this anyway I could, including helping him get up to Connecticut to see his old therapist. But as I have stressed, you just can't make Galen do anything if he doesn't want to do it. Conversely, if he wants to do something, nothing will stop him.

The process of surrendering to the inevitable is truly awful, and I don't think I could begin to describe it. It's like a slow steady drip of worry and unhappy feelings, some of them so vague they are almost beneath the radar of perception, a dripping that initially seems inconsequential, until over time you realize it created a Grand Canyon in your soul. Emotions of this type are like an acid eating through all sorts of defensive layers and uncovering more buried feelings underneath them. A willingness to let this happen is helpful, but surrendering has been hard. In truth, I railed against this the whole way, as loudly as I could.

And then there's the anger. It is beyond infuriating to witness one's child toss away all reasonable opportunities, and spiral downward, due in part to illness but also to obstinate refusal to accept help. It is beyond infuriating to watch them do absolutely nothing about it at all, despite the obviousness of their own self destruction, despite your constant pleading that they wake up and realize they are letting themselves sink into ruin.

A wise person I know contends that all our problems dealing with others can be traced to our having standards and expectations for their behavior. If they do not meet our standards and expectations, we become upset. The trick of course is to lose the standards and expectations and live in a more neutral place, but that is really tough when dealing with one's own children. We do expect them to grow up into healthy functioning people and we also have standards about how they might best behave.

One spring night Galen called me from his college dorm sounding especially crazy and spoke about killing himself, and I feared he was serious. For a mother, this sort of call is absolutely terrifying. Previously, a psychiatrist he had seen a few times had advised me to call 911 anytime I was really worried about him, and ask the police to go pick him up and take him to a hospital. I called 911 after I got Galen's call at about 2 AM and asked the police to go to his dorm and take him to the hospital. The cops went to get him, and Galen turned on his considerable charm, convincing them that his mother really had a control problem and that he was fine. The cops left him at school. Then they called me to report they didn't think Galen had a problem, and in fact made it clear they weren't thrilled to have me calling them at such an hour and that I shouldn't bother them anymore. I suppose there are people who might call the police at such an hour just on a whim, but I really didn't appreciate their complete lack of support for my concern over my son.

Sadly, less than 12 hours later, Galen was treated at a hospital following a suicide attempt. He had swallowed half a bottle of Advil and checked himself in to the hospital's ER when he became very sick. Galen told the hospital not to tell me where he was, but one of the doctors called me anyway, telling me he felt any mother had the right to know when her son was in the hospital.

Now all my worries and fear were taking concrete shape. My child was so mentally ill he was suicidal. And there was nothing whatsoever that I could do about it. What a horrible realization.

CHAPTER 5

Galen and psychosis

In May of 2012 Galen spent a couple of weeks in the hospital after he had checked himself into the ER following a suicide attempt. As he stubbornly resisted taking the medication the attending psychiatrist felt he needed, they transferred him to a mental health facility. He remained at that facility for a month.

From a conversation with one of his doctors, I learned that in New York State if two attending psychiatrists independently believe further hospitalization is required, they can go to court to have a judge decide whether or not to order more treatment. The judge has the right to overrule the psychiatrists, but usually agrees with them, as these court hearings take into account the rights of the community as well as the patient. These court hearings can also be used for a court order for medication.

So not surprisingly, during Galen's stay at this hospital there was a trip to court (the court room, wood paneling and all, was located in another hospital) for an order to remain hospitalized and eventually another trip to the same court for an order for medication. I had to appear, ready to testify if needed, which thankfully I never had to do, as the psychiatrist told me he'd avoid having me testify if at all possible.

While Galen was hospitalized, there were also several instances where he had to be forcefully held down and sedated due to his extreme behavior on the ward. Remarkably, on one occasion he called 911 from the ward demanding transfer to another hospital. When the EMS crew arrived, there was quite a scene, I was told.

He also accused the social worker of trying to seduce him, and told the psychiatrist there that he always knew what everyone was thinking. We had a lengthy discussion as to whether this meant schizophrenia (hearing voices), as there is a rather delicate difference between hearing voices and knowing what people are thinking. There had been an earlier incident, relayed to me by a friend, in which voices told him that he had to pee in his pants on the subway or they'd hurt him, so he peed in his pants.

Desperation is not too strong a word to use about my feelings at this time. I felt like I was moving through life with my body encased in lead, burdened down with heavy bags. I had a son I loved dearly and he'd tried to kill himself. And he was now in a mental hospital. Every day brought a new horror, with new reports from the psychiatrists. Sam was useless, too sick himself to be helpful in any way. In the hospital, patients could use a pay phone to call out. The phone only took quarters, so when I went to visit him, I'd bring a few quarters. Sam always gave in to whatever Galen wanted, and brought him dozens of quarters, which enabled Galen to make a constant stream of ridiculous phone calls to me, all begging me to get him out.

What an indescribable experience it is to visit your oldest child in a mental hospital. Who would ever have thought we'd end up there? Like everyone, I had some preconceived ideas of what such a place would look like, and though it was indeed a lockdown facility, with locked double doors to enter or leave, I was pleased that it was clean and the staff seemed very capable and interested in helping him. The only reason Galen was there as long as he was, in fact that he was there at all, was his refusal to take medication. Because of the court order for medication, the doctors could not release him until he complied with the court order.

The suicide attempt was a reaction to a breakup with a girlfriend. The breakup had occurred the previous fall, but Galen could not stop obsessing about her. He does not take "NO" for an answer from anyone. He wouldn't stop bothering her and stalking her, going over to her apartment at all kinds of crazy hours. The girl involved was 11 years older than he was, a heavy cocaine user, and possibly an alcoholic, though she was employed as an attorney. She may have had a restraining order against him as well.

During Galen's stay at this hospital, he continued to badger me relentlessly about "getting him out". Obviously, I had no power to do this, as he was there due to his suicide attempt and also because of his refusal to take medication, and I wouldn't have gotten him out anyway, because I (and his doctors) thought he desperately needed psychiatric care. But it is worth noting he has at times ascribed great powers to me, powers I simply don't have. His sister has said that it is almost as if he thinks I spend all my time organizing a nation-wide conspiracy against him.

But Galen finally got the message, and when he took some medication for a few days, the hospital let him go. They recommended appropriate after care, as they must by law, and found a place for him to go for treatment that was near his dorm. However, he never went and consistently refused to get any of the recommended follow up mental health care, or take the recommended medication. He wouldn't even take it with him and left it with me.

I tried to send him to a treatment program in late summer of 2012, which was less than two years before his father's passing. He would not go. His mental health was declining rapidly. But with his refusal to enter treatment, there were no good options except going back to college, and though I knew this was a poor, possibly disastrous choice, I couldn't find an alternative solution, and so back to school he went, in the fall. Being forced by circumstances to do something you know won't work, and may in fact end miserably, brings you down to another level of pain you never even knew existed. Perhaps the single most frustrating thing in dealing with someone with this level of deteriorating mental health is the lack of good options.

During Hurricane Sandy, he came home for a few days because his dorm had lost power and school was closed. This became an excruciatingly frightening and unpleasant experience, as he behaved badly and refused to leave when school reopened. I told him that I would continue to pay for tuition, a dorm room, and a meal card, but I would not give him extra cash unless he agreed to get some therapy.

During this fall semester, though he had a dorm room at college, he began coming to my apartment at all hours, in increasingly agitated and angry states, often at times that were not good for me as I work at home and see clients at home. I asked him to phone before he came, so we could find a mutually convenient time for his visit. He refused. I was also becoming afraid of him. His anger was intense, and I didn't feel safe in his presence. Sometimes he would show up with a cop demanding to be let in. I even joked that having Galen visit in the company of a police officer was the best way to have him in the house. Eventually I got tired of all the endless disruption to my life, and because I was afraid of him, I changed my locks.

Who knew it is illegal for a Mom to change her own locks?

Unbelievably, Galen took me to court, and even more unbelievably, he won, on the basis that changing my locks was an illegal lockout. He always said he wanted to be an attorney, and it appears he has some talent for it. I was ordered by the judge to give him keys to my apartment, which I did. I then started formal eviction proceedings, which were successful. No mother, no matter how much she loves her son, should be required to live with him when he is out of control and potentially dangerous, to the point it scares her to have him in the house.

When the hearing for the eviction occurred a few weeks later, the judge had said she'd render her verdict at the conclusion of the hearing. She asked me to speak first and all I said was that I loved my son dearly but was too afraid of him to continue to have him live in my home. Then Galen spoke. He began reasonably enough, sounding clear and sober, which was not surprising because he can often pull himself together for a few moments. Wisely, the judge let him continue to talk. By the time he finally finished nearly an hour later, he had said things that were so crazy and so frightening that the judge calmly said we'd be receiving her verdict by mail. There was no way that she was going to risk Galen's rage or any crazy actions by agreeing to the eviction on the spot.

What a pity that he had to push things to this extent, and what a stupid and foolish thing to do! Rather than respect reasonable boundaries set by his mother, he chose to go to war instead and ended up getting himself evicted from a lovely, large, rent-controlled apartment in a great neighborhood in New York City. Perhaps, for New Yorkers, that alone says volumes about his mental health. Rent-controlled apartments, unlike rent-stabilized apartments, can be inherited, (providing the inheriting family member can prove residence in the apartment for a period of time), and their low rents rise gradually following city guidelines. They are the best housing deal in the city, and my apartment is a gem.

This is typical of the struggles many of us have had with him. He will not accept an answer of NO from anyone, and has to conquer anybody who refuses to do what he wants. He will not even stop short of litigation, if he feels he can get his way. In fact, since then he has brought many frivolous legal actions against me. As I've said, he always wanted to be a lawyer and seems to have an aptitude for it. I've spent a lot of money, more than I'd like to think about, on lawyers in the past few years just to keep my boundaries firm and fend off his legal actions. It would be difficult to describe the wide range of emotions those ridiculous lawsuits stirred up in me. The whole experience felt like torture, endlessly cruel and sadistic, especially so since it was all being instigated by a son I loved so much. And it was so expensive to boot. To have to appear before any court and explain the awful things your son has done, or explain that you are too frightened of him to continue to live with him is both infuriating and aggravating.

In the second semester of his senior year he grew increasingly agitated and unstable. He saw the school therapist a few times, but he refused to continue treatment when it became evident he could not line the therapist up on his side as an ally to continue the battle with me on his behalf. Galen did not finish the semester, or his degree, simply leaving in May of 2013 just before final exams to run away. At that time, he was obsessed with living on the West Coast.

His professors extended deadlines and reduced their requirements for the completion of his degree. First, they changed his major from history to general studies so they could cancel the thesis he was supposed to write. Then they cancelled all back assignments, and asked him to write a short essay for each class within the next six months, take one online class to make up for the missing thesis credits, and he'd have his degree. They could not have been more understanding about his situation, or more willing to work with him. In fact, they were willing to bend over backwards to help him. Sadly, he was too ill to get anything done, so he has an incomplete degree. Should he ever return to it, getting that degree would not be difficult or time consuming.

Pushed to the edge of what I could endure, and utterly fed up with his antics, I applied for a Protective Order (PO) from Family Court, due to HUNDREDS of threatening emails, calls, and texts, which often continued without stopping day and night. I was truly afraid of my own son.

A few days later, on May 8, 2013 Galen showed up at my apartment in an unbelievably angry and out of control state, threatened me with kitchen knives, and asked me to use the knives to kill him. Though the judge had ruled I could evict him, his eviction was a lengthy process that was not yet complete, so he still had keys. And even though I had a temporary Protective Order from Family Court, Galen had not been served the papers yet, and the court hearing to make the PO permanent was still two weeks away.

Galen was screaming and yelling, and kicking over chairs, including the one I was sitting on (I jumped off quickly), as well as smashing his juice containers on the dining room table and the walls, staining the rug permanently. I reached for the phone to call 911, and he said that if I called the police he'd kill every policeman who showed up and anybody else he could as well. I later learned that preventing someone from calling 911 is a misdemeanor.

It is worth noting that his rage on this day concerned his perception that I wouldn't help Sam. As I have written, Sam had been hospitalized at around this time to participate in a clinical study for the treatment of chronic severe depression in older people. He was taking a new medication as well as undergoing shock therapy treatment, which horrified Galen, and he wanted me to get his father out of the hospital. Galen had not been present when Sam's doctors had explained to me that modern day shock therapy isn't like it once was, and with careful, sensitive use, can be very helpful for someone in Sam's condition. However, I recognize that the use of ECT is still horrifying to many, and I don't mean to address this subject lightly. I am fully aware of the negative feelings it stirs up in a lot of people. Still, as I've thought about the tragic way Sam's life ended, and how much his premature death cost him - not getting to watch his children grow up and graduate from college, from medical school, and from graduate school with a PhD, not attending their weddings, let alone not experiencing a possible renewal of his extraordinary teaching and playing - well, if it had been up to me personally, I would have taken the gamble. I would have risked it.

I thought Sam was exactly where he should be and I was not going to make any effort to get him out. Of course, I would not have had the power to do so anyway, something Galen could not comprehend. This enraged him. Ultimately, on that awful day, I got Galen to leave by giving him some cash and promising him that I'd see what I could do about his father. I would have promised him anything at all, just to get him out of the house so I could put the chain on the door.

Eventually, he persuaded his father to leave the hospital, against medical advice. Sadly, Sam had no further treatment for his depression/mood disorder, which directly contributed to his death a year later, on May 6 of 2014.

I filed a Complaint with the police the next day, and when I was filing the Complaint, I showed the police a photo of Galen. They said "That's your kid? He's here all the time asking us how he can make his mother do what he wants her to do. Lady, you have your hands full!" The police served him the papers for the Family Court PO that same day; I'm not sure exactly where.

A few days later, on Mother's Day, Galen came to my apartment again, which was now a violation of the Protective Order. I knew he'd never obey the PO - when had he ever obeyed any other rules? - and I fully expected him to show up, so the police and I agreed on what we'd do when he showed up. We put our plan into action. The police were called as soon as he knocked on the door, and I asked them to take Galen to a hospital for a 72-hour hold, rather than arresting him and taking him to jail.

Unbelievably, he was taken to the same hospital where his father was being treated in the experimental program. Both father and son were now at the same hospital at the same time, on different floors. Even stranger, due to HIPPA laws, their doctors could not confer. The admitting doctor in the ER told me: "The prognosis for this kid is very poor because he has no insight whatsoever into his condition. We can stabilize him, but eventually he will be released, and then he may very well hurt himself or someone else."

Even though Galen had been sent to a hospital, at my request, rather than being arrested for violating the Protective Order, this only delayed the arrest. After his release from the hospital he was arrested, and the judge issued another temporary Protective Order, this one through Criminal Court. After his release on his own recognizance, Galen made his way to Seattle, by bus I believe, where he took up residence in a homeless shelter. Eventually, a month later, a friend gave him ticket money to return to NY.

When he returned, the PO was issued by Family Court, as he had defaulted by not attending court on the hearing date, and when he went to the police to ask them to serve me notice of one of his legal ventures, the police served the Family Court PO. During the summer of 2014, there were a series of court days regarding the Family Court PO and his attempts to fight it. I also believe he went to Washington repeatedly during the summer, as I found many plane ticket charges on his father's credit cards after his father's death.

At some point in the fall he saw a therapist for a few sessions. Typically for him, he did not continue the therapy. When a therapist asks a tough question, or suggests medication, or Galen cannot rope him into believing everything he says, he runs away from treatment.

That Thanksgiving, Galen was hospitalized in Seattle. He was held in a psychiatric ward for 72 hours following an episode of running naked in SeaTac airport trying to get the cops to shoot him (suicide by cop). The doctors at the hospital thought he should remain in the hospital, but after a court hearing, he was released. A month later, he was held at another psychiatric hospital in Washington state after the police picked him up. He was driving his rented car erratically and had knives in his trunk.

When my other kids were home from college on their Holiday break, the police banged on our door at 4 AM one night. They had been sent by the police in Washington state to make sure we were all still alive, as Galen had said things to the Washington police that concerned them immensely. The police also came the next day for the same reason. During the first police visit, the mental hospital in Washington called me, and I asked my daughter to handle the police while I spoke with the doctors at the mental hospital. What an insane situation for a family to deal with at 4 am during Christmas vacation!

In the hospital in Washington, he was held first for 72 hours, and then for a 14-day Involuntary Commitment. There was a court hearing for this 14-day Involuntary Commitment, during which I was asked to testify by phone, which I did. During this hospitalization he was put on medication, I believe. I do not know which one.

When Galen was about to go to court for a hearing that would probably have resulted in a 90-day Involuntary Commitment at a large Washington State mental hospital, he instead signed a Voluntary 90 Day Commitment to avoid winding up at the state hospital. This 90 Day Voluntary Commitment allowed the hospital to transfer him to a treatment facility in Texas recommended to me by a consultant I had hired on the recommendation of one of Galen's former therapists. This particular program was known for its work with treatment resistant adults.

In January of 2014, Galen went to Texas. He agreed to remain and fulfill the Voluntary 90 Day Commitment that was agreed to in Washington. Shortly after he got to Texas, he had to be hospitalized again; he had been hiding his medication in his cheek and not swallowing it. I don't believe he ever took any medication again, maybe not even until the present time.

One night in January, I was awakened in the middle of the night by the fire department and an EMS squad. They had gotten a call that I was very sick and needed help. It took some time to convince them I was fine and didn't need their help. As this was sorted out, it was evident the call had come from Galen, in Texas.

Sadly, a month later, in February 2014, after obtaining a phone and money from his father, he walked out of the Texas facility (and in so doing violated the 90-day Voluntary Commitment agreed to in Washington) and came back to NY to live with his father, both of them severely mentally ill at this point.

In April of 2014, Galen pleaded Guilty to Harassment in the Second Degree (for his non-compliant behavior with the Criminal Court PO and his numerous threatening emails and phone calls to me and others) and I was grateful and impressed that the thoughtful judge imposed a "sentence" of 52 weeks of psychiatric treatment. The judge also arranged that Galen's record will be expunged when he provides proof to the judge that he has completed the required psychiatric treatment. (Of course, even after a judge's ruling, there were no "teeth" in this sentence, because there was no legal way to enforce it. Such a pity!)

The charges had been brought by the DA's office, and I might have had to testify if needed. I didn't want to wait in the courtroom or in the waiting area outside, as I thought it would be too excruciatingly painful to risk running into Galen and I also thought it would be too upsetting and too sad to think about the fact that my son was in a courtroom for threatening me, so I decided to go wait in the Marriage Bureau, downstairs from the court. Though the location had changed, Sam and I got married at the NYC Marriage Bureau, and I sat there wondering what I would have done on the day I got married all those years ago if I had known then even a portion of what lay before me. Of course, most likely, with my naturally optimistic spirit, I wouldn't have believed all these events would be possible in one lifetime!

The parade of characters waiting to get married was a delightful distraction: a military couple in fatigues, with their whole wedding party in full dress uniforms, women dressed in traditional gowns with their mates in tuxes along with those wearing what looked like nightgowns, people in dirty and torn clothes and unkempt hair who had obviously just gotten out of bed and made no prep for getting married whatsoever, very pregnant women towing several kids, gay couples often dressed identically, including one couple that looked so adorable in their matching denim jackets, leopard tights and black skirts, both carrying identical bouquets of white roses.

Flowers are for sale in the Marriage Bureau, and the bouquets were fresh and lovely. I was seriously tempted to buy one, just because they were so pretty, but then I thought that if I were called to testify, it would look very odd indeed if I showed up carrying a wedding bouquet.

CHAPTER 6

Galen After the Death of Sam

On May 6, 2014, Galen's life and the lives of the rest of the family were forever changed, thrown into heart-wrenching emotional and personal chaos, after his father's fall from the roof. The death certificate said he was a suicide. Before Sam's death, he and Galen had been arguing.

Arriving at the uptown St. Luke's Hospital during the evening, accompanied by two policemen, my overriding concern is Galen. I persuade hospital staff to keep him as an inpatient as I thought it was an extremely bad idea to send Galen back to his father's apartment, given his own history of suicide attempts. The doctors agreed, and they held him and transferred him to Roosevelt Hospital in midtown. When he arrived at Roosevelt, the same doctors who had treated him after his suicide attempt three years earlier, including the Russian psychiatrist who knew him well, were deeply concerned about releasing him.

This was my second experience with having my oldest son in a mental hospital in New York, and going there to visit him and meet with the staff. Whatever my imagination might have cooked up regarding this facility before I got there, (as I've said before, mental hospitals do not automatically conjure up benevolent images in our collective minds), I found the doctors and social workers put their hearts and souls into helping him. Obviously, I felt he belonged there, and I was grateful he was there, after so many months running around out of control. At least he was safe.

Safe. What a totally bizarre concept when it comes to how we define it for the mentally ill! Was my overriding concern that he was healthy or productive or even capable of enjoying life or communicating in some sort of reasonable way? No. I was grateful simply for the fact that he was being kept alive, in a supervised, locked environment where he could not harm himself or others, and would have some food and a safe place to sleep.

Once, when I went to the hospital to meet with his doctors and social workers, we were all talking quietly in a small conference room, when suddenly there was a large crashing noise outside in the corridor. As it turned out, someone had accidentally knocked over a snack cart, but I will never forget the flashes of pure terror racing across all the staff's faces, and the sprinter's speed with which they bolted out of the room (truly, I'm not kidding, in a couple of seconds) to confront whatever mayhem might have gone on. What must it be like for them, to work in an environment where a simple, unexpectedly loud noise could send you flying out into the hall prepared to confront something absolutely awful?

There were two court hearings out on Riker's Island (yes the notorious jail - THAT Riker's Island) while Galen was in this hospital, one to obtain a court order for him to take his medication, because true to form he refused to take all their proffered "poison", and the other to order an extended hospitalization, both successful. I went to court twice to testify.

That's another agonizing affair, going to that hell-hole of a prison, which is all by itself a comprehensively traumatizing experience. Riker's is notoriously horrible, and an indescribable mess, in truth little more than a completely outdated penal colony. Seemingly dating to the Civil War Era, it isn't really that old, and in fact opened in 1932. But recently even city government officials have recognized the need to close Riker's, and I believe they have plans to close it within the next few years.

Once I got out there, to the building on Riker's where they hold court hearings, I had to get past the intense security system. I pushed my way through a couple of sets of heavy, rather unwieldy doors, and couldn't go further until I got past a guard in a cubicle made of a lot of extra-thick Plexiglas. (My guess is that the Plexiglas was probably bullet proof as well as generally impenetrable.) I bent

My Life with Crazy

over and shouted at the guard through a small speaking hole covered with steel mesh, inexplicably, not at head height. He wasn't hearing me very well, if at all, so I shouted some more. Next to his cubicle was the first set of the prison's doors, heavy grey slabs with Plexiglas windows and large sliding internal metal plate locks. The guard had to open the locks electronically, which he did (I guess he finally heard me), and I walked in, past the first of them. But then the doors closed and now I stood there, stuck between two sets of locked doors. At this point another guard checked my bag, and scanned me with a metal detector, looking for who knows what. Then Galen's psychiatrist arrived, and the second set of doors opened.

Just getting through security made me feel like a criminal myself. The psychiatrist and I took the elevator with a guard escorting us, up to the floor that held court hearing rooms and waiting rooms. It was so odd to see a nicely decked out, wood paneled courtroom in the middle of Riker's Island, but as you might recall this was actually the second such courtroom I had seen in such an unexpected location. I wonder if there is some tacit understanding that all courtrooms have to have a certain "look", which must include wood paneling. Of course, I had many experiences (more than I like to think about) with Galen at the courthouse downtown, but I expected those courtrooms to look like something out of Law and Order. Who expected to find such a place in a jail?

I had to wait for hours to testify, in the company of a slew of completely deranged people and their families. And I do mean deranged. I am lucky in a way that Galen can present for brief periods of time as the sanest and most rational young man, but out there I was waiting for hours amongst people arguing with imaginary companions, with a woman who said she was thirsty but thought the water fountains were poisoned, as well as the bottles of juice and water a prison guard kindly fetched for her. It was evident another would have tossed herself out the windows, were the windows not barred. After witnessing this up close for hours, I had to testify as to the mental state of my own son, with the son sitting there right in front of me along with his doctors from the hospital. And I recognized that if the hearing were successful, that is, if the judge ordered continued hospitalization, the sorts of people I had waited with were the people he'd be hospitalized with. You really wonder how anybody can get better when everybody around you is just so plainly…mentally ill.

I didn't say much in my testimony. I never do. There's no point. I can say what I have to say in just a few sentences. Many years before, when my family was dealing with the legal issues that arose after my father's death, my attorney at the time told me that when testifying in a deposition or in court "if they ask you what time it is, don't tell them how to build a watch." Good advice, and I always keep it in mind when I have to testify. I said I love my son dearly, and that he needs extended mental health treatment as he is so mentally ill that he is a danger to himself and others. If asked, I give an example or two, as efficiently as possible. Galen sat there, just a few feet from me, just staring at me, though it was rather obvious to me (maybe from the small smirk on his face?) that part of him seemed to enjoy being the center of all this. After all, probably dozens of people (if you count the guards) had been required to find their way to Riker's to hold this hearing. In a perverse way, I felt he liked being the center of all the attention.

Every time psychiatrists in New York have followed proper legal procedures and sought to obtain court orders to treat Galen or give him medication, the judge has agreed with the psychiatrists. This time was no different from the others, and Galen was ordered held. A few weeks later, on a second trip, he was ordered to take medication.

Great care was taken that I didn't have to meet Galen after the hearing was over, which took less than fifteen minutes. I testified and so did the psychiatrist, and that was it. Galen was hustled away quickly, with guards, and taken back to the hospital on a bus with the others who had come out to Riker's for their hearings. I was asked to wait until they were all away. Then Galen's main psychiatrist escorted me out of the building. It's perhaps even more convoluted to get out than it is to get in, for obvious reasons I suppose, with even more care taken with the locking and unlocking of doors, which continued to make the whole day bizarre. The psychiatrist called a car service for me, as there didn't seem to be any other way of getting off Riker's Island easily, and he waited with me until the car came. The psychiatrist is a genuinely nice guy, and he obviously cares a lot about his patients and their families. I still see him once in a while in my neighborhood, usually on a weekend with his young son. When I run into him we just say hello, as he's got more sense than to ask me how Galen is doing.

Eventually though, the psychiatrists at Roosevelt believed Galen was stable enough to leave the hospital. But he was still ill and needed treatment, so the hospital released him to go back to the treatment facility in Texas, from which he had run away a few months earlier. On June 12, 2014, a staff member from the Texas facility came to get him.

Galen remained in Texas for over a month, but ran away again, and came back to NY in August 2014 when he received a check from the Washington hospital reimbursing him for a backpack and computer they had lost. The office staff at the facility tried valiantly to keep the check away from him, watching for the FedEx truck and attempting to intercept it, but the check eventually slipped past them and into Galen's hands.

After Galen returned to NY, he wore out his welcome with various friends, all of whom kicked him out in short order. He was homeless for a period of time, and even tried checking himself into St. Luke's hospital again when he had nowhere to stay. The docs refused to keep him, and he realized he had no options but to return to Texas, which he did in September 2014.

I was very glad he was away from NY and, again, glad he was safely in a facility where people were watching out for him and taking care of him to the best of their abilities. Having Galen without a home, knowing he was wandering the streets, was unimaginably awful.

During his homeless period, I was flat-out terrified of my own son, and I began to develop my own version of PTSD. I was extra cautious wherever I went, because I didn't know how he would react, were I to run into him. Even though I had two protective orders thanks to his antics, I didn't really feel safe. (PO's are incapable of keeping people you are afraid of from coming after you, they only give those people a bunch of trouble once they do come after you. This does not really help you, if they have already attacked you or killed you.) Most of the time, I just used a taxi to get around town, because I knew I'd be safe in the cab, while the buses or subways were public places I might encounter Galen. I warned all the people who worked in my building – the doormen, handymen, super – that Galen was dangerous and unstable and should not be let into my apartment or into the building at any time. The super, a kind man, went so far as to remove my apartment's keys from the pegboard holding the keys for all the apartments in the building, and he put them in a special place in his office where a substitute handyman or doorman who might not have known about Galen could not find them. Galen can talk anybody into nearly anything, (I have frequently said he could sell the Devil fire), so I felt I had to warn all the people I could, because he could surely have talked an unfamiliar doorman into letting him into "his" apartment.

I had hidden the knives the previous year after he threatened me with them, and they remained hidden for a long time. Actually, they only went back in the knife drawer at the time of this writing. I still find myself reluctant to write down where I hid them, in case I ever have to hide them there again. By the way, I'm not the only person who has had to hide all the weapon-like tools, finding some secret spaces to bury these household objects where a mentally ill family member would be unlikely to look. I know of at least two other people amongst my friends and acquaintances who have done this. If you spend a few moments contemplating where you'd hide such things, you might realize that it isn't easy as it might seem, but also, even needing to have to think these thoughts and find such a place is not a fun experience. Nobody wants to remove useful tools like the household screwdriver, the hammer or the sharp knives, but for some of us, they can't be left where they are easily accessible either.

A few months later, in October 2014, Galen ran away from the Texas facility again, accompanied by a fellow patient who lived in Washington State. She was more than twice Galen's age and I don't know if they were a couple or if he was "working for her as her caregiver", which was his story. I believe her family provided the cash for running away, and I was absolutely furious with them. I mean, if you want to sabotage your own child's recovery, that is your business, but why do you have to screw up my son's treatment possibilities?

By the end of 2014, though, Galen was eager to get out of the situation with her and willingly accepted my offer to send him to a working organic farm in the Northwest that is also a treatment center.

During this period, I understand he adopted some strange dietary habits. He became very fussy about what he ate, to the point of becoming very thin, possibly anorexic. His food demands and obsessions were a continuous problem, resulting in numerous confrontations to the point they had to lock some food items away from him. For instance, he insisted that all the tofu in the refrigerator was his, cooked it with excessive amounts of olive oil, and if anyone else cooked something next to him and it spattered in his food, he'd throw it all out and start over. Galen was at the organic farm in Washington for a few months. Even though he went there willingly, after admitting he had problems with anxiety and obsessive behavior, he did not do the work expected of him, whether the work involved farm chores or therapy groups.

After a couple of months at this facility, he began a campaign to find someone to enable him to leave. In order to do that, he made up stories about mistreatment that had no basis in fact (though in his mind, if he tells a tale long enough it seems true to him), and he phoned and emailed literally everybody he'd ever met. For the record, Galen was never held against his will at this facility. He was always free to leave and make his way in the world. I'm sure he irritated many at the facility, because he can be very annoying, and their responses to him may not have always been ideal, because of course they too were there because of their own psychiatric issues.

Galen campaigned relentlessly to find a rescuer, calling every family member, friend of the family, acquaintance he knew even tangentially or had met only briefly at some point years earlier. During this period I had to suffer through (and believe me, suffer is the right word) all sorts of unpleasant emails and phone calls from dozens of friends and acquaintances, all asking me why I'd sent Galen to such a horrible place. I heard from all his old high school teachers, I heard from many of my personal friends, I heard from parents of his old friends, and I heard from relatives, and I even heard from some of his old tutors.

Eventually, he found someone willing to send him money to return to NY. I believe this time his enabler was one of my siblings. It is really hard to describe the extent to which Galen can wear people down with his incessant pestering, and I think my relative gave him cash just to get him to stop. This was such a tragedy, as the director of the program at the organic farm was close to having Galen admitted to a psychiatric hospital. And as a result of leaving that facility, Galen has remained totally untreated for the last several years, from that point in June of 2015 to very recently. Only in the last couple of months has Galen shown any willingness to consider treatment.

I suppose when there are three children in the family, it's pretty typical that two of them pair off and become great friends and the other remains outside their sphere. Such, anyway, is what happened with me and my own siblings. It didn't help that there was a huge legal mess after my father died, and I sided with and stood by my mother, which put us both in opposition to my siblings. Even so, I was very hurt and upset that they would take an action with Galen without asking me. When I asked why they had not talked to me first, before releasing Galen from the facility by sending him cash, one of them said "I don't need your permission to do anything."

While that is obviously true, it was also quite hurtful. It would have been wonderful if my siblings supported my attempts to help my son, and showed some awareness of the need to get Galen into treatment, rather than sabotaging a great opportunity for him. Feeling betrayed by your own siblings is a heartbreaking experience.

After Galen received enough cash to leave the treatment center at the organic farm, he headed back to New York in June of 2015. Upon returning, Galen crashed with different friends in New York City until he had worn out his welcome with everyone. Eventually, with nowhere to stay, he went to a homeless shelter for mentally ill men in the Bronx. Through phone calls with their outstanding therapists, I realized this shelter was also an excellent treatment facility. But again, Galen refused to comply with even simple rules, like keeping the curfew, and he left that program to go to another homeless shelter for mentally ill men in Brooklyn. It is worth noting that when Galen wanted to go to a homeless shelter, the City of New York put him in a homeless shelter for the mentally ill on two separate occasions. Despite his continued claims that there is nothing wrong with him, his legions of doctors, treatment facilities, judges and social workers clearly believe otherwise, and the City of New York has agreed, refusing to house him with the general population.

Though I knew something of Galen's life in the Bronx shelter, as I had some lengthy conversations with two of his therapists, I never found out much about the shelter in Brooklyn. I believe it appealed to him because it was a much bigger facility and the rules were not strictly enforced. I believe he just walked away from this shelter at one point. I don't know why, though I believe it was because sometime during this period he received some money from an IRA of Sam's. Sam seemed to have forgotten he had three children, never adding the twins as beneficiaries of his IRAs after they were born, so Galen was the sole beneficiary. It didn't take him long to burn through it.

A few months later, in September of 2016, after knocking around in cheap hotels, he put his belongings in a storage locker and abruptly flew to Alaska. No one knows why he chose Alaska, though we all remember his obsession with the Pacific NW for many years. Sometimes he expressed a desire to get work on a fishing boat, work that can be lucrative, though extremely dangerous. Although when he actually moved to Alaska, he moved inland, so the fishing boat idea may have lost its appeal. He might also have moved up there because it is really far from New York, or because he anticipated a quieter and easier life than in NYC. I'd like to think he moved there for the gorgeous scenery, the beautiful birds, the wildlife and clean air. But I am not sure any of that had anything to do with it.

Later on, maybe six months later, after he pestered me repeatedly and gave the storage facility his written consent, I got his stuff out and sent it to him. As I packed it all into boxes, I couldn't help but notice the belongings he had stored. Strangely, one item stored in a huge duffle bag were his lengthy medical records from the hospital where he was treated after his father died. (If one is homeless, and has to drag all of their possessions around, why would anyone keep a big file of medical records?)

Because I didn't want to be directly involved, for many obvious reasons, I engaged my attorney to provide an allowance for Galen in Alaska. None of us thought it would be desirable for him to be up there homeless, freezing to death, in the extreme cold of wintertime Alaska. This worked out for a few months, and things with Galen seemed, for this period of time, stable.

But then, suddenly, everything changed. Galen tried to buy a gun – and not once, but twice. When my attorney provided Galen an allowance, Galen would send him credit card statements listing purchases, usually with nearly everything whited out except the company and the amount spent. In one month, there were two separate gun purchases and one for a considerable amount of ammunition, which horrified all of us.

The insane situation with guns in this country, including the ease with which the mentally ill can procure a gun, and the near totality in the lack of enforcement of inadequate gun laws that already do exist, deserves its own chapter. I will address that subject in a chapter later in this book.

Clearly, nobody on my end, not me and not my attorney, was going to allow Galen to purchase a gun. On a strong recommendation from the local police department in Galen's town (who thankfully stepped in and stopped the gun purchases), I engaged a local fiduciary service agency to pay Galen's expenses directly. They gave him only a small cash allowance, as well as checks for other expenses. He did not like the idea at all, but at least they got him an apartment and took care of other expenses, like gas and electric bills. He also got into some other trouble, soliciting underage girls online. He apparently came close to getting arrested, and probably put himself in some danger from angry relatives. (This could have been one reason why he wanted the guns.) In addition, there are also police reports of arguments, petty thefts, threatening behavior, trespassing, and the like.

He had some unsavory characters hanging around his apartment, and there were reports of all sorts of outrageous behavior, such as banging on the walls at all hours and scaring people in the laundry room. He disturbed and frightened elderly neighbors so much that they moved out. He had also caused some damage in the apartment by leaving windows open in the winter (strictly forbidden) so that they froze in the open position and broke when he tried to close them, making their replacement necessary.

Because of his erratic and unpredictable nature, the kind landlord offered him a different apartment in another building, separate from the others so he wouldn't bother neighbors. Typically, Galen refused to move, and continued to refuse to move for six months. During those six months his behavior became so deranged and outrageous that the landlord finally tired of putting up with it and went to court to evict him, which he did, successfully. I've been told Galen left the apartment a complete mess, creating a lot of damage and necessitating many repairs; this landlord, and likely other local landlords, may now have "second thoughts" about renting anything else to him in the future.

People are afraid of Galen. Some of the stores where he shopped refuse to allow him in any longer. Reportedly, he has torn out patches of his hair, wears a hat made out of tin foil (not a joke, and confirmed by a photo provided by the local police department), and speaks so erratically that no one can understand him. He scares people. I understand this fear very, very well - I experienced it firsthand.

Galen desperately needs mental health services, both for medication and therapy. Hopefully, these will happen for him one day. His life depends on it. It infuriates me that this is so difficult to bring about! How can we as a society be so uncaring as to let people sink into increasing insanity without providing a way out for them? It makes no sense.

I cannot make this happen, even as his mother, as I have no legal control whatsoever over what he does with his life. I do have a choice, however, regarding my own attitude. While I could be pessimistic, as it is a fact that this illness could easily kill him or get him into even worse trouble than he has found for himself to date, I am choosing to be optimistic, hopeful that something might occur at some point that will lead him to appropriate treatment, and perhaps with treatment, a more regulated life.

Long ago, one of his therapists put it very well. He said to Galen that if it is true, as Galen contends, that he has no psychiatric issues whatsoever and all his problems are caused by others (mostly me) then he must "suck" at public relations because everybody he meets thinks he's "bat shit crazy". Galen agreed that is so!

I love Galen dearly. There is very little I would not do to help him. However, I have to face the fact that I have also done all I can do. At this point I must set him free to follow his own path, wherever that leads. I must also set myself free, as the worry and concern I have had for him does neither of us any good. He does not want anyone telling him what to do, so I won't. Wherever he goes, though, he has my deepest love, always.

I have concluded that there is no other way to cope with his current condition other than to accept it.

(As this book is going to press there have been some dramatic new developments with Galen. At long last, after years of resistance, he has accepted a recent diagnosis of paranoid schizophrenia, has begun taking medication, and wants to enter a treatment program. This is a huge development and tremendously fortunate. Though none of us know what will happen or how treatment might help him, I am adding this good news as a reminder that there is always hope, and things can unexpectedly move in a positive direction.)

CHAPTER 7

Ella, my daughter

I suppose it might make sense that a family with so much mental illness would produce a child intensely interested in the study of neurology and psychology, and that such interests might appear at a young age. Currently, Ella is a PhD candidate in Clinical Psychology and Neuroscience, which seems sort of pre-destined, given our family history; she genuinely loves science and clearly has the talent and aptitude for it. She also absolutely loved math as an undergraduate, and even TA'd for a couple of classes, so her ability as an analytical thinker is not limited to biology. She sees patients in several clinics and is involved in some interesting research. I have no doubt she will put her heart and soul into trying to help others, and I intuit she will have some rewarding professional experiences. That would be wonderful for her.

From birth, this was a self-assured young woman who knew where she was going and how to get there, starting with getting born. It's almost as though she had asked "what do I have to do to get an A here?", and then she was delivered rather easily. Her twin, by contrast, was a breach birth, a far more complicated affair.

Her first few months were a little rough on her, and on us, because she was a colicky baby and cried (make that screamed) for hours a day. I have an adorable picture of Ella with Galen: she, bright red with her mouth wide open, obviously wailing away at the top of her lungs, and Galen, with his arm around her, patiently putting up with it all but not very happily, as evidenced by the pained smile on his face. Thankfully, she grew out of the colic phase after several months. Even with colic, though, she was so cute and adorable, born with a full head of dark curls, and the sort of lovely little baby that everyone cooed over.

I still have a mental picture of her at a carnival ride when she was about a year and a half old. She was so excited to be at her first carnival! Carnival workers were taking children in groups, a dozen or so for each ride. I could tell she had her sights on a mechanized miniature train ride. Ella waited in line, patiently and confidently, and when it was her turn, even though she was probably the youngest and shortest child, she climbed into the engineer's seat of the small kid-friendly train and began to "lead" all the other children on their ride. I'll never forget the look on her face, which I can see in my mind's eye to this day, self-assured, confident, utterly delighted with herself, and having a wonderful time. This hasn't changed in the twenty-five years since that ride. That little girl, proudly doing what she wants to do, knowing where she is going, is still the same today.

When her father first cracked up, she insisted on staying home from pre-school in order to try to help him, convinced she could do or say something useful, something that hadn't occurred to any of the adults involved. I found this moving, and worrisome, but let it ride, as she was quite determined and I do not believe in squashing determination in young children. Indeed, my daughter may have felt she could do a better job of caring for her father than her mother was doing. It was heartbreaking to witness her lack of success, the changing expressions on her sweet little face, and her dawning awareness that her efforts weren't having any effect at all, and that she - just like her mom and all of the other adults - couldn't think of anything to do to make things better. After a few days of this, she gave up and went back to pre-school.

She was such a sweet and sensitive little girl, and we always had such fun together! We loved the art projects she and I worked on, and she was so thrilled, along with her brothers to learn to cook. She became a master baker, a craft she continues to perfect, much to the delight of everyone around her. And Ella was always up for running around in the park. In every way it was a pleasure being her mother and I enjoyed every minute of the time we spent together.

And she absolutely loved animals. We always had pets of all

kinds, and one day her pet parakeet got out of its cage and ended up in the mouth of one of our cats. Though the little fellow was rescued quickly, she was sobbing inconsolably, so Sam took her and her pet bird over to the Animal Medical Center to see what they could do. Now this is patently ridiculous, as any parent would tell you – taking a bird that cost $12 to an internationally famous (and expensive) animal treatment center, where even a short exam was guaranteed to cost a few hundred. But Ella was crying so much, and Sam was such a soft-hearted guy, so off they went.

Of course, the little bird was a goner. But the vet was so kind, considerate, and patient, and she was so wonderful with my daughter. I had an idea. Ella's birthday was coming up, and I phoned the vet and asked her if she would consider giving my daughter and all her classmates a tour of the Animal Medical Center for a birthday gathering. The vet was terrific and readily agreed.

When the day came, all the kids were treated to a phenomenal tour of the pet hospital, which rivals advanced human hospitals in its equipment and technology, and even keeps donor animals for blood transfusions. The vet had arranged for the kids to "examine" and listen to the heartbeats of a variety of animals - bunnies, cats, dogs, birds. As party favors I'd purchased some kid-sized stethoscopes and animal-printed scrubs from a party store, and quite unbelievably the stethoscopes actually worked. After all the animal fun was over, we took them all for pizza nearby.

My daughter's love of animals, or "aminals" as she said when she was tiny (once in a while even today I ask her to say "aminals" for me, just so I can hear it again!), was a bit challenged when feeding time arrived for her big brother's snakes. Snakes require live food, pretty much, so for some of them that meant dropping a cute little fuzzy white mouse, with pink ears and toes, right into the snake's cage. What happens next is not pretty, and my daughter really hated it all, often ending up sobbing in her room. We took pity on her and fed them when she wasn't around, sometimes using frozen mice, which seemed more palatable. Still, I have some adorable pictures of her holding the snakes, whose company she clearly enjoyed, in spite of their eating habits.

Ella often brought to life significant plot aspects of her favorite books. For instance, we lived for a whole summer with a virtually impassable deck at the PA house, because after reading Charlotte's Web she led her brothers in creating a web out of string, covering the whole deck. String was everywhere, from chairs to rails to posts to drains, and there was nowhere to sit!

Ella was an absolute dream of a child for so many different reasons. She always thrived in any school we sent her to, never having the issues her older brother had. Ella always made awesome grades, maintaining a stellar GPA through her last year of college. She graduated summa cum laude from undergrad and won scholarships all along the way. Her sweet agreeable nature made her a wonderful friend. She was, however, then as well as now, thoroughly passionate when it came to injustices she saw around her, reacting strongly to what she saw as unfair policies at school, or the behavior of others, or anything that she thought was not based on fair treatment of all.

Like her brothers and the rest of the family, she, too, was a gifted musician; according to her father, she developed a perfect physical set-up for the violin. In a school program, she actually played in a concert in Carnegie Hall, with her twin, when they were in the fourth grade. She also played guitar, later bass guitar, joining her brothers and her friends. I don't remember if she was ever involved with a specific band, but she was always involved in music projects, and participated in school orchestras through high school.

In addition to excelling in math and science classes, Ella loved pottery and creative writing. I still have some essays she wrote. Here's an excerpt from one, written at age 9:

> My favorite time of year is Christmas because of all the dessert supplies that are easier to find. I like to make pudding and pies. Also I like to sled and make snow forts and snowmen. I like snowball fights too. My favorite thing to do in the

Winter is to go on the roof deck at our country house and rest on my back on the lounges and let the snowflakes fall onto my eyes and face. Another thing I love to do is to look out the window to the sky during a blizzard and watch the snowflakes fall because of the way the white snow runs away from the gray storm clouds. And fall ever so gently into the pile of flakes with no two alike. Someday I will ski because I have always wanted to and also because we live close to a ski area. We snow tube there a lot and go to the water park in the summer. The snow tube lift is fun because you ride up in the tube and on the way up if you reach your hand out you can scoop up some snow which means that on the way up we have snowball fights."

Sports were always a part of her life, too, especially soccer when she was in grade school (and track later on). We have active youth soccer leagues in NYC and she participated in them with great pleasure. As I've been writing this chapter, I came across an email I got from her soccer coach when she was ten. He summarized Ella's work ethic and lovely personality very well:

"She is definitively a pleasure to coach. She never says no to anything and always goes about her business. She is a very advanced player. I try not to take her out in the last quarter because I want my best players playing in the last quarter. She is one of six key players. Tell her how much I appreciate her contributions, good nature, and willingness to try and keep trying again."

All my kids were in school during the biggest event of our time, the terrorist attacks of September 11, 2001, and all of their schools were outside Manhattan. In all the horror, chaos and uncertainty, we had to deal with the reality that our kids could not get home from school, as all inbound roads to Manhattan were closed indefinitely.

The only solution was to pick everyone up with our car and head out to our Pennsylvania home. Of course, once we left, none of us would be allowed to return until the roads opened up again. I grabbed all the non-perishable food and drinks I could find in the pantry, quickly packed up the animals, and we headed out. I did leave the snakes, after filling their water bowls, as they don't eat frequently and I thought they could manage on their own, no matter how long we had to stay away. (The kids, however, were very upset I left the snakes in New York, and I never heard the end of it!) Traffic was virtually at a standstill, and every few feet it seemed like there was a professionally dressed person covered in dust, attempting to hitchhike a ride out of the city. Public transportation was shut down as well.

Eventually we made it to Galen's school and picked him up. Crossing over the bridge into the Bronx we were reminded that we were leaving Manhattan and couldn't go back. Next, we had to figure out how to get to the twins, normally a 15-minute drive from Galen's school. A few hours later, as we approached their school, we were met with members of the army, rifles trained on the approaching cars. (This is also a unique experience, having members of your own country's military aiming a rifle at you.) As we weren't allowed to drive any further, Sam turned around, did some creative maneuvering through all sorts of little side streets, and we arrived at the twins' school at dinnertime. We were the last parents to pick up our kids.

The trip out to Pennsylvania was easy, with no traffic whatsoever. As many have commented, the weather that day was gorgeous, with a deep blue late summer sky. And they grounded all the airplanes, so it was also very quiet. We were out there quite a few days, until they opened the roads back into the city and we could return.

Ella was the only one of my children who had a connection to someone killed in the towers, the father of a good friend of hers, so it did hit her on a personal level. There is no question that the event itself produced tremendous anxiety in everyone in the country, if not the world, but perhaps especially so for those of us who lived in NY. You couldn't get away from the awful smell, or the smoke that would drift by you occasionally, like the whiff you got from someone standing 10 feet from you smoking an especially noxious cigar, only far worse. My daughter had to see her childhood dentist whose office was way downtown, where the smell and smoke were especially bad.

It also affected her socially. Many people, including parents of some of her friends, became fearful about coming into Manhattan. Some never got over it, and those friends stopped coming for play dates at our home. She went to theirs, but she said she didn't understand why her friends, and their parents, were so scared to cross the bridge into Manhattan because she crossed it twice every day, going to and from school, and nothing bad ever happened to her. This is so typical of her. She's always had such a practical, common sense attitude about life, bless her heart.

However, I have often thought the antics of the guys in our family must have been quite a burden to Ella, and must have provided her with some extra pressure to excel academically and stay out of trouble. She has so much personal empathy and I really believe she didn't want to cause me, the only other woman in the family besides grandma, any extra anguish. Ella really worked hard at everything and her grades were an absolute priority for her. While I found this admirable, I worried that this nose-to-the-grindstone attitude may not have allowed her as much freedom as she should have had as a young person.

When we were looking at high schools, one of the school interviewers mentioned Ella's flawless academic record, and expressed some concern about the pressure she must have put herself under to create such a record. The interviewer said that if she elected to attend their high school her first assignment would be to do no homework in any subject for one week, in an attempt to get her to lighten up about her academics. On our way home, my daughter begged me not to send her to that school if she got in (which she did). She said she didn't think she could manage to ignore all homework assignments for a whole week without freaking out completely.

Yet her interest in the arts remained strong, despite her determination in her more traditional academic classes. The most memorable sculpture classes at the high school where she wound up always had a fabulous annual fashion show that challenged the students to create clothing out of any material except cloth. She had several very original and interesting projects, but her final one, in her senior year, was the pinnacle. Believe it or not, she made an entire dress out of tape from the inside of a VCR cassette, and then molded the plastic cassettes (because, why waste?) into an artfully arranged bodice. A picture of her in that amazing dress even made it into Teen Vogue.

In high school, influenced by teen culture and undoubtedly by some of her brother's behavior, Ella began to drink. And the extent of her drinking was worrisome. But once this was pointed out to her, she immediately stopped and it never came up again. I had written down some of the other incidents she got herself involved in, but upon reflection, I deleted them all. It doesn't seem fair to her to give equal weight to behavior that she managed to correct on her own in short order in a book describing the antics of others in the family with very serious psychological or addiction problems. She provided me with some worry and stress that came at a time when I was dealing with the serious issues of her father and her older brother, and a few very substantial problems that had recently materialized with her twin. However, looking back over the years, I can say she had an awesome ability to evaluate her own actions, and when faced with an important decision, always chose the better path going forward.

Ella has grown into a wonderful, kind and generous young woman, with an exceptional work ethic, and I am so proud of her. As she nears the end of her PhD, she is already seeing patients in her departmental clinic. Recently she got engaged to a wonderful young man who is a close friend of her brother Zach, and they are creating a terrific life together. Still, all of us were molded by Sam's deterioration, and layers of buried or unacknowledged feelings will have to get dug up sometime, by her and the rest of us. This journey is tough to get through, and it takes time. Recently, on her father's birthday, we both mentioned how much we are still processing and sorting out our feelings about his life.

My daughter also developed into something of an athlete, which balances her intense grad school life: she climbs mountains, bikes everywhere, snowboards, and runs marathons. In fact, she won a contest to participate in the 2019 NYC marathon, all expenses paid. Though there is obviously a lot of healthy self-care involved, perhaps running also gives her ample opportunity, when she's out in the fresh air and alone in nature, to work through some family history. I have no doubt this helps her and that she will figure it all out magnificently, in her own good time, just like she always has. I feel the most interesting part of her life's story has yet to happen, but it will be a fascinating journey for her.

CHAPTER 8

Zach, my younger son

Zach, my younger son and Ella's twin brother, has quite a different and far more convoluted story; a story that involves struggles with alcohol and drug addiction. I'd like to tell you about him and about his childhood, but first I'd like to make some comments about the journey of addiction and recovery. I am so proud of him. His story is scary, but he has turned his life around, and he is an example of everything that is wonderful about an effective rehab program.

Though it might sound perverse to say it, in a way Zach was extremely lucky to go through the long journey of addiction rehab. After all, the months he spent there involved a lot of introspection, private and group therapy sessions, and an intense commitment to the 12-step program, a highly effective way to come to terms with miserable events that can sometimes make their way into someone's life.

His story is truly one of hope and inspiration. His life could have gone in a totally different direction. Indeed, it is possible, had the rehab not "taken", that he would not be leading a productive life today, or even be in a very good place at all. He is so smart, with stellar grades, but intelligence might not have prevented him from trying ever more dangerous drugs. He might have gone on to dealing, or who knows what. His recovery is a precious gift to himself, his sister, and to his mother, one I appreciate daily.

Zach made the right choices. It was a bit of a struggle, but today he is a true success story, in every way. One of his counselors at his first rehab told me that he could hardly wait to see the remarkable person this young man would become in ten years. Sadly, that counselor is no longer with us, but after Zach was married I marveled that the wedding occurred just about ten years after the counselor's comment, around the time that he and his wife graduated from medical school.

Looking at the members of my family who have suffered from some aspect of mental illness, the unanswerable question is what makes one person refuse to accept their illness and refuse all treatment, and another person come to realize how sick they are and what they have to do to get well - and then, most essentially, what makes them actually commit to it and work at it? I don't pretend to have an answer, but in my case, I am grateful beyond any ability to put into words that Zach got the message and turned his life around.

When I wrote about Galen, I spoke of how actively he moved in utero. Zach was the complete opposite. I rarely felt him move. He was so quiet, in fact, and moved so little, that I went to a couple of routine sonograms half expecting they'd tell me he hadn't made it. Happily, that was not the case and he was always fine!

As I mentioned in the last chapter he was a breach birth, meaning he was crammed up under my rib cage with his head next to my heart. After his sister was born easily (by the book, so to speak), he had to be turned, a procedure involving a whole bunch of doctors and nurses pushing and pulling my stomach; I remember joking at the time that it might be easier to reach down my throat and grab him. The doctors also needed forceps to deliver him, and the awful bruises on his face were horrible to see. I still wince when I think about them today.

As a little boy, Zach was just so darn cute and adorable! I called him the "smush", or sometimes velvet head, because his hair was just that velvety. Quite literally, every woman who ever met him, of any age, teachers, classmates, grandmas, fell in love with him. He was so painfully shy, but while peeking out from wherever he was half hidden, he could come up with the most endearing expressions! He could make your heart melt. Most of my friends remember him hiding under my skirt for hours, which is hard to imagine today as he is now so tall. He didn't say much. He didn't have to.

Zach showed great interest in music from the beginning. We

always had, not surprisingly, a large collection of recorded music and as soon as he could manage it, he'd play the records all day long. I remember the day he found a Beethoven Symphony LP, I don't remember which one, and it absolutely mesmerized him. I must have said something about it, and Zach replied, incredulously, "you mean there are more of these?" I assured him there were and he asked me to find the others. The following day, believe it or not, he listened to all nine Beethoven symphonies, plus the Choral Fantasy, one after the other, in order. It's hard to imagine how many small children would ever do that.

He also showed an early interest in math and computers. Way ahead of me from the instant he first sat down at a desktop MAC, he taught me how to use our first family computer - when he was four! That's a uniquely humbling experience, being taught how to use a computer by a four-year-old.

He found his way to the piano and wanted to learn to play, so I engaged an ex-student of mine to teach him and the other two as well. (I personally don't believe parents should teach their own children to play musical instruments.) Sam also arranged for cello lessons for all the kids, though the twins later switched to violin. He too found a student to teach them, and we were all amazed by this young man's ability to get them to practice - a lot - until we realized that he'd been bribing them with chocolates (it worked, and we didn't care). Zach became good enough to minor in music and piano in college. He also played guitar, like many teenagers, and played in bands all the way through school. He continues to play to this day, both piano and guitar. Sometimes he even plays in public, at benefit concerts organized by his medical school, the most recent a pediatric AIDS benefit concert. His wife, a lovely woman whom he met in medical school, is also a talented musician, and she joins him, singing and playing her guitar.

Zach always had a devilish streak about him and a tremendous sense of humor, and always took part in some practical joke or other. Thinking back over his childhood, I remember especially a school play where he played Ms. Marple, in drag. Even then he was taller than everyone else, and in costume, faking a British accent, he was a riot.

And I also remember when his middle school teachers asked him if he could please come up with something they could play at a school assembly the following day that would encourage his fellow students to contribute to a local food pantry, the food drive to that point having produced only a few pitiful contributions. He worked with several other students, quite literally all night (yes, I'm that permissive as a mom!), and created an animated cartoon video that was so funny several teachers told me they were laughing so hard their sides hurt. Apparently, he and his friends delightfully mixed up items about their studies, remarks typical of teachers, bits from the evening news, and characterizations of personalities at school, and the final product brought the house down. Zach and his friends were invited to go with the donations, which now filled a large truck, to drop them off at the food pantry.

Animated cartooning was something he got into fairly seriously. Frustrated that he couldn't find any other young friend to help him explore this hobby, Zach found a friend on the internet, a young man in Holland. The only problem was that this young fellow spoke little English, so my son decided to learn Dutch. We were all amused when he went around the house calling things by their Dutch names, and speaking it at family meals.

All of our children were born at a time when Sam and I were functioning as well as we ever did as a family, were happy together and enjoying our lives, were successful professionally, modestly prosperous, and our lives flowed on uneventfully. Galen had about 7 years of this pleasant and enjoyable family life before Sam had his first deep depression, and the twins, Ella and Zach, about 4 years.

When the twins were babies, they were in one room in separate cribs. Eventually, Zach moved in with his big brother and the two boys shared a room. Of course, I was unaware of what was developing with Galen, but in retrospect I realize (hindsight is so frustratingly perfect) that this was very difficult for Zach, asked at a very young age to share his living space with a person slowly overrun by mental illness. I feel really awful about this, and can't believe I was in such a state of denial or distraction that I allowed it to go on. I can't even begin to imagine how hard this must have been for Zach. Siblings can tussle and even fight, which is normal, but the emotional burden placed upon Zach was really not fair to him.

Our younger son is in many ways the opposite of Galen. While Galen is loud, energetic, and in your face, with an emotional life that is plastered all over him at all times for the world to see, Zach was quiet, sensitive, and soft spoken, felt events deeply while hiding them in the depths of himself, as if in a well locked up behind a wall. He was a natural "lark", which meant he would just curl up on the floor and fall asleep even before bedtime, which was completely the opposite of the other two, and especially his older brother, who tried to keep, as I have always joked, vampire hours. During Zach's first year in nursery school, he barely said a word, with his twin sister piping up for him when he needed something. "He needs some juice." "He wants to play in the sandbox." Zach was always a deep thinker, and he just stood back quietly while the rest of the world, and Galen, carried on.

In his first year of pre-school, Zach broke his leg. He had jumped off a merry-go-round on the playground just as another child came running around it and crashed into him, twisting him as he fell, creating a torque that broke his leg in two places. The orthopedist said the break was similar to what occurs when slalom skiers break their legs. They had to put the leg in a cast in such a way that he could not put weight on it or walk on it, and he sort of scooted around on his bottom, using the leg that wasn't in a cast to propel himself. The school was concerned about how he would get out of the building in case of fire, as his classroom was up several flights of stairs, so they asked me to hire a babysitter to stay with him. Not a bad idea, certainly, though the whole experience began to create some deep anxieties in him (he had nightmares about not being able to leave his school because of a fire), and this became his first experience with the sort of anxiety that would eventually lead to his addiction problems. The day this all happened and I was called in to the school, Galen had also hurt himself, falling over backwards in a chair and getting yet one more "eggie" on his head. Galen didn't seem as badly hurt as his brother, so I left him at school under the nurse's care and carried his brother to the doctor.

Zach was in a huge amount of pain, and screamed whenever I moved even slightly. Clearly the leg needed to be X-rayed, and so I carted him in my arms from the pediatrician's office to the radiologist. Wouldn't you know, their equipment was down, so then I carried him again, trying not to jostle him, to another office blocks away. I don't think I ever experienced such back and neck pain as I did that evening, from holding a heavy child in one position, for hours, as I walked with him in my arms from office to office and continued to hold him until he could be examined.

Zach developed his own issues with school, mostly because he caught on to things quickly, and he got bored and impatient waiting for the class to move on. He had special aptitudes for math and science, in addition to his talents for music. We had some difficulty finding the right school for him, like we had with his brother; eventually, in 3rd grade, he ended up in a school with Ella, where he was fortunate enough to have a true master teacher for her final academic year before retirement. Having that marvelous teacher that particular year was one of the luckiest events of his life. Both he and his sister stayed at that school, very happily, through 8th grade.

But the dual toll of living with Galen, as well as Sam's frequent depressions began to create some deep anxiety, severe enough that by middle school I felt it necessary to find Zach a psychiatrist. At the time I was completely ignorant about possible treatments, but later I learned that with childhood anxiety there are quite literally dozens of options, and I also learned that experts agree you should exhaust every single one of them before you prescribe a young person potentially-addictive medications. Nonetheless, around the age of 14 his doctor prescribed Klonopin, one of the Benzodiazepines. At the time this did not cause me great alarm because Sam had taken these with no ill effect. But such meds do have addictive potential, and it seems as though his psychiatrist would have been more responsible had he tried any of a number of alternatives, first. In rehab, they gave the parents a list of anti-anxiety alternatives that should be tried before the benzos, and this list was 9 pages long. Later, Zach told me that he knew he was addicted after he took just one pill. No one who has raised a teenager will be surprised to learn that he also began to experiment with other substances, including alcohol and other drugs (not all of them known to me), but especially marijuana, as it is another highly effective anxiolytic substance, that is, a substance that relieves anxiety.

The first incident that alerted me to a problem came about when straightening his room, and I found a backpack that I didn't think belonged to any of my kids. (They were all at school and had their backpacks with them.) Many of my kids' friends hung out at our house, something I encouraged and was always happy to host, and I assumed somebody had left it behind. So I opened up the backpack to see if I could figure out which of his friends had accidentally left it.

I got a huge wake-up shock, as I found quite a large bag of either pot or hash, some pills I later learned were Ecstasy, other pills I never identified, and a very weird scale. I was beyond stunned, but I knew what at least some of it was, and I wanted all that stuff out of my house, immediately. But I also wanted to know what I was dealing with and what the various pills were, and wanted to find someone who could tell me. Perhaps I intuited that if I asked my son about this backpack and its contents I'd get a ridiculous story; I also didn't want to argue with him as to what to do with it, because whatever he said, it was going to be out of my house and thrown away, regardless. Whatever collection of worried mom factors went into my less-than-optimal decision, I can't say, but I had an idea to take the backpack to the nearest police precinct, just a few blocks from my apartment and ask them to tell me what this stuff was, and ask if they could dispose of it appropriately. Now, whether I was really stupid or naïve or just desperate, I don't know, though all would seem to apply. But I walked into the local police precinct to speak to them about what I'd found, expecting help, facts, and a measure of sympathy.

Well, talk about learning from experience. I was not treated as the worried and frightened parent I was, alarmed by what I'd found in my home. I was treated like a criminal, and I almost got arrested. It turned out the scale was a professional dealer's scale and simply possessing it was cause for great alarm on the part of the police. They told me what the Ecstasy was, but like me they didn't know what the other pills were either. After several hours of questioning they let me go, and I can truthfully report I was dizzy and shaking from head to toe as I left. I was almost unable to walk down the sidewalk, because I was scared, almost to the point of being terrified. I had to force myself to keep going and quickly get as far away from them as possible. They kept everything.

I told Zach what I'd done after he came home from school, (and my instincts were right as I got a nonsensical tale about the origins of the backpack and he professed, vigorously, to know NOTHING about its contents). He must have shared the story with his friends because after this, none of them ever came to my house again, and I mean that quite literally. A few weeks later as I went to put away some clean socks I found another device in a drawer. This was some sort of elaborate wooden and glass gizmo intended to take the impurities and the smell out of pot smoke, so you can smoke the stuff in your room without your mom figuring out what you are doing. This time I took the thing down to the river and tossed it in. The river isn't very deep along the edges, which I hadn't factored into making this decision. No one is going to sign me up to pitch for the Mets, but I thought with my best toss it would reach the deeper water past the rocks at the edge. Alas, the gizmo ended up crashing on some barely submerged rocks 20 or 30 feet from the riverbank. The next time I had to get rid of drug-related paraphernalia, I went to a different river, where the current runs fast and deep, and I could just drop it in from a walkway that juts out over the water's edge.

Common knowledge says, or so I'd heard, that if a kid has a drug problem, his grades will tank, his friends will change, and everything will generally roll downhill. I never saw any of that. His friends remained the same, his girlfriends were lovely, and I saw no change in the quality of his schoolwork. In fact, he maintained his very high GPA while constantly stoned, and eventually got a near-perfect SAT score, also while stoned.

Perhaps this young man would have become addicted anyway, due to the prevalence of drug and alcohol experimentation with teenagers in our culture, but I personally believe the main reason Zach began using was a search for relief from all the anxiety at home, replete with its dramatic emotional experiences: a home he shared with a brother well on his way to mental illness, and a beloved father who had already taken a turn into mental illness ill and was repeatedly falling into deep depressions.

Soon he began to fall apart too, in his own quiet way. Zach was becoming someone I didn't know, someone comfortable with lies and deceptions of all kinds, inconsistencies, sneaking around, and hiding what he was doing from me. His outlandish behavior included stealing my cash, and I found peculiar charges on my credit cards. One day he locked me out of my apartment. I had told him I was going to be gone when he got home from school, but would not be out long.

When I got home, the door was locked. He had also put the chain and dead bolt on, and, trust me, the police dramas on TV are wrong - you can't break the door down by crashing into it, you just end up hurting your shoulder. I even had our doorman try to get the door open, without luck, as he couldn't break it down either. Eventually, after I'd stood in the hall for at least an hour trying to get his attention by shouting his name, and walking around to the side of the building, shouting up from the street, he came to the door and opened it. He was so stoned he could barely stand.

I got calls from other parents about his behavior in their homes, and calls from parents who announced they wouldn't let their kids hang out with him anymore because he was becoming a bad influence. All sorts of mysterious events got explained away with whatever far-fetched tale happened to cross his mind in the moment. This was causing me increasing fear for his safety, as well as upset and rage at his increasingly unpredictable and erratic behavior.

Many other strange things were yet to happen, most of which I only learned about later. Consider for example how you might hide drugs if you wanted to get them past your mother and the TSA agents and onto an airplane for an extended family vacation with grandma, aunts, and uncles in Florida. Yep, you are right, that's how he did it! For those of you who can't figure it out, trust me, you don't want to know.

Here's the most mind-boggling part of all of this. Even though I didn't fully comprehend the extent of the problems at their outset, my pediatrician had known all about my child's drug use for two or three years. Blood tests had confirmed what he suspected, but the results were not shared with me. I do not have words to express how furious and betrayed I felt upon learning of this. After all, I had carefully selected this pediatrician based on his compassionate treatment of my newborns at the hospital, and even though getting to his office was somewhat inconvenient for me, I had faithfully taken all three kids to his practice their whole lives. That apparently counted for nothing, in terms of helping a mom figure out the best way of saving her son's life.

I do understand that he may have felt bound to the letter of the HIPAA law, but if so, that law is not in the least bit helpful to a mom in my position. There's a lot about HIPAA laws that most of us parents do not know. I will write about this elsewhere, in its own chapter, but I want to continue telling this part of my son's story here.

One day, I got a call from the school nurse asking me to come get Zach. She said he had come in to her office not feeling well and she was having trouble waking him up; she was afraid to send him home on the bus and wanted me to take the responsibility of getting him home safely. I went to school and dragged him directly over to the pediatrician's office, arguing with him and restraining him so he couldn't jump out of the taxi on the way. (Not an easy task, since he was nearly a foot taller than I am, and much stronger.) I was freaking out and scared about what was happening and wanted some answers.

Testing was done, but Zach started screaming about confidentiality and both the doctor and my son told me I wouldn't be told the results. And in fact, I never did get to see the results, and haven't to this day, more than ten years later. However, I got the message and began looking into treatment options, wasting time initially with an outpatient program. To give you some truly time-saving information, I would advise parents who suspect drug use to skip outpatient treatment altogether and head directly to inpatient treatment – you'll save yourself a lot of lost time, grief, money, and anxiety. Plus, if you have a smart kid like mine, all those A's in chemistry will not go to waste, as they will be put to good use figuring out how to outsmart the urine tests, so you'll think progress is being made when it isn't.

Discovering all this and getting Zach into treatment was quite an adventure. It became obvious we needed a referral to an addiction specialist. I found one, and when we went I took his sister along too. The specialist said they both had a problem, he with benzos and pot, and she was drinking too much alcohol; for my son, he recommended getting him into a treatment program immediately. My daughter was really ticked off that I dragged her and her brother to this appointment. But for whatever it is worth, as far as I could tell, that was the end of my daughter's excess drinking. I give her immense credit for this.

At his first program, the outpatient program, they insisted on urine tests every time the kids came in, which was nearly every day. Zach's solution to this problem was to purchase a fake penis online, so he could put somebody else's clean pee or some other creative concoction in the attached pouch, and pass the drug tests. This entire charade was necessary because the program actually, physically, looked at their patients as they collected their samples. As a result, he was easily passing his drug tests, using a friend's pee or some other brew (as I've said, he was an A student in chemistry and biology), but he was still actively using. Wow, did I give the folks that sold him the fake penis a piece of my mind! And I reported them everywhere possible, as this was not something they were supposed to have sold to a minor.

Eventually the outpatient program caught on to what Zach was doing and it became apparent he would need inpatient rehab. I cannot overstate what a lonely, miserable journey it is for a parent to explore residential treatment programs. If there are a few things most of us are hopelessly uneducated about, finding the right rehab for your own child would certainly rank highly on that list. I was totally confused, I didn't know which ones were any good, I had no idea where to look or how to choose, but to the best of my ability I continued to sort out options.

Zach continued to see his psychiatrist, and this doctor continued to prescribe Klonopin, as well as similar medications. Unbelievably, like the pediatrician, he too knew full well my son was addicted to the stuff, and knew it for months, though I didn't know anything at all. I really don't even have words to describe my feelings about this and I cannot understand how HIPAA rules hold a physician hostage to the point a parent has no information about the drug use, prescribed or otherwise, of her child. I can hardly believe I didn't have the presence of mind to delve into the pluses and minuses of the drugs he prescribed, which also included an antidepressant, but I didn't. Possibly, I didn't look into the drugs because, as I mentioned, his father had taken most of them (including Klonopin) without addiction issues. I do not know if his father's history played a part in selecting the medications my son was prescribed.

Just before rehab, though, I'd begun to wonder if the benzos were a problem, so I also took Zach to a highly recommended psychiatrist for a second opinion. This other guy, unbelievably, doubled the amount of the prescription, instead of helping figure out how to get my son off the stuff. In retrospect, I honestly believe that neither of these doctors truly understood the scope of addiction possibilities with benzodiazepines, to the detriment of their young patient.

I was completely in the dark, and didn't know what to think. I figured it all out when Zach was in rehab, when the truth came out. And wow, did the first psychiatrist ever try to cover himself when I pressed him about why he continued to prescribe these medications even though he knew about the addiction. In retrospect, I have even wondered how forthright he was with me, because when I asked for a copy of my son's records, (the rehab wanted to see them and Zach had given me permission), the records were sparse.

One day, in April of his junior year in high school, Zach mentioned to a teacher at his high school that he was thinking about suicide. The school told me he couldn't come back until his psychiatrist had written a letter saying Zach was not a danger to himself or others. The psychiatrist saw my son that same day (for me, this was another mad dash up to school to retrieve Zach and then another trip from hell to drag him to the doctor, where I was forced to sit and listen to my son spout more wild stories) and he wrote the requested letter, stating that it was safe for all concerned for my child to return to school. In retrospect, this was an absolutely foolhardy and stupid thing for this doctor to do, possibly bordering on malpractice. And no, I never even considered that – I was far too busy getting through all the messes in my life to get myself bogged down in a lawsuit. I've been involved in a few lawsuits, over which I had little choice or control, and I know for a fact they basically wreck your life, taking it over for months at a time. I had to concentrate on other things, more important things, including finding help for my son.

My son never saw this doctor again.

That very night I found Zach reading Kurt Kobain's suicide note, and making active plans for suicide. Could any discovery be more frightening to a mom? The pure terror is hard to describe, and I think I was just about as terrified and anxious as I had ever been in my life. But I couldn't let those emotions out at this time; the situation required control until I could get him to the safe haven of rehab. It was, in all regards, a truly miserable experience. The day after I caught Zach reading Kurt Cobain's note, I booked professional transporters to take him to rehab, only a few minutes before my son came to me and volunteered to go. He had been speaking with his girlfriend and I believe she had strongly urged him to take this step. When these capable professionals arrived I was so relieved, as I knew he would get to the residential rehab safely, and within a few hours. But his behavior had become so bizarre and I was so scared and worried about him that I did not sleep at all while I waited for the transporters to arrive. Quite literally, I was afraid to close my eyes or let him out of my sight.

This residential program was outside a large city in a nearby state. It was a good program, but I knew before Zach went there that it really wasn't going to be long enough, as the maximum stay in their program was 4 months. I didn't believe that would be enough for him. I also knew in my heart when he left my home that April night more than ten years ago that he'd never live at home again, which was so painfully tough to take in emotionally, as he was barely 17, and I was not ready for him to leave home for good. It was like he was going off to college, but earlier than I expected; he left in a sick and vulnerable state, and not for the right reasons. But I had to get over wallowing in my unhappiness about this, though, as I was also aware that his life depended on getting to rehab.

In rehab, they detoxed Zach in their hospital, as coming off Benzos is medically dangerous, but they weaned him off of them successfully and he completed his first month without issue. He needed another three months, and I signed him up for those extra months. He had an absolutely wonderful therapist there, who was not only great at his job but a gem of a human being, and even though my son seemed to be making progress, neither the therapist nor I felt he was taking rehab seriously.

Later on, but only after my son had spent some time in rehab, I learned that my child's drugs of choice were those same Benzodiazepines: medications such as Klonapin, Xanax, and Valium. In a memorable discussion during a family weekend in rehab, the kids were sharing how they were able to get the drugs they had used. My kid said, with perfect truth, "my psychiatrist was my dealer." And, like the pediatrician, this psychiatrist knew my son was becoming addicted and said nothing to me. This, I firmly believe, needs to change.

As his time at the program neared the end, the counselors informed me that one way of finding out where he was in his recovery was to allow him home visits on 24 hour passes. The therapist at the rehab told me that only home visits could say whether their treatment program had loosened the stranglehold of addiction and would allow him to return home for his senior year of high school. He asked me to be patient and said it would all become clear toward the end of August. He was right.

Just to set the scene, wouldn't you know the last of his three 24-hour home visits would occur on the hottest, most humid, most miserable day of the summer, with polluted, unhealthy air on top of temperatures exceeding 100 F. It was the kind of air where they advised people to stay inside if possible. News reports said people literally died on the streets or in their own homes. Going around the city was awful enough just on its own, let alone as a background to my rehab-prescribed never-let-him-out-of-my-sight chaperoning. The plan was to pick Zach up at the bus station, have dinner with him, go to an AA meeting together with him and a potential new AA sponsor, have a family meeting at some point, and then put him back on the bus the next day.

We had some strict rules about this home visit because, during a previous 24-hour home visit my son pushed the rules about computer use, phone use, and a few other things. The point was not that his behavior was so extreme, but that his attitude of wanting to get away with something or being above the rules had not changed. Now that it was time for another visit, a couple of weekends later, we hammered out an even more precise statement of rules for the visit among all of us, at home and at the rehab center.

I picked my son up at the bus station, and immediately I knew something was off, though I couldn't specifically label it at that moment. Zach was quietly hanging out with his twin sister a few hours later, watching a movie, I think, when the phone rang and one of the counselors from rehab called with some startling information. Another patient had confessed that Zach said he was going to sneak out of the house in the middle of the night, either through the front door or through the window, buy weed, smoke some, and bring some back to the rehab facility to share. The counselor thought I should know about this.

They asked me what I planned to do, and I admit my first reaction was to try to figure out how I might prevent the relapse. But a few seconds later I told the counselor that I was completely fed up with the way I had been living with Zach for months, with all the stealing, lying, conniving, and cheating, and that I was not going back to living like that, ever again, under any circumstances. Therefore, if he was determined to sneak out, buy pot, and relapse it would be solid proof that he was not ready to come home for his senior year and that he needed further treatment somewhere. It was obvious that I should not interfere and so I decided to wait and see what he actually did. At this point there was at least the possibility that it was all talk, though I honestly didn't think so. I told them I was going to go about the home visit as though everything was just fine, and let whatever was going to happen just happen. As I told them, if Zach could not refrain from relapsing less than a day after coming home, I didn't want him to go back to his high school that fall. He would need to stay in rehab.

Zach made a big fuss about a "wound" he had gotten on his leg, supposedly while horsing around with the other kids, and it had a great big bandage on it. I have a sense what that bandage is really for, but we go about our evening, picking up his new AA sponsor in a cab, and head out to a Saturday evening teen AA meeting at a hospital way downtown. I sat there quietly reading a book in an internal state of incandescent fury, blended with indescribable pain and sadness, and the occasional tear, and I waited patiently while he went off to the hospital cafeteria to get food with his pals from the meeting. I was extra nice to his sponsor even though every instinct in me said this particular gentleman was not a good sponsor for him. I listened to my son carry on SO convincingly about what a great experience the meeting was, how inspiring and uplifting. I heard all about the incredible joy of getting a 90-day keychain and how great it was to see friends, and how pleased they all were about his stunning progress and his 30+ pounds of weight gain, blah, blah, blah, etc., etc.

Remember, I know what is up, so I have to listen to absolute rivers of "you must think I'm stupid" lies coming out of him, as he spouts everything he thinks he should spout when he is with me. I don't know what happened during the AA meeting, as outsiders and parents weren't allowed in. But I surely can relay that when he was with me, and with the sponsor, he was into across-the-board dramatic role playing. It was completely surreal, and nearly unbelievable, and even at times almost funny, given what I knew was likely to happen. There were a few times I had to really get myself under control not to laugh. I mean, how dumb did he think we all were?! What a performance! Although honestly, in retrospect, the Oscar should have gone to me, for keeping my cool and not letting on, at any point during the entire visit, that I knew what a charade he was putting on.

During the previous pass we'd not found time for the required family meeting, so we got to it after we got home from the teen AA meeting. Zach carried on and on about how great he was doing and about other things I don't even remember. I do remember saying that there were very important things I needed to say to him but couldn't say to him until the next day. I just couldn't talk about anything until a day later. It was late. I was tired. I couldn't listen to any more of it or subject myself to his attitude about the way he thought his act was conning me. Sitting through this family meeting was where I came the closest to losing it. It would have been so easy to start screaming at him, but I didn't, and sat there with total composure.

He also wanted to call his girlfriend. Later I found out that he half told her what he was going to do, (leaving out the relapse part), saying something about leaving the apartment by the window to sit outside. She told him that did not sound like a good idea and he should stay in his room. When she found out later what he'd done right after he spoke with her, she was hurt and angry, just like the rest of us.

I pretended like everything was just fine. Later, when it was all over, Zach's rehab therapist gave me a hard time for what I had put myself through, though later he apologized and said I had done exactly what needed to be done, and that he admired my courage. He even said that he had never had a parent display the courage and self-assurance I did that night, and didn't know how many other parents could have carried this off, which I thought was one of the most supportive things anybody ever said to me. However, it would be impossibly difficult to try to explain to anyone else, and it is hard doing this even now, just how absolutely painful and upsetting this whole day was. I felt I had done what needed doing. I figured if he was going to relapse, he'd need further rehab, so we'd better find out what he had planned.

It was bedtime. For hours I had known he only had one thing on his mind – having the opportunity to sneak out of the house and cop some weed and pills. I was tired. It had been a really long day. I went to bed and amazed myself by falling asleep easily.

I woke up at six, more or less when I usually get up, and immediately went into his room to see if he was there. I thought I detected just a tiny trace of pot smell, but wasn't sure. I sat down on his bed. He opened his eyes and I knew for sure what he had done.

There is a look Zach gets when he is caught up in this behavior that is utterly blank and black. That look is so dark, so lost, so profoundly empty and soulless, I didn't need to see anything else. I knew.

I looked around the room. The first thing I noticed was the window screen. It had been cut and a pair of scissors was lying on the windowsill. Yes, the screen was slightly torn already, but this was a deliberate straight-line cut, diagonally across the whole window. I asked him about it, and typically, he concocted a big elaborate lie about trying to open the window and accidentally cutting the screen with the peen end of a hammer, with which, supposedly, he was trying to open the window. Sure. Right. His explanation of that was that he needed to get some cool air. The screen itself, apparently, did not provide enough fresh air, and the 100-degree air outside being somehow cooler and more refreshing than the air-conditioned air inside, as well as the fact that the screen in question belonged to a window six inches away from one with an excellent air conditioner.

Then he had the idea to go in and tell his sister how the screen got cut, elaborating and embellishing the story in the short distance from his room to hers. I had not told her what was going on, as I didn't think I should put the burden on her of knowing her twin was relapsing. I didn't want to tear her in two like that – divided between loyalty to her mom and disappointment for her twin. I did tell her I wanted to talk to her as soon as I got back from taking Zach to the bus. However, she came in and told me she thought his screen-cutting story was just ridiculous, though that wasn't the word she used.

Fortunately, with breakfast and showers and some laundry and all that needed to happen, the morning passed relatively quickly and it was soon time to take him back to the bus. Just as we left the building, in his sweetest, nicest voice, Zach asked me if he could please just have a few minutes to go to the park which is just outside our building's door and sit under one of the beautiful trees communing with nature. I told him that the rehab center said I had to be physically with him every moment he was home (with the exception of the AA meeting), so if he wanted to go I had to go with him. He declined my offer.

In the bus terminal he had to go to the drug store to buy some soap and other supplies. He showed me the shelves of cough syrups containing DXM, explaining that he didn't abuse that stuff TOO much. I don't know if he picked up on my mood, but he didn't buy the cough syrup, and I was never so glad in my life to drop someone off for a bus. At the end of a weekend from hell, I wanted nothing more than just leave him in the line, but I waited until I saw him actually board the bus, and then I waited some more until I saw the bus pull away. I came home and told his sister all about this. To say the least, she was stunned.

People have asked me why I didn't confront Zach that morning, before he was back at rehab, as it was so obvious what he had done. There are many reasons, but primarily I was well aware that rehab was the safest place for him and I didn't want to risk that he wouldn't return to rehab. He had so clearly underlined that he needed rehab more than ever, and if he had decided to run away or disappear in NYC, the whole situation would have become exponentially more complicated and dangerous. Also, I was angry about being put through this experience, and I knew I wasn't the right person to take him through the inner journey of facing up to what he'd done, certainly not at that time. I am also not physically as strong as he is, and I am certainly not strong enough to hold him if he had decided to fight me or run away. Most of all, I thought the whole process would be easier if his relapse were sorted out in rehab.

Somehow, Zach passed the physical inspection back at rehab, which is pretty amazing because they were looking out for him to bring something back. He also did whatever it is that he learned to do so well, and cheated again on the urine screen, so he passed the drug test because "somehow" no THC appeared, although later they did find benzos in another more sensitive test. But the most amazing part is that he did succeed in hiding some pills and weed, by taping it to his leg under the bandages for his "wound". (He had asked me for more bandages just before we left for the bus station). At rehab he enjoyed his new supply with another patient there.

Shall we say it all hit the fan when it occurred to them to unwind the leg bandage, where they discovered some joints and some pills, and he confessed to sneaking out of the house via his bedroom window for a rendezvous with his dealer. His dealer's nickname, and I am not making this up, was "Light". What an ironic and astonishingly ridiculous name for a drug dealer. Remarkably, he had not only brought goodies back for the rehab kids, he'd left some in his room; anticipating another home pass within a week or two, he hid a stash in an old VCR. His brother and sister spent several hours, with great amusement, trying to fish it all out. When they did, I took it with me over to a different river on the other side of town, where a friend and I could drop it in the water, improvising a little ceremony and asking the Universe to help him end his drug use. Heck, a mom can try! He said he hid more pot somewhere in the park near our apartment, which was probably what he hoped to retrieve when he wanted to go commune with nature. If I had known where it was, I'd have gone to find it long ago and dropped that in the river as well.

I feel I need to make a few comments about marijuana use. With marijuana now legal in numerous states, many consider it benign. While this may be true for some people or even most people, there are those for whom addiction may develop. There are those who say addiction to marijuana can't happen, but I disagree, as it certainly proved so with my son. And I have seen other young people in rehab who were also addicted. This does not mean that I do not appreciate the medical value of THC, as I have two friends, both healthy and productive, who have controlled their cancers without chemotherapy, only by using oils with a high THC concentration. And I am not talking about CBD, as that has very little THC, which is the part of marijuana that makes people high. Personally, I believe teenagers with growing bodies and brains, as well as sensitive people who are not using marijuana for a medical purpose, need to remain conscious of the addictive potential, and proceed with caution.

Getting the entire truth about all this out of Zach took many days. He didn't call me until five days later to admit the relapse and I didn't find out about bringing the pot back to rehab until ten days later. Most amazing of all was his angry reaction that the rehab staff and his Mom had "allowed" him to relapse. He was enraged that we hadn't prevented it.

Besides the relapse, the other thing he did – leaving an apartment in NYC by a window at night – was physically dangerous. Had he slipped and fallen, he might have gotten hurt or even died. We are only on the second floor, but there is a deep "moat" around the building. I'm guessing that the drop from his window to the bottom of that moat must be thirty feet. There are iron rails and the window ledge is narrow. The building is made of stone. If he had gone by somebody else's window, they might have become alarmed and called the police. And his counselor pointed out a neighbor might have thought he was an intruder and he could have been shot. Also, he gave no thought that his actions might have endangered my relationship with my landlord. As I had gone to bed and to sleep, he easily could have avoided all this and left by the front door. I asked his therapist why he hadn't done that and the therapist said that the rituals around a drug purchase are like foreplay: they make it all more exciting.

I was actually extremely grateful for this relapse. I had grown deeply concerned whether Zach would ever expose the depth and severity of his addiction and his lying at the rehab facility. He is a genuinely nice guy, polite, charming, well-mannered, sensitive, extremely likable, and pleasant company. He can read people well and say to them what he thinks they want to hear. People like him, a lot. He was doing this rehab program well and making lots of progress. All he had to do was control himself for another couple of weekend home visits and the counselors might have convinced me to let him try coming home to school in the fall. What a disaster that would have been and how grateful I am for the relapse, which led to a longer, more successful treatment program somewhere else!

Because when all this blew up, the treatment center realized Zach needed longer term rehab.

After the rehab program thankfully threw the book at him, there were not going to be any more home visits or phone calls, and we collectively decided to transfer him to another program, ASAP. We picked a program in the southwest, chosen because it was way out in the wilderness, so far from anywhere or any city that running away or escaping to find drugs was virtually impossible. If he did attempt a relapse or decide to run away there, he'd have to walk at least an hour across a rattlesnake and scorpion infested desert to find a city. This new program asked me to leave him there a year, and I agreed.

In addition to the expected therapeutic aspects of the program, as well as school, they also offered equine therapy, and the program considered its horses among its best therapists. The day Zach arrived, the program assigned him a horse, Ace, as I recall. I got calls from my son complaining about this horse, as he reported that Ace was completely uncooperative, absolutely stubborn, wouldn't do anything he asked him to do, and was rebellious and difficult in general. He said to me that I had no idea how tough it was to deal with a creature who never did anything you wanted him to do! I would listen politely, but I was tempted to reply, "wow, ain't karma a bitch".

Eventually he figured out how to deal with Ace, by building a relationship with Ace, letting Ace take the lead, and becoming sensitive to what the horse was telling my son to do, (not the other way around). As soon as he figured this out, they gave him a different horse, with whom he was to learn different lessons. Over his time there, he had a number of horses, all different, each requiring a unique sensitivity lesson on the part of the rider. The lessons that were learned involved another being, obviously delivered powerfully, via a great big awesome creature they couldn't "control".

For a period of time, even out there, my son still wasn't getting the message, and he kept demanding I send him some expensive headphones, called Beats, to listen to his music. I had no intention of indulging him. Then I had an idea. I found a box about the size of the box Beats headphones came in, and I filled it full of beets, the vegetable. When my son opened the package, I was told it created quite a stir. Apparently, this became a notorious tale at rehab, one that is repeated to this day, so kids still hear about it!

The program also had a strong service component, believing the young men in its care would do better with their recoveries if they considered the desperate needs of the impoverished and made some attempt to help them. Essentially, they were being taught to think of others, and not just themselves. The kids were always involved in various activities designed to raise money for poor families, like fund-raising car washes and golf tournaments, or selling their student-created art projects, and they helped local families take care of their homes, yards, and children.

Every year, some of them went on an international service trip, and my son went with a group to Nepal. During the month there, the boys taught orphans in a local orphanage for half the day, and the other half of the day they helped out Buddhist monks around the temple, did yoga, meditated, and spent time with an English-speaking monk, who was also a rising political leader in Nepal.

I have some terrific pictures of my son in the most improbable settings during this trip, like sitting among people at a funeral pyre who had just smeared themselves with the white ashes of the dead, or playing with orphans with the peaks of the Himalayas in the background, or riding on an elephant.

For my son, I believe this trip was life-changing. He wrote a powerful article for the rehab's March 2011 school journal about this experience, crediting the trip with a spiritual awakening and eye-opening awareness about his addiction. Here's a quote:

"In Nepal, I made the decision to be freed from shame and not carry around negative feelings anymore. Instead, I put my focus into doing whatever actions I can do in the present moment to help someone.

Surrounded by the spiritual magic of Nepal and caught by surprise on bumpy bus rides in between sightseeing and cultural events, I experienced moments free from the mental torments of this life, moments where I was granted total serenity and freedom from all thought, except those simple thoughts pertaining to the present moment."

In that amazing Himalayan setting, he resolved to stay sober and be of service to others in the future.

The rehab program also included a requirement that their students get training in a useful profession of their choosing, one that didn't require college or further education, and one with immediate post-rehab employment prospects. My son became a certified sous-chef, which served him well when he worked in restaurants all the way through college. Today he is an excellent cook and we all enjoy his culinary creations.

The program also encouraged the young men in their charge to learn to have fun without drugs or alcohol. They were offered many options, such as snowboarding, rock climbing, paintball, flag football, hikes, horse treks, and positive peer culture weekends. In addition, they attended AA meetings off-site as well as sober conferences in a variety of cities. The emphasis was on demonstrating that they could have a lot of fun, and still remain sober.

After a few months in the desert, the program moved him to their transitional program in town, which allowed more freedom, though there were still many rules and therapy continued. He made some good friends in the program, and after a few months, they moved into an apartment together, and having now graduated from high school through the program, began attending the local university. Remarkably, he even began working in the rehab program, as a student counselor. Zach and his roommates lived a normal college life. They had signed an agreement that if one of them relapsed, he'd have to move out. Zach told me the police had shown up at a party at his apartment one Saturday night, after the neighbors had complained about the loud music. When the police arrived, they asked how much everyone had been drinking and what drugs they were using. My son and his roommates told the police that this was a sober party and they could search the premises if they wanted to, but they'd find nothing at all except for food and sodas.

During his time at this program, Zach got the message loud and clear. And since then his life has continually evolved into the life that he, and his mother, once dreamed about.

While I am eternally grateful to my son for his amazing progress, I am never far from remembering that some of his friends, young people I knew and cared about, didn't make it. There were several, but especially I think about a young man I'll call John. He was one of my son's best friends in this desert program, as well as one of his roommates in college. I will never forget his kindness to me on several occasions when I was at parent gatherings. Most memorably, one evening I had just arrived from the airport for a parent weekend. It was hot and I was tired, and I got to the rehab center just in time for dinner. The young men cooked dinner themselves, and when I took my place at the table I saw a selection of Diet Coke, Dr. Pepper, and Diet Ginger Ale. John must have seen my face, because I was really quite thirsty but didn't want to drink soda. Quietly, without fanfare, he came over with a few bottles of water and said he thought I'd probably prefer drinking water, which I most certainly did. All during the dinner he paid attention to me, and the other parents as well, and treated us with great kindness. He was an exceptionally thoughtful and lovely young man.

A few years later, after he had returned home to live with his family, John relapsed and began drinking again. One New Year's, he went with some friends to a lake house in a neighboring state, and under the influence of who-knows-what, he and three other young men decided to go for a canoe ride on the icy lake in the middle of a bitterly cold night. They were not even wearing coats, and there were four of them, all large guys, in a three-person canoe. Nobody knew where they had gone or what they were doing. The canoe overturned and they all drowned in the freezing water.

There were others who didn't make it as well, including a young man who ran away from the first rehab, got drunk, and was hit and killed by a car, and a couple who overdosed with their baby asleep in the same room, and others who went directly from rehab to relapse and died. Still, I remember John most vividly, possibly because he was such a good friend to my son and so kind to me and the other parents. The loss of a young person like this is so utterly senseless and tragic.

I am very well aware that Zach might easily have had a similar story. He and I were both very lucky. But truthfully, it involved much more than luck. Whatever inner journey it took for him to decide to walk a sober path, he started walking and hasn't stopped. He gets the credit for making this happen and continuing to nourish his recovery.

Today he has over 10 years sober, has finished medical school and is working in the Emergency Medicine Department in a large teaching hospital, has married a wonderful young woman (herself a physician), and in every way has a very bright future ahead of him. He maintains his activity in AA, and frequently runs off to meetings, even with his demanding schedule. He has my deepest respect and gratitude.

I should also speak about a battle I had with an insurance company over payment for Zach's treatment, as my success might encourage others. When he entered the first inpatient rehab program (and all of these programs are very expensive), I called the insurance company and asked what they would cover. They said they would cover 80% of the first month, and if he needed to remain in the program longer, they'd cover most of that at the same rate as well.

As promised, they reimbursed much of the first month of treatment, especially the portion he needed to spend in the hospital, but they balked when asked to reimburse for the longer period. I asked for a review, and again, we were turned down. On the advice of the rehab's business office, I put together a large packet of materials and sent it off to the NY State Insurance Board. My materials included information from all the well-known rehabs affirming that 28 days of treatment is not sufficient, various supporting articles written by leading experts, my son's full and complete medical records including those from the rehab center, and so forth. The package was huge – as large as the old New York City phone book. The rehab folks had also pointed out that the insurance company's reviewer was not an addiction specialist, so I made a big deal of that.

I did not pursue this insurance review believing that I would win. I pursued it because I thought it was the right thing to do. It made me very angry that insurance wouldn't pay for my son's treatment when it was so clearly needed to save his life. I figured that somebody had to start squawking about this problem, and that if I began, perhaps others would follow, hoping that eventually the collective voice might compel insurance companies to pay for more than the first few weeks of a medically required extensive stay.

Imagine my surprise when I won, and the State's review overturned the insurance company's decision and required them to reimburse me for 80% of the extended treatment fees! I kept my successful packet of materials for several years, offering it as a template to anyone else who might want to take a crack at getting an insurance company to pay for addiction treatment, but no one ever took me up on my offer. Eventually I threw the thing out.

PART TWO

Guns, HIPAA, Legal Issues, and Beacons of Hope

CHAPTER 9

Guns

Guns. Why did it have to be guns? I always thought my oldest son wouldn't be able to buy a gun, due to his well-established history. I always thought this was one problem we'd never have to deal with. Boy, was I wrong.

About a year after moving to Alaska, using a fake name (a choice so laughable it should have aroused suspicion immediately) and a credit card also issued in a fake name, he bought a handgun from one online store, and large amounts of ammo from another. He also tried to buy a second gun at a local gun shop in Alaska. Though I do not know a lot of specifics about gun possession laws, it is rather obvious that if Galen has the ability to purchase one, our current gun laws do not do enough to keep guns out of the hands of the mentally ill. We are fooling ourselves if we think otherwise. I would not have thought these purchases possible, and certainly not by him. But I was wrong and it was possible, and easily done.

I'm not against all guns. I grew up in the West, after all. If responsible, sane people have guns, and they keep them safely locked up, gun possession isn't going to cause any problems. All my grandparents and great-grandparents were Westerners who owned guns and needed guns. My maternal grandparents lived on a ranch and used a rifle to hunt animals for food, as well as to protect their chickens and livestock, not to mention themselves. One of my aunts married a Navy Commander who loved skeet shooting. She got involved in his hobby and skeet shooting became an important part of their social lives, especially after they retired. Meals at our family gatherings often included venison, pheasant, and duck provided by the hunters in the family. And I hear it is a lot of fun to shoot tin cans off fence posts.

But that's not what we are talking about here.

Gun ownership should assume that the person owning the gun is sane, and will use a firearm responsibly. In my son's case, neither is true. If he were to own a gun, someone, himself or someone else, would get hurt or die; that much is a near certainty. People die because of guns every day, every hour of the day. Even among my parents' reasonable, sane, gun owning friends, there was a suicide with a gun, when one of my father's friends received a serious medical diagnosis.

When I first heard about Galen's attempted gun purchases, I called the local police in his town in Alaska. They provided all sorts of solid help and information, and a terrific local policeman personally saw to it that the guns Galen tried to purchase never got into his hands. I don't know the details, but it seemed that online purchases had to be sent to a local gun store, where Galen could pick them up. The policeman stopped the sales. This officer told me, and I'm quoting precisely, "gun ownership is not a right, but a privilege that has to be earned and kept with responsible behavior" and that furthermore "having a gun should require a license just like having a car requires a driver's license, and that individuals should only be allowed to keep a gun and license as long as they handle the responsibilities safely." I could not have put it better and I couldn't agree more.

I am incredibly grateful to this thoughtful police officer. This experience certainly underlines an immense national need for the sort of gun control laws that would make it impossible for someone like my son to own a gun. When I asked my son why he wanted a gun, he told me that he needed it for personal protection (his illness makes him super-paranoid and his temper creates arguments and fights with others constantly), and also because guns are a "common household item, like a kitchen sponge".

I was convinced he'd be in deep trouble with ATF, as it is illegal to buy a gun with an alias, just as it is illegal to lie about one's mental health history, or arrest history, or use a fake credit card for a gun purchase. But there wasn't so much as a peep from ATF! I was shocked. Recently there was an interesting article in the Washington Post about how very few gun purchase violations were ever pursued and prosecuted by ATF; in fact, almost none of them are. If you want to read the article for yourself, it's called "Lying to buy a handgun? Don't worry about the Feds". It was written by Joe Davidson, and it was published on September 12, 2018.

Here's an excerpt from the article:

"If you lied to buy a firearm, fear not the feds.

Your chances of being prosecuted by the Justice Department for falsifying information to illegally buy a gun are almost zero.

Reviews by the National Instant Criminal Background Check System in fiscal 2017 led to 112,000 gun-purchase denials because people were in forbidden categories, according to a new report by the Government Accountability Office (GAO). The Justice Department's Bureau of Alcohol, Tobacco, Firearms and Explosives (ATF) investigated 12,700 of those cases.

How many of the investigated cases resulted in prosecutions?

Twelve.

That's 0.09 percent of the cases ATF investigated.

That means the crooks, the wife beaters and the homicidal maniacs who lie to get a gun have little reason to worry that Uncle Sam will get them for faking on Form 4473. It lists nine questions designed to cull those who should not be strapped. The questions include: 'Have you ever been convicted in any court of a felony,' 'Are you a fugitive from justice,' and 'Have you ever been adjudicated as a mental defective.'"

It's pretty horrifying that the culture of gun ownership runs so deep in this country that out and out crazy people are buying guns effortlessly. Does this not occur to gun advocates? We see evidence of this all the time, in the relentless mass shootings we are all dealing with. Surely any sensible person would agree that this is an unbelievable situation.

People with mental illness should not have the right to purchase a gun, period. And I am profoundly grateful to the policeman who stopped my son from acquiring a firearm. It is a safety issue, for my son and all concerned, not a violation of his civil liberties. He should absolutely, positively not be allowed to buy a gun, ever. He's too volatile and just plain crazy. On several occasions, if he'd had a gun, he would have shot me. It's too easy, and quick, to vent anger by pulling a trigger.

As a society, we will continue to suffer mass shootings and family tragedies until we come to our senses about guns. For years, I've had a deep fear that Galen and I could find ourselves in the middle of a mass tragedy, with our faces plastered all over every front page in the nation, glowing out from every TV, if he ever got hold of a gun. Whatever comes to pass in the future, over which I have no control, I will do anything and everything I possibly can to prevent Galen from ever owning a gun.

The kind officer in Alaska also helped me find the local fiduciary services agency that helped oversee my son's affairs. They manage his finances, allowance, and monthly expenses, his housing, and most importantly restrict Galen's access to cash so that he never has enough on hand at any one time for a gun purchase. Those of us living through these horrendous situations have to remember that even awful circumstances can bring positive and unexpected gifts to us and to our family members, and introduce us to some wonderful people.

As of this writing, there is a bill in congress that would require universal background checks for gun purchases. The need for this law is so clear, and the proposed law makes so much sense, but it isn't going anywhere as of now, and its future is bleak. There are many other great ideas proposed by sensible leaders and impassioned gun violence victims. Still, nothing ever gets done. This is horrifying. Whenever we have a mass shooting, which often happen one right after the other, everyone is shocked and upset. Would it be too much to dream that perhaps something could finally get done? Most people have had enough, and a large majority of us believe we should have greater gun control laws than we have now, but who knows whether that will be enough to make changes.

It has been widely reported that the mother of the shooter in the El Paso incident in August of 2019 had asked the police for information about whether her son had been able to purchase his assault rifle legally. On August 8, 2019, CNN's Scott Glover and Majlie de Puy Kamp filed a report with the headline "El Paso shooter's mother called police concerned about gun":

"The El Paso shooting suspect's mother called the Allen, Texas, Police Department weeks before the shooting because she was concerned about her son owning an 'AK' type firearm, lawyers for the family confirmed to CNN.

The mother contacted police because she was worried about her son owning the weapon given his age, maturity level and lack of experience handling such a firearm, attorneys Chris Ayres and R. Jack Ayres said.

During the call, the mother was transferred to a public safety officer who told her that based on her description of the situation -- her son, 21, was legally allowed to purchase the weapon, the attorneys said. The mother did not provide her name or her son's name, and police did not seek any additional information from her before the call concluded, they added."

It appears that no one knows precisely what she asked them, but even so, why wasn't her phone call enough to merit an investigation? And if the answer to her questions was that her son "was legally allowed to purchase the weapon", so the police could do nothing and "did not seek any additional information from her before the call concluded", then we have a very serious problem.

At a minimum, we need enforceable laws that prevent the mentally ill from owning or having access to guns. Lives depend on this. When are we going to wake up, folks? How many more people have to die in mass shootings? Several dozen every week? Hundreds every year? That happens a lot already. Do we need even bigger numbers? Why can't our nation's lawmakers do something to help families prevent a deadly situation, before it unfolds? If I can attest to the nature and quality of my son's mental illness, I should have some help, and some say, in keeping him away from guns. Why is this so hard?

From what I can determine, the State of Alaska has some of the most permissive gun laws in the nation, and very few regulations regarding their sale. For me, it is astonishing to realize that no permit is required to purchase or own a gun in Alaska. I wonder if Alaskan lawmakers have any idea of the ongoing nightmares these permissive laws create for families of the mentally ill?!

Given these laws, and the fact that my son lived in Alaska for a number of years, I am incredibly grateful to the policeman who helped me keep guns out of his hands. Much of the information about Alaska's gun laws listed below is from the Giffords Law Center website, and the information is current as of November 1, 2019.

Alaska's Gun Laws

Universal Background Checks

Alaska does not require a background check on the purchaser of a firearm when the seller is not a licensed dealer.

Alaska prohibits any person from knowingly selling or transferring a concealable firearm to any person convicted of a felony or whose physical or mental condition is substantially impaired by liquor or controlled substances.

Comment: "knowingly" is perhaps a key word here. It is perhaps difficult to prove that someone "knowingly" sold a concealable firearm to a person convicted of a felony, especially since no background check is required.

For the same reason, the following law also lacks teeth:

The state also prohibits any person from knowingly selling a firearm to anyone under age 18.

Concealed Carry

Alaska does not require a permit to carry a concealed firearm.

Open Carry

Alaska does not prohibit the open carrying of firearms in public.

Guns in Schools

Alaska has no specific statutes or regulations restricting firearms on college or university property.

Gun dealer licensing

Alaska has no law requiring firearms dealers to obtain a state license or permit.

Comment: There is a federal law that dealers must get licensed through the Bureau of Alcohol, Tobacco, Firearms & Explosives (ATF), but if you wonder about their track record on such matters, please refer back to the Joe Davidson article in the Washington Post earlier in this chapter, where he writes "Your chances of being prosecuted by the Justice Department for falsifying information to illegally buy a gun are almost zero" In fact, as he calculated, 0.09 percent of the cases that the ATF investigated resulted in prosecutions.

Alaska has no law requiring dealers to conduct a background check on prospective firearm purchasers.

Licensing in Alaska

Alaska has no law requiring gun owners or purchasers to obtain a license.

Waiting Periods in Alaska

Alaska imposes no waiting period between the time of purchase and the actual physical transfer of a firearm.

Categories of Prohibited People in Alaska

Alaska prohibits a person from possessing a concealable firearm (i.e., handgun) after having been convicted of a felony or adjudicated a delinquent minor for conduct that would constitute a felony if committed by an adult by any court. However, this prohibition does not apply if the felony was not an offense against a person and a period of 10 years or more has elapsed between the date of the person's unconditional discharge and the date of the violation.

In 2010, Alaska repealed a law that prohibited a person intoxicated by liquor or a controlled substance from possessing a handgun.

Alaska has no state law prohibiting firearm purchase or possession by:

- Violent misdemeanants;
- Persons with mental illness; or
- Persons subject to domestic violence restraining orders.

Child Access Prevention in Alaska
Alaska has no law specifically penalizing allowing children access to firearms.

Assault Weapons
Alaska has no law restricting assault weapons.

Large Capacity Magazines
Alaska has no law restricting large capacity magazines.

Ammunition Regulation in Alaska
Alaska does not:
- Require a license for the sale of ammunition;
- Require sellers of ammunition to maintain a record of the purchasers.

Fifty Caliber Rifles
Alaska has no law restricting fifty caliber rifles.

Trafficking & Straw Purchasing in Alaska
Alaska does not:

- Penalize a firearms dealer for failing to conduct the federally required background check on a purchaser;
- Prohibit any person from giving false information or offering false evidence of his or her identity in purchasing or otherwise securing delivery of a firearm;
- Prohibit obtaining a firearm with the intent to provide it to someone the person knows is ineligible to possess a firearm; or
- Have any other laws aimed at firearms trafficking.

Bulk Gun Purchases

Alaska has no law restricting sales or purchases of multiple firearms.

Design Safety Standards

Alaska imposes no design safety standards on handguns.

Comments: There are problems here. One, when you add all of this up, almost anybody in Alaska can buy a gun. Also, that anyone over 21 can carry a concealed weapon. While we can debate the merits of this, imagine the possibilities when an unstable or mentally ill individual procures a handgun that they can carry with them at all times. And then one day while in the fog of psychosis they see the person sitting quietly at the bus stop as an imminent threat.

Also, there is the law that a convicted felon cannot possess a gun until 10 years have passed since the day they are out of jail. This is a great law. Unfortunately, as we see, no state permit is required to possess a rifle, shotgun or handgun. So why would anybody selling a gun have any reason to ask the potential buyer how long it has been since they were released from prison?

So amongst other problems these laws introduce, police will have no idea of who has a gun, or how many guns that individual may possess. And as we discussed earlier, a gun seller has no legal obligation to know the mental state of the person seeking to purchase a gun. These are issues that present real problems, that will only lead to more senseless killings.

CHAPTER 10

HIPAA, Your Child, and You

Part 1, when your child is under 18

There is a moment in every parent's life, when your child is maybe 12 or 13, and your pediatrician says, "Today you ought to remain in the waiting room during the physical exam, as it is appropriate at this age for your child to do this alone." It seems innocent enough, and, looking back, I can even remember thinking it was yet another milestone reached on the way to growing up. Few parents understand that something dramatic has just happened, an event with potentially chilling, even life-altering implications, a development that has taken place in secrecy, or at least without any attempt to clarify to the parent the full breadth of how the relationship between the parent and the pediatrician has just dramatically changed. 12th birthdays slipped quietly past one by one while my kids continued to see the same pediatrician they saw since birth.

But here is something I didn't know: from this point forward, if your child has not given specific written permission allowing their physician to share information with you, including permission for you to see results of tests, even basic tests like blood tests, you will not see the results.

When I speak of HIPAA regulations, what comes to your mind? What understanding do you have of these laws and what they might mean in your life? I have never spoken to a single parent who comprehends the full extent of what HIPAA laws mean, with regard to your relationship with medical professionals and what HIPAA laws permit them to tell you about your child.

HIPAA regulations and other similar laws were created to protect the privacy rights of patients, which is absolutely laudable. They also protect the rights of minors to seek advice about birth control, drug use, and other similar topics without their parents finding out, and possibly going ballistic. I do understand the desirability of protecting young people, so that they might have a safe place to talk about drugs, sex, and maybe family issues. I understand that many parents wouldn't be empathetic to a young teenager seeking birth control, or honest discussions of drug use. I totally agree that it is better for a young teen to obtain birth control from a physician than the alternative of not asking for it, if he or she is worried about their parents finding out they have become sexually active. Perhaps with these issues, one can empathize with the tough situations that the HIPAA laws cover, but it is more difficult to understand when we are talking about burgeoning, imminently life-threatening mental health or addiction issues.

I thought, like most parents (and probably like you) that these privacy laws kicked in when kids turn 18. Indeed, when I tell other parents about the true facts of the situation, everybody is completely surprised. I've never met another parent, no matter how well educated or sophisticated that wasn't surprised, and this is true even for physicians who do not treat children. Most parents, even smart, hip parents, do not know about this. They do not know that doctors will provide them with absolutely no information about their child's medical or mental condition without written permission given to the doctor by their child. Information can be shared only if it is of an immediate life-threatening nature, such as an active desire to commit suicide at that exact moment (which means only at that precise moment, not five minutes ago or with a potential for feeling the same way later that night).

I certainly didn't know this.

It is possible that many doctors still see drug use as a personal choice, about which they can educate their young patients and steer them in a different direction. Perhaps they simply do not pay attention to when it becomes addiction, even though full-blown addiction is a life-threatening, but treatable, medical condition.

When my younger son began experimenting with drugs, I didn't fully comprehend the extent of what was going on, as his behavior didn't immediately change all that much. However, my pediatrician had known all about his drug use for two or three years, and blood tests had confirmed what he knew, but the results were not shared with me. I had no idea that we were flying into a cyclone as a family, and had no concept of what I needed to do to prepare. I don't think this is fair, not to me or to other parents.

And this situation happened so quietly, so subtly, that it was only possible to perceive it in retrospect. Had I known that I was being kept in the dark, at the very least I would have recognized that I needed to learn more about HIPAA, including precisely what a physician was or was not able to tell me and under what circumstances. I would have then explored my options based on that knowledge. Other parents can wise up about this and be proactive, but first you have to know the truth. Physicians should explain to parents, clearly, what and when they will or will not tell them. If I had an inkling that it was possible for my kid's doctor to withhold medical information about him from me, I would have become a good deal more aware and watchful.

With HIPAA as it presently stands, the first checkup without a parent in the room established an impenetrable wall: a legal shield that will bar parents, from that day going forward, from accessing information about anything discussed between the child and the clinician, about anything learned by the medical staff during the visit, about any concerns that are revealed, no matter how serious, no matter the potential consequences for the child's life or the parent's ability to look out for the well-being of that child.

I needed to get written permission from my kids in order to have access to everything the doctor knew about them. I had no idea. Sometimes parents ask me what a parent should do if the child says no. For things that are important, and for me it is vitally important to converse openly with my child's doctor, you have to stand your ground. This boundary needs to be clear. Even if the doctor was convinced he or she was dutifully following HIPAA regulations, I believe the interpretation of those regulations may have been different if my kid had been sick with some other disease. If my son needed an appendectomy, for example, would the doctor have refused to tell me, even if my son had told him not to tell me, maybe because he didn't want to go to the hospital? Or what if my son had done some teenage shenanigan and had really hurt himself, receiving a hospital-worthy injury in the process? If he had told the doctor not to tell me because he thought I'd be mad about what he'd done, would the doctor still have kept his mouth shut and refused to tell me my child needed to go to the ER?

I'm confident the doctor would have shown more sense in these situations, and would have told me he needed immediate treatment. I can't actually imagine, HIPAA or no HIPAA, a situation where a teenager needs in-patient hospitalization for a life-threatening medical condition without informing the parents, unless the life-threatening condition is one related to addiction. My son did require hospitalization at the beginning of his first inpatient rehab for withdrawal from benzodiazepines, as withdrawal from these drugs is medically dangerous. But his pediatrician never told me a thing. How much better would it have been if we might have worked together to get treatment for my son!

However, as the laws stand now, children have all the privacy protections and rights and the parents have no access to information needed to make decisions, which makes parenting extremely difficult if your child presents with any number of issues out of a whole spectrum of problems.

I'd like to make it clear I do not know enough about the fine points of HIPAA regulations to understand precisely how following these regulations might impact a doctor's license or if there are any other considerations of which I am unaware. In this book my concern is how the laws that we currently have, including HIPAA, have impacted me and impacted my family, not always in a positive manner, and to initiate conversation about their possible change.

Dr. E Fuller Torrey, the founder of the Treatment Advocacy Center in Arlington, VA (TAC), said in his excellent book, *Surviving Schizophrenia*, on pages 257-258:

> "In recent years it has become increasingly clear to everyone that the HIPAA law, as currently written, is impeding the treatment of individuals with schizophrenia and other serious mental illnesses. In 2016, members of Congress introduced legislation to amend the HIPAA law and, although such legislation has not yet been passed, it is likely to do so in the near future. It has also become clear that HIPAA is protecting public officials more than it is protecting patients. Whenever a high-profile homicide occurs in which a mentally ill person is thought to have been the perpetrator, public officials invoke the HIPAA law to justify not giving out any information, including information about how they failed to provide treatment to that individual. Indeed, the greatest utility of the HIPAA law to date is in protecting the backsides of public officials."

I would add that this law protects the backsides of physicians too, and though Dr. Torrey's book was written about schizophrenia, these statements surely apply to all forms of mental illness, including addiction.

I have met some doctors who have told me that they are up front with parents about everything learned in exams with their young patients, insisting that all young patients sign releases or other needed paperwork. These doctors are rare. But in order to find one, first you have to know you need one.

Here's how the situation I am describing can play out. Let's say your child tells someone at school he is thinking about killing himself, a situation that I am all too familiar with. The school will call you, alarmed, and insist you come to the school to pick up your child, telling you they are afraid to send him home on the bus. They will insist that your child seek psychological help immediately, and make it clear he or she cannot come back to school until he or she no longer presents a danger to himself or herself or others. If your child tells his or her pediatrician, however, instead of the school, the doctor can do nothing and you will be told nothing unless the doctor feels this is an immediate threat, meaning that the suicide will take place now or within a few minutes. Both of these experiences have happened to me.

Until my younger son was in rehab, I didn't learn the full extent of his drug use. And I also didn't learn, until then, that my child's drugs of choice were Benzodiazepines, including Klonopin and Ambien, that his psychiatrist prescribed. Unbelievably, just like the pediatrician, my son's psychiatrist knew my son was addicted and said nothing to me. Even more astonishingly, he continued to prescribe the drugs! I can't think of anything more horrifying, except perhaps my son's statement, when he was in rehab, that he considered the psychiatrist his dealer.

After my son was in his first inpatient rehab, I confronted this psychiatrist. Zach had seen him for years, and he had prescribed the Benzos and other medications. So when I discovered my son's "drugs of choice" were Benzos, I was very upset. The rehab center had asked me to obtain copies of all Zach's medical files and prescription history, and with Zach's permission, the psychiatrist dutifully provided me with a couple of sheets of paper. Now, while I am not saying he fibbed to me, I am saying the brevity of his file on my son surprised me and even stunned me. I have to admit I was annoyed with myself too, for trusting these professionals so much, and never questioning what they were doing. It feels very strange and unsettling to realize I dutifully filled and paid for all those prescriptions for years, thinking I was helping my son, when I was doing the exact opposite.

Learning about my son's biggest addiction problem, and the dangerous benzodiazepines, *only after* he was in rehab, shocked me. Once my son was admitted safely to rehab, I decided to call the other doctor who took care of Zach, his pediatrician, a doctor who had taken care of all my children since birth. I asked him how he thought I was feeling about his secrecy all those years. He said he could certainly understand my anger and frustration, but the most important thing for him, as a doctor, was to maintain his credibility with his patients. I told him I thought my child's life was far more important than his credibility, and I felt he had put my child's life at risk.

Obviously, I never wanted to use this pediatrician again under any circumstances, but wouldn't you know we needed to get more blood testing done quickly before a medical school deadline because Zach had a false positive TB test during the first testing. The easiest solution was to ask this pediatrician to do the tests, and that's what happened. He asked my son "Is your mom still mad at me?" My son said that I was. Actually, that's not true. I'm not mad at him at this point, because I don't have time or energy to devote to being mad at him, and I also don't believe staying mad at someone is very healthy. But I am fearful for the harm his all-knowing attitude might cause in the lives of his current patients, and for the harm HIPAA laws can do, in general.

Here are my questions: Under what circumstances is it OK for doctors to keep silent and "maintain their credibility"? Is it really OK for a parent to find out what the pediatrician has known for years, only at the point a minor child is seriously ill and in rehab? Don't we send our children to professionals so that that those professionals "have our backs", and can help us do the best job possible raising our kids? Don't we expect our docs to keep us informed, so we can make the right decisions for our kids?

Doctors see our kids for a few minutes, and we are with them all the time. We need physicians to help us keep our kids healthy, advising us based on their professional knowledge. I believe it is wrong for the medical community to assume responsibilities and rights that justly belong to parents, and think it is rather incredible that whoever wrote the HIPAA laws assume clinicians know how to handle issues like drug or alcohol use better than parents. If physicians have to follow the current HIPAA laws or risk losing their licenses, then those laws need changing.

If parents recognize this situation exists in advance, they could search for pediatricians and psychiatrists with whom they might communicate more openly and have a different kind of relationship. I have met a few doctors who are horrified by the extremes of HIPAA, and who tell their patients and families up front that in their practice consent forms are required so that information of a serious nature will be shared with parents, making it possible for medical professionals and families to work together. Some clinicians are adamant there will be no secrets in their practices. But again, we need to emphasize that in order to begin looking for such a doctor, first you have to know you need one. Unfortunately, if we are discussing parental rights in the current situation, given the laws that currently stand, the only right we parents have is the right to pay the bill. And yet you still have to parent as best you can, minus all the facts. What do you think? Is this right? Or fair?

Inform yourself. Ask your children's doctors how they would deal with this issue. Ask them whether they will tell you everything they learn in an exam or from tests. And prepare to be surprised.

Part 2, when your child is over 18

Sometimes I get calls from other parents whose teenage children are in trouble. Almost invariably, the parents are reluctant to deal with the pressing realities for the health and future of their child, as they can't bear to tear them away from the ongoing high school experiences or the social framework their children hold so dear. They want to let their kids finish high school before dealing with treatment or rehab. There's the dream of playing on a beloved baseball team, or going to the prom, or taking AP Bio, or whatever else.

Parents, get a grip! Every day without treatment for a minor who needs treatment is a wasted day, and potentially another day towards problems that might degenerate rapidly. Few parents realize that the only time you can legally force someone to get mental health or drug treatment is before they turn 18. And even if you can get them into treatment, they can walk away on their 18th birthday, because no program can hold them without their consent. There are rare exceptions to this, but they are extremely difficult to pursue. The best and easiest course of action is to get them into treatment at least a year, or as soon as possible, before they turn 18. The treatment program is less fun than the prom, but is probably more fun than getting a late-night call that your child is in jail, or worse.

In my opinion, as a society we have really messed up the application of civil liberties for the mentally ill. Without question, individual liberties are precious, and all of us hold them dear. But it is foolish to honor the civil liberties of a seriously mentally ill adult over 18 to the point they don't receive treatment because they refuse to accept it. As the psychiatric nurse from Washington said, "The laws of Washington state firmly protect your son's right to remain crazy." Sadly, this logic applies in the rest of the country as well.

Once a teenager has reached his or her 18th birthday, you have no "rights" to know anything at all. Many have commented about the absurdity of this situation with regards to college, that a parent's only "right" is to pay the tuition bill, to not even know what classes the student is taking, or whether they even go to class or what grades they earn. And much has been written lately concerning colleges and universities that do not inform parents about a depressed or even suicidal student, information sometimes kept from parents who first hear of it, sadly, only after it is too late. One article on this subject, "His College Knew of His Despair. His Parents Didn't, Until It Was Too Late.", by Anemona Hartocollis, was published on May 12, 2018 in the NY Times. Another article, written by Jane E. Brody, "Preventing Suicide Among College Students" was also published in the NY Times, on July 2, 2018. These are only two examples of many, easily found in an internet search.

Given the now common university requirement for parental

access to records through written student permission only, many parents have wised up and said "if you want me to pay for college, you have to give me permission to have access to your files and records at school, and to speak to faculty and staff about you". Perhaps some parents would abuse this privilege, even annoy some college administrators or faculty, and undoubtedly annoy their children. But in the case of a child with demonstrated addictive or depressive behavior, parents should not hesitate to insist. Do it. Not for the purpose of spying on your child, but for the purpose of watching for any signs of self-destruction.

However, because parents cannot legally compel their adult child or any other adult relative to seek treatment, families are left to cope the best they can. Quite often, this will involve the police.

For example, a friend of mine told me of her struggles with a relative. Her relative has a variety of physical and psychiatric illnesses and as a result takes a lot of medication. He gets violent if he doesn't take meds, or if he mixes up the combination. One day she received a phone call and he told her that he was going to go to the mall and kill people. She starts talking to him, keeps him on the phone, and gets in her car and drives a couple of hours to his home. On the way, she calls the police and tells them they need to pick this fellow up, due to his threats. When the police get there, he's calmer, so he is not at that exact moment a clear and present danger to himself or others, so they leave without taking him to a hospital.

In some of the recent mass shootings, family members are quoted as trying to phone employers to express concern, or calling the police, or appealing to their relative to please get some help. And yet there was nothing – literally nothing - they could legally do to compel a clearly deranged person into treatment, and possibly prevent a tragedy. Isn't this crazy, in itself??! One can imagine the personal torture these family members must go through afterwards, and yet there was nothing they could have done to change the destructive path they resolutely feared their loved one might, sadly, embark upon.

In Galen's story, I spoke about calling the police to go check on him in his dorm, and that they did not take him to a psych ward because he didn't appear to be a danger to himself at that moment. This is a common experience when you have a mentally ill relative. You might also remember that my son ran stark naked through an airport trying to get the police to kill him (called suicide by cop), and after being held 72 hours in a psychiatric hospital, was set free because he was deemed no longer a danger to himself or others at the time of release. But remember 3 weeks later he did another crazy thing when he made a high-speed U turn across a double yellow line in his rented car, right in front of the police. They stopped him and questioned him, determined he needed psychiatric care, and sent him to another psychiatric hospital. And as you may also remember, they also found knives in the trunk of his car.

The police are all too often in the thick of all this, and I have been very lucky to have had relationships with wonderful policemen in several towns where Galen has lived. But they tell me their hands are tied, just like the doctor's, both from HIPAA laws and existing laws about mental health care. I will discuss some possible changes we could make to those laws in the next chapter.

We need to wise up and change some of these laws, to protect ourselves, our children, and society. It is just so stupid not to do this! As a society, how can we all be so dumb?

CHAPTER 11

The Legal System and Mental Illness

If you set out to design terrible, ineffective, even useless laws regarding mental health care, you might end up with something like the ones currently in place. The system we have right now makes things incredibly difficult for families of the mentally ill, and getting a loved one into treatment is nearly impossible. Some states may do better than others, but in my own family's life, and the lives of so many others, we've had to sit by and watch our loved ones get sicker and sicker, and in the case of my ex-husband, die - all while waiting helplessly, unable to get them properly treated.

As I mentioned in an earlier chapter, a mental health professional once said to me "the laws concerning mental health treatment in this country are sicker than the sick people they are supposed to help" and "the mental health laws of our state firmly protect your son's right to be crazy." These quotes are worth repeating, because they say it all.

What on earth can anyone say about this mess? Looking through my family's history will provide many points where anyone might well wonder how things might have turned around were we able to enforce treatment. Admittedly one might make this point about other illnesses, such as families that make efforts to convince a diabetic to take insulin, or a heart patient to stop smoking. Clearly, families come up against habits that are hard to change. Mental illness is different, though, because the nature of the illness prevents the sufferer from comprehending accurately the nature or seriousness of their situation. Many severely mentally ill people suffer from the diagnosable condition Anosognosia, which means they have no ability to recognize that they are ill.

I'm not a lawyer and can't parse out the legal aspects of mental health care like a lawyer with expertise in the field. However, I can tell you how the laws play out every day in a family's life. After every big tragedy, Aurora, Sandy Hook, the Naval Yard, and so on, everybody always says the same thing. Why wasn't something done to prevent this? The shooter was clearly a deeply troubled young person, so why didn't somebody help? Why didn't somebody stop him (they are mostly young men), before he got to this point? Parents are often tacitly blamed for their offspring's tragic behavior, though legally their hands were tied and they had no options for intervening.

But the sad answer, the truth, is that nobody can do a thing. Nothing, perhaps with the obvious exception of keeping one's personal weapons safely locked away. As discussed, compelling anyone over 18 to undergo psychiatric treatment or hospitalization hovers somewhere between extremely difficult and completely impossible, and such a compelled hospitalization is nearly always for a short time. The maximum time frame is usually 72 hours, nowhere close to the lengthy treatment that is almost always called for. Nobody would think a 72-hour hospitalization would cure diabetes or heart disease, but nobody is thinking clearly, obviously, if they expect a short hospitalization is going to cure someone with serious mental illness.

If you surmise you are dealing with a problem that needs professional help, then getting a diagnosis, finding treatment, convincing your child or relative to submit to the necessary treatment and testing is all very overwhelming and emotionally draining, as well as expensive. And you are facing a nearly insurmountable series of obstacles if you want to place an adult into long term treatment, should they resist. And there are no clear-cut guidelines or established procedures for doing so.

As I've searched over the years for ways to discuss the lack of helpful legal options for families traumatized by SMI, I was grateful to discover an organization known as the Treatment Advocacy Center, whose work I have mentioned before. The TAC is located in Arlington, Virginia and was founded by Dr. E. Fuller Torrey, a psychiatrist who is the author of several excellent books including *Surviving Schizophrenia, A Family Manual*, which I have quoted elsewhere. For further information, there is much useful information on their website (www.treatmentadvocacycenter.org), and it is worth your time to explore it. I'd heartily recommend getting on their mailing list as well. This is a great organization and it deserves our support in every way.

In the fall of 2018, the TAC sent me their Catalyst Newsletter, which contained an article laying out 12 policy recommendation for mental health laws. I think their 12 policy recommendations nail it, as they are clearly laid out and easy to follow. For me personally, their sensible recommendations - especially about inpatient commitment - hit closest to home, as the inability to commit either my husband or my son against their will has caused immense suffering for both of them, and for me, and for the rest of the family.

If there might be just one thing I personally would like to see brought into the world by waving a magic wand, it would be more humane laws on this topic, as well as gun control laws and their enforcement, which are related to this topic because they would keep weapons out of the hands of the mentally ill.

I'm going to list the TAC's 12 policy recommendations, which I've done in bold type, and have also added some comments below the first 7 of them. They have divided their recommendations into three sections: Emergency Psychiatric Evaluation, Inpatient Commitment, and Assisted Outpatient Treatment.

Emergency Psychiatric Evaluation:

1. "The duration for initial emergency custody should be a minimum of 48 hours with a strong preference given to holds of 72 hours or longer."

I would personally like to stress the importance of allowing emergency custody to extend as long as judged necessary by the clinic staff, even longer than 72 hours. Whatever the actions that caused admittance, that person most likely calmed down considerably during the hold, if only from the stability of a safe warm place to get some sleep, some good food, and, possibly, appropriate medication. However, that doesn't mean their problems are gone. To let someone who is mentally ill go free after 72 hours is often really unadvisable. I also believe, based on my own experience, that if the hospital doctors believe the patient should not be released after 48 or 72 hours, they should have the legal grounds to continue to hold the patient.

I am intimately aware of problems that may appear with the absence of such rules. When Galen ran naked through the airport trying to get the police to shoot him, he was initially hospitalized for a 72-hour-hold. The facility went to court to keep him longer, because the doctors felt he wasn't well enough to leave. A kind nurse told me about the court hearing and found a fax number for me, so that I might send the court a message, but the court ignored my message and would not allow me to testify by phone. They set him free. He was hospitalized again only a few days later, in another city. Why couldn't he have just been held in the first hospital, because he clearly needed treatment?

2. "Any responsible adult or, at a minimum, guardians and family members, must be able to petition the courts to seek a court order for evaluative custody."

This is such a reasonable and helpful suggestion! My son Galen's life is littered with people who cared about him but were helpless to act. This was also true of my husband. As a spouse and parent, I had no control over the train wrecks careening out of control in front of my eyes, and friends and colleagues found their attempts to help my husband and Galen shut down as well.

As things stand, it is really tough to get another adult into treatment, no matter how desperate the illness. Changing this would affect so many lives for the better, and provide the mentally ill a chance at recovery.

3. "Emergency Evaluation laws should provide clear guidance for initiating a petition."

This is so obvious that it almost seems as though it would require no further comments. If there are clear steps to follow, and figurative boxes to check off, then caring friends and family can work through those steps and get a petition underway for their friend or loved one. But as things exist right now for the family and friends, it is almost impossible to fight one's way through the thicket and get help. I have consulted several different types of attorneys who were at a loss to suggest any possible paths forward. If even legal specialists can't figure out what to do, how can the rest of us? We desperately need these clear guidelines!

Inpatient Commitment

4. "Any responsible adult or, at a minimum, guardians and family members must be able to petition the courts to seek a court order for inpatient commitment."

Surely this is completely obvious. Laws like this would permit any concerned persons, including family members, to ask a court to put a mentally ill person into inpatient treatment. At the present time, this legal possibility does not exist and the amount of anxiety and despair that comes along with doing nothing is beyond comprehension. And all the while, the mentally ill get sicker and sicker. Remember that this can go on for years, and part of treating the mentally ill also includes some peace of mind for the family.

I've often compared this situation to the swift remediation that sometimes takes place after a fatal traffic accident, when a community jumps into action to put up a stop sign or traffic light at a dangerous corner, though the dangers of that intersection were known for years and many had complained. Often, such stop signs or a street lights actually do get installed after a tragedy. Why is it so different to change mental health laws? If our loved ones die (or kill others) nobody listens to us. No matter what horrible things happen, the situation does not change.

It is always possible that it will, and I think minds are beginning to change. The media folks are moderating a national debate as to whether mass shootings are terrorist attacks or the deeds of a seriously mentally ill person. I'm not going to get into that discussion, but I would like to ask one simple question: would our nation, and the dead and injured, be better off today if the young men who committed horrible acts had been locked up and in the process of psychiatric evaluation rather than free and out in society, able to roam around and carry out their mayhem?

5. "Statutory language defining the 'danger to self or others' standard should not require imminence of harm."

Even mentally ill people can sometimes pull themselves together for a few minutes. My oldest son is a master of this, and has fooled the police many times. This particular recommendation, that the "danger to self or others standard should not require imminence of harm" is absolutely essential. My son will never be able to get treatment if one requirement is that he must be imminently in danger of hurting himself or others.

6. "Statutory language defining the 'grave disability' standard should not require imminence or an unreasonably high risk of harm."

As I've said, Galen (like many with mental illness) can hold himself together long enough to present himself for a few minutes as the most sane and reasonable young man. If you recall my story about the eviction proceedings I regrettably had to take, Galen initially spoke quite calmly and reasonably when the judge asked him to testify. And while he eventually broke into a rambling angry mess that carried on and on, his initial presentation would convince even the most discerning of his sanity.

With the current stringent legal definitions of "grave disability", my mentally ill son can't get the help he needs. And neither could my husband.

7. "Statutory language defining the 'psychiatric deterioration' standard should expressly allow consideration of treatment history and the likelihood of future psychiatric deterioration without treatment."

Again, from the perspective of a family member, this is so reasonable and important. In my experience, every time a judge was called upon to determine my son's fate, neither my son's history nor a reasonable projection of his likely future without treatment was ever considered.

Assisted Outpatient Treatment

Assisted Outpatient Treatment (AOT) was never a possibility for my son. Because of his Anosognosia, he has never been able to accept that he has psychological problems and is convinced all his medications are poison. Many people with bipolar illness or schizophrenia suffer from this, and it makes them poor candidates for AOT. Perhaps if one could require treatment, as per the previous TAC suggestions, especially if medication could stabilize the mental illness, then AOT might have potential.

All of the remaining TAC suggestions listed below would be invaluable to many people. I list all of them here because I'm sure they are vitally important, but they just don't apply to my situation with my son, nor would they have with my late ex-husband.

8. "For states using one standard for both inpatient and outpatient civil commitment, statutory language authorizing AOT should be allowed consideration of treatment history and the likelihood of future deterioration without treatment."

9. "For states using separate criteria for both inpatient and outpatient civil commitment, statutory language authoring AOT should allow consideration of at least three years of treatment history and should not place unreasonable limitations on eligibility."

10. "Any responsible adult or, at a minimum, guardians and family members, should be able to petition the courts to seek a court order for AOT."

11. "AOT procedures should be described in sufficient detail to provide guidance to practitioners and to make maximum use of the "black robe effect"."

12. "The duration for an initial AOT order should be a minimum of 90 days, and renewed orders should be for a minimum of 180 days."

Thank you, Treatment Advocacy Center, for outlining all of this so clearly. Now the question becomes how do we get it all implemented. Creating laws that reflect these suggestions is a reasonable, clear goal toward which we can all work. We'd create a different world for families like ours if we succeeded. That would be quite a legacy for those of us who have lived this misery to leave behind us.

Recently, following my son Galen's eviction and subsequent homelessness, the wonderful policeman who has helped me in Alaska sent me the following email. I am quoting it verbatim, with his permission, leaving out identifying information.

"I see where our officers went to the apartment Galen was residing in to execute a court order to remove him. The property owner has not filed any sort of complaint about damage. Our prosecutor's office will rarely review instances of damage involving landlord/tenants which I suspect is why he was not arrested. The other issue in Alaska is we cannot arrest on certain crimes we do not observe. I agree with you that arresting him is not the answer. At times, however, it can lead to court ordered treatment and evaluation which would be the one positive point.

Our mental health evaluations are covered under Title 47 in Alaska. Below is how the law reads. It's also very frustrating for us because it really ties our hands with who we can take against their will. I can't tell you the number of times I've contacted individuals talking to themselves on the sidewalk, wearing unusual clothing (from tin foil to cardboard boxes) and have been unable to involuntarily commit them. We tend to have an easier time during the winter because it's much easier to document they are a danger to themselves being out in the elements. Judges have ruled over and over in Alaska that we are not to take anyone against their will just because they appear or sound as if they have mental health problems.

If Galen is willing to go voluntarily we will absolutely assist in getting him to the proper facility however. The other option is to have a physician complete Title 47 hold paperwork. We have assisted in getting folks to treatment facilities for evaluation many times with that paperwork. If he gets picked up on a Title 47 hold then the courts have a few days to have a hearing and determine if he is going to be sent to Anchorage for further treatment. That's usually when the psych evaluation comes in since we do not have a facility like those in Anchorage.

Do you think he'd be willing to speak to me if I called him? I can try and evaluate where he's at and offer him some assistance. If you think that would work and have a good working number for him, I can certainly try. Just let me know.

Our homeless population is quite large here. The temperatures have been in the 80's recently so he should be ok for now. Biggest issue is the large wildfires burning all around that have blanketed the city in smoke and ash. Makes breathing very difficult. Maybe he'd be willing to go to Anchorage since the air is better down that way.

I'll be in and out of the office the next few days for court proceedings but will work on contacting him if you thing that would help.

Thanks Nan and I'm sorry you're having to deal with this."

He also sent along copies of the language of the laws for Alaska.

As you have just read, this officer and I were both frustrated by the difficulties of hospitalizing Galen, due to the laws in Alaska pertaining to emergency detention or evaluation for persons who are suffering from mental illness. The officer sent me a copy of the laws and as they are long and written in legal language, perhaps it is best if I summarize them in this way: these laws sound reasonable enough, but, in brief, the rigmarole surrounding the initiation of involuntary commitment procedures in Alaska was never in alignment with the realities of how my mentally ill son lives and acts. In terms of getting some treatment for Galen, this was never possible, in spite of his frequently outrageous behavior. For anyone wishing to read the exact language of the laws, they are AS 47.30.700 and AS 47.30.705, and can be found with a simple internet search. The laws are pretty clear, and the police are frustrated too. The laws in Alaska are no different than in the rest of the country.

I also found it heartening to get this email from the officer:

"You're quite welcome for the information. I'm glad it helped shed some light on the current state of affairs in Alaska as they pertain to mental health treatment. Even with the lack of services offered in our city we will continue to march forward and help those we can. As the old saying goes, sometimes it's better to ask for forgiveness than permission. I've used this over the years when dealing with individuals with mental illness that clearly cannot care for themselves. I've found once an individual is taken for treatment against their will there is always time later for a conversation once they are stable and more rational. That's where the apology for forgiveness comes in, although it's also been my experience that the majority of those individuals are thankful and realize they were unable to properly evaluate their condition at the time. It's good to see them get help, repair relationships and move forward toward a better path in life. Our department has been proactive in providing CIT (Crisis Intervention Training) to many of us and it has served me well over the years. Developing rapport is so important when dealing with individuals who don't know or trust you.

I checked our calls last night and there were none involving Galen. I've spoken to the two officers that assisted the landlord with his removal the other day. They stated the apartment was pretty trashed but no real damage. There was nothing they could articulate to take Galen to a medical facility so he was permitted to leave. They did express he appeared to have clear mental health issues and seemed paranoid but again, nothing that fell directly under Title 47.

I did try and reach out to Galen this morning at that number. I could hear the phone being manipulated for a brief second but then it goes to voice mail. I called both from a blocked and unblocked number and let him know who I was. I'm going to touch base with the Housing and Homeless Coordinator this morning and bring him up to speed on Galen's situation. I'm hopeful the number is still valid and Galen will reach out to me. I will also place what we call a "locate" under his name in the statewide system asking for current contact information next time law enforcement encounters him.

With regard to the information I provided you and being quoted. That is just fine. If there is but a small chance it helps someone else, I'm happy to lend my voice. Reading is such a relaxing pastime and I love it.

I'll be retiring next year at some point. My family wants Dad out of the game after a few decades of this work. Or maybe they just want to move closer to their relatives in the Midwest where it is also warmer. It will be great to read your work someday which I hope has the happiest of endings.

I'll be in touch if something urgent comes up. As always, thank you and take care."

Can any of us begin to imagine the levels of frustration found everywhere regarding the current mental health laws? I am frustrated, because I can't help my son, and couldn't help my husband, and the police are frustrated because they'd love to step in and help, but they can't. If those of us who have mentally ill relatives could pull together, maybe we could get some of the laws changed. I'd love to be a part of that. It's just a crying shame to let things stand as they are.

CHAPTER 12

Beacons of Hope

The way we treat the least among us, the poor, sick, mentally ill, unemployed, and so forth, says a lot about the health of our society and its values. When it comes to the mentally ill or substance abusers who break laws and are sent to jail, we haven't done very well. I believe a great society works for the health and wellbeing of all its citizens, no matter their condition, social standing, race or any other metric that can be used to separate us one from each other.

I've written a lot, and complained a lot too, about problems in the legal system that affect all of us with mentally ill family members. Sometimes those of us who are frustrated by the shortcomings of the system might feel like screaming "W*HY DOESN'T ANYONE JUST TRY TO FIX ANY OF THIS?*" Well, some people are doing just that, and it is only fair to include a chapter about some of those extraordinary efforts. It is always hopeful to know that there are people who are doing remarkable work, creating unusual programs, and overseeing projects that are genuine, long-lasting solutions to deep social problems.

The people I write about in this chapter are all people I have met, so I can personally vouch for what I am saying, as well as for their brilliance and determination. I have not set out to compile a comprehensive list of all the good people trying to make a positive difference for the mentally ill and their families. I'm not qualified or knowledgeable enough for that, and there are undoubtedly many I have not heard of. I'm just sharing with you some exceptional people and programs that I have come across in my life.

Mentally ill people often do strange things, either because they have an unbalanced view of the world and don't understand why their behavior is not socially acceptable or because their illness causes them to hear voices or see things that aren't really there. My son Galen was arrested a few months ago because he threw some rocks through a window trying to defend himself from people he thought were trying to hurt him, people that existed only in his mind and weren't actually there. Sometimes, like in this window breaking incident, the strange things they do are actual crimes, and understandably those crimes often involve injured parties wanting restitution or justice. So the next thing that happens is that sick people find themselves arrested and incarcerated, instead of getting the treatment and understanding they desperately need.

It is really horrifying to contemplate the extent to which our society treats the mentally ill as though they are criminals, rather than as sick people in need of treatment. And surely we might all recognize that jail populations, which include hardened criminals and others adept at taking advantage of vulnerable people, are absolutely positively not good company for an unstable person.

The Treatment Advocacy Center states on its website www.treatmentadvocacycenter.org that "in 44 states, a jail or prison holds more mentally ill individuals than the largest remaining state psychiatric hospital" and "individuals with psychiatric diseases like schizophrenia and bipolar disorder are 10 times more likely to be in a jail or prison than a hospital bed."

In terms of attempting to fix this truly horrendous national problem, there are two individuals that I know about whose work stands out, Francis Greenburger in New York City and Judge Stephen Leifman in Miami. I've never come across anything more spectacularly aimed at genuine change than the work these two gentlemen are doing, and would like to tell you a bit more about each of them.

Francis Greenburger

Francis Greenburger, a New York real estate developer, has created the Greenburger Center for Social and Criminal Justice, through which he is working to reduce prison rates and create treatment programs as an alternative to jail for addicts and the mentally ill. Cheryl Roberts is the Executive Director of the Greenburger Center, and it would be hard to imagine two more dynamic or committed people.

The Greenburger Center's Mission Statement says: "The Greenburger Center advocates for reforms to the criminal justice system. We believe the criminal justice system should focus on rehabilitation and not only punishment. Laws should protect society, not penalize poverty, mental illness, or underlying substance abuse. Judges must have the ability to fashion sentences that do justice while preserving human dignity, and the potential for reentry, and include alternatives to incarceration."

Mr. Greenburger came to create the GC after his own experiences as a father with a mentally ill son who got into trouble and served a jail sentence. The New York Times published an article about Francis Greenburger's search for a treatment center for his son rather than having him serve a jail sentence. The article, titled "From a Father's Anguish Comes a Plan to Help Mentally Ill Inmates", was written by Matt A. V. Chaban and published on October 6, 2014. The article states "Mr. Greenburger had been researching the criminal justice system and learned how detrimental it could be for the mentally ill. He began pleading with the district attorney for alternatives, and the district attorney responded that if Mr. Greenburger could find a secure treatment center for his son, he would consider placing him there instead of prison. 'I didn't know it at the time, but he was sending me on a wild-goose chase,' Mr. Greenburger said. 'There were literally none.'"

And from the same NY Times article: "the Greenburger Center, which is envisioned as a think tank and a treatment facility, has even greater ambitions: to cut the United States incarceration rate of 2.3 million in half over the next decade."

Remarkably, Mr. Greenburger not only recognized the enormous need for alternatives to jails, he decided to take the initiative to create these treatment alternatives, and that is what he is doing through the Greenburger Center.

Can any of us imagine what this man is actually trying to do? Could the incarceration rate really be cut by 50% in a decade? Or could we dream that we might actually have a society where only truly dangerous people are in jail and the mentally ill and addicted are in treatment? Bravo to Mr. Greenburger for thinking this might actually be possible and for doing the hard work necessary to create a path to a better future for mentally ill people incarcerated in prisons!

Here are some staggering facts, quoted from the Greenburger Center website www.greenburgercenter.org:

> "People in America suffering from mental illness are 10 times more likely to be in jail than in a psychiatric hospital."

> "In the US, we have 25% of the world's prisoners, but only 5% of the world's population."

> "In 2012, there were 350,000+ severely mentally ill people in our prisons and jails."

> "People with severe mental illness are more likely to be jailed repeatedly, to cost more while they are in jail, to stay in jail longer, to be more difficult to manage in jail, and to be far more likely to attempt to commit suicide in jail."

As if all those facts aren't enough, according to reporting by Ben Chapman in The Wall Street Journal on December 8, 2019, a report prepared by New York City Comptroller Scott Stringer states that a single inmate in a New York City jail costs the city $337,524 for the fiscal year! Surely with such high sums, and quite possibly far less, inmates with mental health or substance abuse problems could be treated and prepared to return to society, which would not only save money but save human beings as well. There is something really wrong with a society that goes along with spending blindly on keeping people in jail without considering whether there is a more humane alternative, which might even prove to be cheaper to boot. The present situation is just plain stupid and makes no sense at all!

Treating the mentally ill like criminals is clearly not the answer. They get worse in jail, not better, and not only because there is little or no treatment in jail. Jail is full of people who are not a positive influence for someone with a mental illness.

The Greenburger Center's first alternative to jail treatment facility, Hope House on Corona Park in the Bronx, is scheduled to open in 2021 or 2022. In every way, this project is unique. It will house equal numbers of men and women. Clients will be carefully selected from inmates who apply, and they will undergo a screening process. They will receive residential care, clinical care, and medication management, as well as daily program instruction in life management skills.

With all my heart I wish the Greenburger Center well with this pilot project, and I also look forward to watching many more Hope Houses pop up all over the country. This program could completely change the experience of incarceration for mentally ill and addicted people, which would be a blessing for hundreds of thousands of these people, and their families.

Judge Steven Leifman

For the past 20 years in Miami-Dade County in Florida, people accused of a crime and on their way to jail have had the opportunity to be treated very differently than in many other municipalities in the United States. Thanks to the efforts of Judge Steven Leifman and the groundbreaking Eleventh Judicial Circuit Mental Health Project, consideration is given as to whether the crimes that were committed, especially if they are low level offences, might have resulted from mental illness. And if the offenders are found to have mental illness or substance abuse issues, they are given the opportunity for treatment instead.

Judge Leifman is an eloquent spokesperson for the current situation. On March 26, 2014, he testified before the Subcommittee on Oversight and Investigations of the Energy and Commerce Committee of the United States House of Representatives concerning people with mental illnesses in the criminal justice system. I couldn't improve on what he has said, so I'll quote at length from his remarks:

> "When I became a judge two decades ago, I had no idea I would become the gatekeeper to the largest psychiatric facility in the State of Florida.
>
> Of the roughly 100,000 bookings into the jail every year, nearly 20,000 involve people with serious mental illnesses requiring intensive psychiatric treatment while incarcerated. On any given day, the jail houses approximately 1,200 individuals receiving psychotherapeutic medications, and costs taxpayers roughly $65 million annually, more than $178,000 per day. Additional costs to the county, state, and taxpayers result from crime and associated threats to public safety; civil actions brought against the county and state resulting from injuries or deaths involving people with mental illnesses; injuries to law enforcement and correctional officers; ballooning court caseloads involving defendants with mental illnesses; and uncompensated emergency room and medical care.
>
> Several years ago, the Florida Mental Health Institute at the University of South Florida completed an analysis examining arrest, incarceration, acute care, and inpatient service utilization rates among a group of 97 individuals in Miami-Dade County identified to be frequent recidivists to the criminal justice an acute care systems. Nearly every

individual was diagnosed with schizophrenia, and the vast majority were homeless at the time of arrest. Over a five-year period, these individuals accounted for nearly 2,200 arrests, 27,000 days in jail, and 13,000 days in crisis units, state hospitals, and emergency rooms. The cost to the community was conservatively estimated at $13 million with no demonstrable return on investment in terms of reducing recidivism or promoting recovery ... Five percent of all individuals served by ... courts targeting people with mental illnesses accounted for nearly one quarter of all referrals and utilized the ... majority of available resources.

Community mental health infrastructure was developed at a time when most people with severe and disabling forms of mental illnesses resided in state hospitals ... People who would have been hospitalized 40 years ago ... are now forced to seek services from an inappropriate, fragmented, and unwelcoming system of community-based care ... Their only option ... to receive treatment is .... through the some of the most costly and inefficient points of entry into the healthcare delivery system including emergency rooms, acute crisis services, and ultimately the juvenile and criminal justice systems.

According to the NAMI, 40 percent of adults who experience serious mental illnesses will come into contact with the criminal justice system at some point in their lives. The vast majority of these individuals are charged with minor misdemeanor and low level felony offenses that are a direct result of their psychiatric illnesses.

Over the past 50 years, the number of psychiatric hospital beds nationwide has decreased by more than 90 percent, while the number of people with mental illnesses incarcerated in jails and prisons has grown by 400 percent. Today, it is estimated that there are nearly 14 times as many people with mental illnesses in jails and prisons in the United States as there are in all state psychiatric hospitals combined."

Whew. What a lot of sobering facts. Let's carefully consider what all these mind-numbing figures and stats mean. They mean that our overcrowded jails are simply stuffed full of people who are sick, and should be in treatment and not in jail.

To their enormous credit, Judge Leifman and his team have been addressing these problems concretely for many years, through their efforts to have mentally ill prisoners treated rather than jailed. After years of planning, they now have a 200 bed Mental Health Diversion Facility; the "MHDF" is specifically designed to treat mentally ill people who are frequently in and out of jail.

On April 14, 2020, Judge Leifman and the Miami-Dade Criminal Mental Health Project were featured in a PBS documentary, *The Definition of Insanity*. This is a superb program and anyone interested in this topic would find it both interesting and inspiring. During this hour-long program the filmmakers show how dedicated public servants are working with Judge Leifman and others in the courts to steer people from incarceration to recovery. It is incredibly interesting to observe the intricate choreography of so many different participants in the legal system and their respective departments, some of whom should theoretically oppose each other, but who work together seamlessly toward the same goal – giving sick people a chance to learn to manage their illness and build an independent and productive future. I was struck that watching this film was like watching a war effort from behind the scenes, like having access to Winston Churchill's War Room. All of it was awesome, including the behind the scenes discussions, hard work, and organizing that produce any large-scale success.

The phrase "the definition of insanity" is of course a reference to a famous quote attributed to Albert Einstein: "The definition of insanity is doing the same thing over and over and expecting a different result." What a perfect quote for a film dealing with how the mentally ill are treated so often, over and over, by the criminal justice system. I really enjoy the irony in the title.

With my oldest son's history in mind, witnessing the care given to not let anything fall behind the radiator was what impressed me most about Miami-Dade's Criminal Mental Health Project. In the film we saw staff members of all types, including someone who had been through the program himself, actively involved with making sure the inmates got their meds, that young men on probation actually showed up at their jobs, that mentally ill subjects knew what they had to do, or where they had to go, and when. I could only shake my head as I remembered so many times when nobody ever checked to see if Galen was actually taking his court ordered meds (he wasn't), or if he ever went back to see the psychiatrist (he didn't), or followed up with him in any number of small but important ways.

I wish Judge Leifman and all aspects of his programs the greatest success. I can also dream that these programs might be a template that other communities might follow. This would be a remarkable development for all of us, and for our mentally ill relatives.

Police

We are witnessing a reexamination of the role of policing in our lives and communities. Anyone who has seen some of the body cam footage that brought us to this reexamination will likely agree that steps are needed to ensure these tragic incidents do not occur again, ever.

The mentally ill are frequently involved with the police, because they do not understand reality the way the rest of us do. In the chapters on Galen, I have written about a wonderful policeman in Alaska who helped Galen, and helped me with Galen, immensely. More recently, Galen has had issues in a town he's living in and ended up involved with a special police program set up to deal with the homeless and mentally ill crowding that city's streets. This task force was set up with members of the police department as well as social workers. A policeman is assigned to find and contact each homeless, mentally ill, or addicted individual in the city each week. And they take situations into their hands actively. Coming across Galen once in a bad state, he scooped him up and took him to a hospital for a short involuntary commitment.

Recently, in another city Galen did something that really reflects his level of illness. After he couldn't convince a couple of patrolmen to take him to a psych ward for an involuntary commitment, he asked them if they'd do that if he tried to steal their guns. The entire incident ended, with nobody hurt, and Galen was sent on his way safely. A few days later I got a call from a member of that police department. He told me he'd been going over the body cam footage, and he was asking me, Galen's mother, if there was anything they might have done differently, for a better outcome? I told him that since everyone was uninjured and the incident ended well, I thought they'd done a fine job.

My point in discussing these examples is to show that the experience that my son and I are having with the police has been generally favorable. Of course, let's say it out loud, Galen is white, well-spoken, and obviously educated and intelligent. No doubt this has made a clear difference in how he has been treated. But what is absolutely true, for all of us, is the depth of support those of us who are dealing with this issue day in and day out can draw from knowing that we have an excellent chance of finding useful programs, or at least meeting people who are as frustrated as we are by the current situation and willing to work to change it. I think we can all take heart from that and keep on striving for a better future. No question, much has to change, but we can have glad hearts about those who are already fighting for a better future for us all.

PART THREE

OK, Let's Be Practical and Look at Where We Are

CHAPTER 13

Cleaning Up the Mess

Mental illness is often called a mental disorder. That word, disorder, is meaningful, because the chaos or disorder in someone's mind can manifest itself in a similar chaos or disorder in their physical surroundings. Dealing with this particular side-effect of mental illness can be one of the toughest parts of our journey as family members.

Even people who are seemingly well-adjusted can have weird problems with their "stuff". When I was a child, we had an elderly relative who lived in California. She was a delightful, friendly old soul, and everyone in the family used to love to be around her and go visit her. She was also a great cook, and always had delicious treats to feed her many friends and grandchildren and anyone else who came to her home. Cookies were her specialty, and she always had a large variety of different kinds readily available in tins and boxes. Her home was neat, clean, and well-cared for, as she was herself. We all knew she'd had rough times in Italy before she came to the United States, but nobody ever brought that up, so she never spoke about it. This is a long-entrenched family habit, by the way, and one reason I am writing this book is to do my part to end the multi-generational family habit of never, ever talking about difficult times or unhappy family circumstances.

Imagine our shock when it was discovered, after her death, that she'd kept several large freezers in her basement stuffed full of nothing but butter! I'm talking about more butter than anyone could possibly use in a lifetime of baking cookies for grandchildren. We had many family discussions about what all this butter meant to her. Why she needed to have so much, and what did this butter do for her emotionally – did she need to know she'd never run out? And why butter? Why not something else? She was a happy, seemingly well-adjusted person, who'd raised a family and had a long, seemingly happy marriage. But still, she needed...all that butter. Nora Ephron once said in an NPR interview "You can never have too much butter – that is my belief. If I have a religion, that's it." My guess is these two women would have gotten along famously.

Thinking about this lovely old lady has helped me to see how even people leading reasonable lives can sometimes have an irrational need to horde excessive amounts of something. This trait seems especially pronounced for the mentally ill. And for them, the sicker they get, the less control they have over their lives and their organizational skills, which includes where they keep their belongings, and if they hold on to belongings that outlived their usefulness. This is obvious to anyone who has lived with someone suffering from mental illness.

Less obvious, to me at least as I went through this journey, was that their stressed to the max family members can also lose control, to some extent anyway, of their own organizational skills as pertaining to their personal belongings. On a practical level, there is not enough quiet time to stay well-organized about many of life's regular details. (And when you find quiet time, you may want to do something more fun than sort your belongings.) In reality, you've got a whole family of people who are either stressed or ill, and it is inevitable that we will "lose control" over our belongings and end up with way too much of everything.

While I wouldn't categorize the rest of us on Sam's level as accumulators, every parent knows how frequently kids outgrow their clothes, or their school books, or their winter boots, not to mention the art supplies, pens, and notebooks. They all get replaced annually, and in our house, the old ones didn't always get tossed. Sometimes I rationalized keeping them, as for instance, when I kept at least a dozen random-sized pairs of snow boots in the PA attic "for the children of guests". But as Sam got sicker, people stopped coming out to our house, and at that point I thankfully had the sense to donate them all. But I couldn't keep up, as extremely stressed out people don't stay on top of sorting and tossing.

Of course, many have commented that this problem is endemic in modern society anyway, or else organizing consultant Marie Kondo wouldn't have made such a name for herself. Although for a situation like mine, I believe one aspect of her method is perhaps a tad difficult to apply. She advocates dumping everything you possess from one category of belongings on the floor and sorting all of it there. I can get the giggles when I think of the heights we might have reached for certain categories of Sam's possessions if we dumped them all in a pile! Surely some of those piles would have been many feet high; I would have needed a small airplane hangar for the sorting. I had to discover a different method.

Remember, we lived in two homes, a lovely New York apartment, not large but near a park and in a wonderful neighborhood, and a normal-sized house in northeastern Pennsylvania with a full attic (the attic was twice the size of the NY apartment) and a big garage, as well as a garden shed and a large unfinished area in the lower level. In other words, there was a lot of space to fill with "stuff".

I cannot overstate how overwhelmed and overloaded I felt by every aspect of my life by the time Sam moved out of our apartment. And remember, he took nothing he owned with him except some of his clothes, leaving everything else behind for me to cope with. Clearing this out was been a wonderful exercise in self-knowledge, because I saw how much of my personal power I had given up in my life, first to a demanding and difficult father, and then to Sam, all done in the name of keeping the peace. But done at a huge cost to me personally.

Sam was a born pack rat. He kept literally everything. I'm still not done with sorting out all his belongings, even though I have tossed out or given away several hundred large contractor sized bags filled with his belongings.

The most difficult, seemingly impossible task, was dealing with the immense quantities of printed music. I'm honestly not sure I could begin to describe the extent of what he accumulated. To give one example, he loved Shostakovich, and he owned the composer's complete chamber music works in the original first edition, which was in Russian - and neither of us spoke Russian. This alone took up about six linear feet on a bookcase, but as far as I knew, he never played anything from it. He just liked having the original editions around, buried on the top shelf of the bookcase. When we played a composition by Shostakovich, we used other English editions.

He also had music from the estates of several older cellists, all in the rattiest condition imaginable. (Having his own huge collection wasn't enough, he had to add on the big collections of dead cellists as well!) In the end, some music was thrown out, and well over a hundred boxes of music and scores left my living spaces and went to libraries and schools. Maybe more than that. I lost count.

After we divorced, I sorted out quite a bit of his music in the NY apartment (which he kept crammed into a built-in cabinet the width of a large room), and I rounded up about 20 boxes I thought I could give away. It wasn't everything (it didn't include the Shostakovich, which eventually went to the Lincoln Center Library), but Sam got so upset that he came with a friend to get the music, which he dragged out to Pennsylvania and put in the attic. Of course, a few years later, I had to drag it all back down from the attic, drag it back to New York, and proceed with my original plan.

There were also boxes and boxes of career-related memorabilia, which I didn't want to throw away, but also didn't want to keep in my house. Fortunately, I learned about the cello archives at a wonderful university in the south, and they were delighted to get everything from Sam's career. And I do mean everything – recordings, publicity materials, photos, papers, reviews, correspondence – all of it. Future cellists can look at any of these materials and listen to Sam's concert recordings through their terrific Archive. For me, this was an absolute blessing, as none of this had to stay in my house, and I did not need to save it for the kids. If they want to see or hear anything, they know where they can find it.

I also burned a lot of the music out at the country house. Sam had a practical system for working within the limited orchestral rehearsal time available for a visiting soloist. He purchased copies of all the needed orchestral parts, then made a copy of each of them and marked up the copy thoroughly with indications for dynamics, bowings, or any special instructions not printed in the music. These marked parts saved an incredible amount of time in rehearsals. Sam would send this batch of marked parts off to the orchestra, and they would send it back after the concert was over. And that's when the problem began, because then he'd stack up these large packets of marked-up orchestral parts in the basement of the Pennsylvania house. There were dozens and dozens of them, in multiple six-foot piles. He never seemed to reuse any of them, always re-thinking and re-marking everything fresh for each performance, like the great artist he was.

I had asked around for someone who might want them, but got no interest whatsoever. So finally, by the light of a gorgeous full moon, a friend and I burned them all up in a bonfire. The flames shot up high in the air, in multicolored DNA-type spirals, like no flames I'd never seen before. The flames were really bizarre.

Sam also loved computers and electronic gear and was always upgrading to the newest and latest model. There was nothing wrong with that, but the problem was that the old ones never got tossed, even when they no longer worked. It took several trips to the local electronics recycling center, with the car loaded to the max, to get it all out of the Pennsylvania house.

Then there were bigger things than computers or music scores to deal with. Sam's mother had an old Mason and Hamlin piano, a real beauty, with everything that was original to the piano still intact. In many ways, it was the best piano I ever played. But Sam didn't want it and I didn't want to keep it either, due to all the emotions centered around it, and around the unhappy relationship Sam's mother and father had with music, as well as their unhappy relationship with each other, and with Sam. And with me. In addition to an unpleasant habit of shedding its ivories if played too aggressively, it had one serious flaw, as the pin block had moved at some point. When I had the piano appraised I was told it would almost inevitably move again, even though it hadn't moved in decades. For any buyer, that would be an expensive repair. I sold the piano to one of my best students, a highly accomplished pianist, conductor, and organist, for the appraised value minus a price adjustment for the eventual repair of the pin block. Sam was furious, as he felt I let it go for too little.

And then there were his cars. I gave him an ultimatum to come get them by a certain date, but of course he didn't, so I had to get rid of them myself. The ancient BMW was sold to a dealer who was going to fix it up and display it in his showroom, as it certainly was a relic, dating to the early 70's, as I recall. Another car was sold to a friend. Sam thought I'd sold that for peanuts as well. But when the thing died not long afterwards, and the car was found to be full of mold (the symbolism of this wasn't lost on me), it turned out the price was just about right, as the new owners got more or less the purchase price when they sold it for parts. Another car was totaled by my oldest son, when he drove it in an ice storm, against my wishes - what else would he have done. Fortunately, no one was hurt in the accident, and it was determined the accident was not his fault.

Still, there is a lot I've had to examine in my own behavior in all of this. While this stuff was Sam's, the truth is I allowed the mess to accumulate. Overriding all else was my own desire to keep my family together, as peacefully as possible. I gave my own tacit permission for the hoarding, even while grumbling to myself, because I didn't want to rock the boat. In retrospect, everyone involved would have been far better off if I had set some firm boundaries and stuck to them. Would there have been fighting and arguing? Absolutely, but I am capable of fighting fair, capable of setting clear boundaries, and I would not have been left with so much of this mess (emotionally as well) had I made more of a point to stand up for myself.

My own desire to make everything as smooth as possible and avoid arguments overrode my desire to give myself fair treatment.

With the passage of time I have determined not to be such a pushover. This has been an important personal development point for me, part of what I'd encourage others to explore, because I doubt I'm the only spouse who ever made this compromise. Anyone involved with someone with SMI has done a lot of adjusting and bending, perhaps excessively so. We put up with much just to keep things on an even keel, in order to maintain some minimum level of stability. Is this really the best way to handle difficult situations, now or in the future? Having tried this method, I can say unequivocally that I don't recommend it.

And what is there in our upbringing that makes this the default method of handling a tough situation? It is worth thinking about. In my case I believe it is because of behaviors I learned as a child. I had a difficult, rough-cut father who made it clear that you did not cross him. This meant I learned to devalue myself and everything I felt, as I had to make sure nothing I did pushed my father to anger and rage. I grew up learning to please people and make them happy, and to never set anybody off. I know this is a survival issue for a small child, and that at such a young age it is too risky to react if there is a sense of danger or even the hidden sense of separation from your family. I watched my mother adapt to my father the exact same way I did, so I learned from both of them, my mother through example and my father through intimidation, that this is how you kept yourself in good graces with your family – shut up and don't push the river. Of course, this is another very long story, but I believe it formed the roots of how I got here. I also believe this is why I married a gentle, kind, sweet guy like Sam, because I thought he was completely different and far more considerate of my feelings than my father. In the end, though, that didn't exactly work out as I thought it would.

More interesting than the saga of removing all of Sam's stuff are the questions about why he kept it all. I understood that it wasn't the physical music scores that mattered so much to him, but what they contained within them as possibilities - the great concerts, the excitement of the whole experience of playing the music they contained. His whole professional life was represented within those boxes, and understandably it was really tough for him to let it go. Only now, with the task almost done, do I perceive some of the real meanings behind why he did so. Excess possessions symbolize memories to those who keep them. If your performance life is crumbling, but it was dear to you, of course you wouldn't want to give away your music, as the music represents so many wonderful concerts and experiences. An honest realization is not possible - that the music isn't being used, that it is in fact quite literally crumbling to bits, that it will most likely never be used again. Or, the realization that storing so much music is doing awful things to your, or your family's, living space, and even that it could all be purchased again or checked out of the library if needed. That rusty old BMW represented Sam's carefree youth, and even though the thing didn't run anymore, (and had no seat belts), Sam allotted it space in the PA garage and insured it for years. I can't believe, in retrospect, that I actually allowed that to continue for as long as I did.

Again, though, I have had to take a good hard look as to why I participated in this or put up with it. Becoming more aware of what I actually experienced was key here. Though I have said that Sam couldn't bear to part with all reminders of his marvelous concert life, the truth is I also had an emotional connection to them. Actually, I think it was even harder for me to let go of any hope that he would one day play concerts again, because I envisioned a path for him that would have made that possible, one he didn't choose in the end.

I realized this recently when there was a televised concert by a major orchestra, and when I was watching it I realized that one of the cellists, to whom we had sold Sam's best bow, was most likely playing the concert with this bow. I was inexpressibly happy to witness this, to realize this magnificent bow was in use once again making gorgeous music! And it brought home to me that I, too, may have subconsciously agreed to hold some of this endless pile of music for him in the hopes that Sam would one day be back in action.

To clear ANYTHING, even a trash can, or old food in the

fridge, requires some degree of a healthy, want-to-move-forward life attitude and openness to living in the present. Anyone who has ever kept a house knows this very well. Doing simple acts of cleaning up and sorting out also help all of us feel freer and more in control of our lives. But if we can't bear to look at the feelings going on in the space between the creation of the mess and the initiative required to clean it up, well, the result is just a bigger and bigger mess. That mess, whatever makes it up, is just more emotionally-protective padding that drags us farther and farther down, into a spiraling descent.

There were other ways I cleaned up the mess as well. In a perfect world, needing to "start over", I would have moved to a different apartment, either at the time of the divorce or by the time Sam died. But I am lucky enough to have a beautiful, relatively inexpensive apartment, which is rare in New York City, so I didn't want to move. In fact, it would have been stupid to move. What I could do was repaint every surface, toss some furniture or have it recovered, have the floors done, and buy some new furniture and rugs. I tossed our old bed and bought a new one, putting it on the other side of the room. In truth, not one square inch has remained untouched in some way, or remains the way it was when Sam lived here. And when people I haven't seen for a while walk in the door, they almost always ask if this is really the same apartment or if I've moved! I did the same thing in the Pennsylvania house, gradually upgrading everything.

"Gradually" is definitely the right word. I have found, for me, that doing LESS is more important than attempting to tackle a lot and getting bogged down. My mantra has been very simple - toss/sort/give away/repurpose one thing every day. I am really serious about this, and it is OK to deal with something really tiny and even as insignificant as one paperclip or one page of music. Truthfully, if you deal with one small thing, you will probably find you get drawn into dealing with a drawer or shelf or more. But I always felt I was finished for the day and off my own internal hook if I decided what I would do with one item, even a small one, and then executed the decision.

There is actually a Japanese business organization system called Kaizen that advocates doing exactly this. I was quite pleased with myself that I discovered the value of moving through the nearly overwhelming task of sorting and clearing out a lifetime of pack-rat Sam's belongings in this way, by taking one tiny step at a time, before I ever heard about Kaizen. Whether you want to make this way of working your own or call it Kaizen, either way I highly recommend it.

CHAPTER 14

How About Cutting Ourselves Some Slack?

When we sort out our feelings about all that went on in our families, if we are open to digging deep enough, we end up face to face with some dark and shadowy emotions (though let's face it, they pop up even if we avoid the digging).

Guilt: I must have done something wrong here. Failure: one of my kids is homeless in Alaska, so I must have failed somehow. Blame and shame: this mess must be my fault, somehow, someway. Embarrassment: why me, why can't my family be more like other families? Fury: how can my husband, or my son, refuse treatment and fall apart? And I'd throw perfectionism in there, too: if I could only make everything perfect, things would go so much better.

I've yet to meet a parent or spouse of a mentally ill, addicted or alcoholic family member who has not asked him or herself, over and over, what I could have done differently? But then we must ask ourselves, what would have made a difference? Is there anything at all we might have done, even the smallest change, so that things might have gone another way?

All of us who are parents and spouses are doing the best we can, and blaming ourselves or each other for things that go awry is really non-productive. Looking back, I can't imagine what I might have changed, and what this change might have entailed, or which alternatives I might have explored. Even the things I might have been able to change, (given the benefit of 20/20 hindsight), were not substantial enough that they would have had much of an impact. Was there something I should have done? I surely do not know. But I sure heard a lot of "Can't you do something? Can't you make him take his meds or go to therapy?" from Sam's immediate family and a lot of his friends, even while not knowing what else I might have done.

Life is an imperfect experience lived by imperfect beings. We carry on, living, dreaming, and hoping, and as we go along, we come to have some expectations of how things will turn out, some standards that people ought to uphold, some understanding that if we function with care and love, ethics and honor, life's events will flow like we've planned. And then these illusions drift away, and life's events slowly present us with other options, options that are radically different than the ones we've come to expect, and our standards and expectations give way to reality. What is that wonderful old saying – life is what happens after we've made other plans?

Once it is clear to us that we are in the middle of an indescribable mess, whether it is mental illness, addiction, or alcoholism, we inevitably look to figure out why. And almost as inevitably, we look to assign blame. What caused this and how it came about are tough questions, without clear answers - frankly, without any real answers. Even so, we keep returning to the question, even when it pains us to ruminate over it: whose fault is it?

While all of us would heartily endorse the value of loving our children and spouses, we must realize that no matter how much we love our family members, we are not responsible for whether our spouses or offspring develop mental illness or addictions. And once they do, we are not responsible for their actions. We are not bad spouses, mothers, or fathers, and we are not failures, if our mentally ill children do not turn out well or cause a lot of trouble or our spouses go off the rails.

Let me say something that took me a while to come to terms with: our biggest responsibility is to take care of ourselves. We need to cut ourselves some slack. Here's another radical thought: we need boundaries as much as we need to be a loving person. We need to define our boundaries clearly, and what we can do for our children and our spouses. And what we can't. Most of us do not have clear boundaries, because we fear the reaction of others when we advocate for ourselves or say no. We don't want to deal with other people's anger or irritation, because, frankly, who needs it and we've probably had way too much of it anyway. Ultimately, though, we fear that if they don't like the way we handle things, they'll ignore us or leave us, or we'll lose track of them.

The situation with my mentally ill son frequently provides a test of my own boundaries. The possibility of losing track of him, of having no idea where he is, or if he is still alive, becomes one of the most terrifying nightmares imaginable for a mother with a child who is often homeless. But that doesn't mean I ought to cave into all of his ridiculous demands, just because I'm afraid of losing track of him. After all, I know I have provided for him, and even if he doesn't like anyone telling him what to do, this doesn't mean I have to violate my own boundaries. My oldest son is capable of the most dramatic blowback imaginable when things don't go his way, but I still don't have to do things I don't think are right. It's OK to say no.

When we are dealing with the mentally ill it is easy to slide into making their problems bigger than ours. In order to keep them unruffled, we put up with a lot. (You have read all about how I did a bit of that along the way.) Consider though, that this becomes how we ensnare ourselves into taking responsibility for them and their actions, that is, taking responsibility for things we didn't do. We walk on a high wire with this boundary issue, and balance is the key, and it is difficult to maintain. For me, I have found it helpful to ask myself, again and again, whenever I waver within my boundaries, if the requests are at all reasonable and if I should grant the request, will it help my son get help, keep him out of immediate harm, or in some way look out for his long-term essential care. If not, it is OK to say no.

With blame, unfortunately, I think it is just human nature to want to find someone to dump the blame on. Few people are mature enough to take real responsibility for themselves and their actions. How often do you actually hear anybody say, "sorry, that's on me, I screwed up", when there are any real consequences to them saying so? And if you have heard that recently, consider how unusual this event is in your life.

Here's my take on this: if something really is somebody's fault (for example, leaving a door unlocked, or forgetting to take out the trash, or not feeding the dog), then the person who truly is at fault is capable of fixing the problem. And they are also capable of cleaning up any mess they created. But a malfunctioning brain does not have the capacity for this, and we can't fix the mess caused by a malfunctioning brain. A malfunctioning brain and the chaos it randomly generates is not something we can remedy, like we can remedy something if we just screwed up. Let yourself off the hook! It is not your fault. It is nobody's fault. Serious mental illness is a disease caused by a malfunctioning brain.

But even if we know it is not our "fault", that doesn't stop us from automatically feeling responsible or guilty. This is almost irrational. Part of our journey through our relationship with someone so ill is taking a long hard look at this and letting go of the guilt. We don't have anything to feel guilty about, and even if we are not happy with how things have turned out, we are not a failure as a parent, a spouse, or a human being.

I know it is built into mothers, especially, to believe they must do all sorts of things to encourage and support and even "train" their children. In my experience, this only "works" when the child in question actually wants to do whatever it is you are supporting and encouraging. So our child does not adhere to the program we set out for them, and does so in a way that does not exactly make you swell with pride. It is only natural, and a purely motherly instinct, to ask "What did I do"? Well, the answer is, maybe I did nothing! Maybe I did my absolute best to help both my husband and my son, spoke to every specialist doctor I could find, researched all I possibly could and read every imaginable article, and found that the deteriorations progressed despite my absolute best efforts? How about some understanding for ourselves, and what we are coping with? We deserve it and we'd readily give it to others. We've done our best, however it all worked out.

When I first thought about writing my story, my ever-alert inner critic pointed out that it might be really embarrassing to have the crazy things in our family right out there in print, for the whole big wide world to see. I have decided that nothing will change with the unhelpful mental health laws, or with treatment options, until those of us who have lived through family mental illnesses and addictions are open about our experiences. I believe this is the only way real change can happen, because most people won't know what needs to change until it is out in the open, or unless it happens to them personally, a fate I wouldn't wish on anyone. Still, I can remember a few incidents where I felt totally embarrassed, and yet in retrospect I should really have been more proud than embarrassed, and more open about what I was doing: helping my family get through a big, big problem.

Just before my younger son went to rehab, I was sorting out what to do about his addiction, and I was also wondering how to figure out how bad his addictions were and what were his specific drugs of choice. (Remember, due to those HIPAA laws I wasn't given access to any of the medical tests from his pediatrician, and while his doctor knew he had big problems, I did not.) I was at my local drug store, standing in front of a shelf filled with drug testing kits for various substances, wondering if I ought to buy one of them, and if so, which one. I thought this might help me determine where things stood, what my son was actually doing and what drugs he was taking.

I'm standing there and along comes the mother of one of my daughter's best friends, a lovely woman and a dear friend herself. We greet each other warmly and then she looks at the shelf I'm standing in front of. I'm not sure she even registered what I was doing. But I know that my inner critic was so eager to get out of there as fast as possible that I said I was in a hurry and had to run, and I found myself almost literally flying out the door in order to avoid an embarrassing discussion. At a gathering at this same friend's home a few weeks later, all the other mothers were discussing their kids' options for the summer, as the summer before senior year of high school was especially important, and all of these young people were bright and headed to college in a year. After hearing about all the plans for trips abroad, language immersion, service programs, internships, and extra pre-college courses, did I have the nerve to say, when they asked me what my son was doing, "my kid's going to rehab this summer!"? Absolutely not. I just said I didn't know yet, which was true, but certainly far short of the whole truth.

It has taken a lot of inner stretching to come to the point where, at least most of the time, I don't care if others judge me or think badly of me. Or if they think badly of my kids, or criticize any of us because my husband went crazy, or because my first-born has so many, many problems, or because my other son had addiction challenges. Besides, whatever problems Zach may have had, he has graduated from medical school, married a lovely woman, and is doing his residency in a major medical center. This does seem to say he is doing very well now, thank you very much!

But I have to admit that even today, when I run into an old acquaintance on the street who hasn't heard all this yet and doesn't know me very well, and asks "How's Galen?", mostly I side-step providing an honest and far-too-long answer and spit out something neutral, like "He's much the same" or maybe, if I'm feeling adventurous "I have no idea, he's just doing his thing and I haven't seen him for a while".

Unfortunately, I find that making an intentionally obfuscating answer like this only ends up making me angry. I can almost count on finding myself in a very grumpy mood a few hours later, and I sometimes have to ponder what happened during the day to bring that dark mood about. Of course, many things make us angry, and in truth, most of us find we do get very angry, sometimes even furious, about unfavorable circumstances that befell us that we had no control over. How could we not?! It can be tough to know how to process raw emotions, and try to move through them. But it doesn't change anything to rail against our fate. Getting angry at your situation, or at your husband or son or anyone else, doesn't accomplish anything. It just makes you upset and angry, which is the last thing any of us need. That is all it does. Getting angry or furious at someone, because you find yourself in a difficult situation that is not of your making, doesn't really do anything. It just gets you angry. It is something to watch out for, because it doesn't help at all.

Let's be clear, though, you do need to acknowledge anger. Don't just try and shove it under the rug. That isn't healthy and neither is stewing in it for days at a time.

It has helped me to find healthy ways to release some anger that fell short of behaviors I would prefer to avoid, like breaking all my dishes by throwing them against a wall, or screaming at the cats. I actually almost went through with breaking some dishes by throwing them against a wall, and even had some old dishes sorted out for this purpose, but then I realized I'd just have to clean up a whole lot of broken bits of china and it didn't seem worth the bother. The last thing I need is one more thing to do. If I can ever find a place to execute this plan, without making a giant mess I have to clean up, I still might look into it.

To help myself get through all this anger when it was at its worst, I took up pottery a number a years ago. When you first have some raw clay to work with, you need to wedge it. This means you have to work with it, knead it, mash it, and squish it, until it becomes pliable and smooth, and the air bubbles are worked out of it (so it won't blow up or break when it is fired). The status of the air bubbles is checked by slicing into the clay with a string, and then you wedge it all again to get the pieces of clay back together.

I became a master of wedging, by banging and bashing, as well as throwing the clay on the table as hard as I could (my favorite!), ultimately smashing it thoroughly into complete and abject compliance. Once, I was making such a racket and going at it with such abandon that another potter asked me if it was really necessary to wedge clay with such fury? I told her it was nothing less than essential, as it was therapeutic for me. She had the good sense to back off, quietly change tables, and let me continue to take out my anger on the clay.

Bread making can be equally effective, as you can go about kneading with an immense release of angry energy, but the problem is that you are left with lots of bread, too much for you to eat all by yourself, (especially if, like me, you don't really eat bread). Also, I found I didn't like bread that had been kneaded with anger, nor did I want to give away fury-filled food. No food should be made with any emotion but love; it doesn't taste good otherwise. Energetic floor scrubbing can work too. I've done that as well. For me, I seem to need to use my hands and my body when I am getting anger out, and it also helps to do something that doesn't involve any thinking at all.

In addition to the most obvious emotions such as anger and rage that result from our experiences, there are other shadowy areas, also ripe for introspection. Though at first glance perfectionism does not seem to belong on a short list of our concerns (relative to the extreme problems we are discussing in this book), the topic bears examination, because it lurks in the background and does affect how we feel. In fact I believe it is at the heart of why our journey is so hard.

Parents, perhaps especially mothers, have a lot of inner imprinting about what we expect of our families, and what we ourselves ought to experience as mothers. This imprinting happens all our lives, whether we realize it or not, on many levels including some we are barely aware of. Advertisements do not help, because this is a big source of all the images we saw as we grew up: the Norman Rockwell worthy family Holiday gathering, a happy family gathered around a dinner table, with a perfectly cooked turkey and nobody misbehaving, or families enjoying a beautiful outing at the beach, replete with smiles and plenty of laughter. Our psyches are crammed full of this sort of thing. I know I wanted my family to have all these happy experiences. In some ways, we have all bought into this, and advertising that promotes these images has virtually brainwashed us.

Indeed, these Norman Rockwell type images permeate our society. But there's a truly big problem here, because Rockwellian images usually don't reflect real families, whether they are families dealing with serious issues like ours, or families dealing with other serious issues, or families just living their lives. Real families and real people are nowhere near perfect. But still, it happens that if we don't live up to this subconscious imaginary ideal (and families with mental illness REALLY fall short), we feel terrible about ourselves, and none of us deserve this. As our very real children, spouses, or parents are not conforming to our wholesome ideals and inner slide show of images, this creates more opportunity for other shadowy emotions to arise, like shame, which we will get to later, in its own chapter.

Personally, I feel neither you nor I can get through this mess until we face perfectionism and all those inner images head-on, as they surely play into our desire, and our expectations to achieve "perfection" ourselves, to have "perfect" children, or a "perfect" marriage, set a "perfect" table, and to have "perfect" holidays. Because when we fall short of the Rockwell painting, we think we are failures. We need to get over ourselves.

I think it is also worth noting that consumerism is at the core of these advertised images of perfect experiences, as they become the bedrock of encouragement to buy more than we need. These visual images always beguile us with beautiful possessions. "Maybe my holiday table would be perfect if I bought some new china, or matching glasses?" or "Maybe our beach outing would go better if I bought us all new swimsuits, or an umbrella, or scuba gear?" or "Maybe my uncle would be nicer and maybe he wouldn't get so drunk at Christmas if I bought him an expensive present?" The act of purchasing something is never going to solve this problem of perfectionism, or assuage the anxiety that comes from feeling we are not good enough. The problem is artificially created; it doesn't actually exist. But advertisers would like to convince us it does. Don't buy into this! (I mean that literally!) Don't listen to them; they don't have your best interests at heart. Advertisers don't care how miserable they succeed in making you feel, they just want your cash.

Intellectually, we all know perfectionism is unattainable across the board, and because it is unattainable, aiming for it will leave us perpetually unhappy. We know this and we know we need to love ourselves just as we are, while we care for others to the best of our ability. But I'm not so sure that genuine self-love and self-acceptance, with all our imperfections, comes very easily to any of us. It surely hasn't come easily to me. This is a big topic, and maybe it is easiest to think of self-acceptance as a long journey through a series of moments when we consciously choose to accept ourselves, just as we are. I think self-acceptance has a lot to do with accepting others, even accepting Galen as he is, along with his illness.

Sometimes it helps me to remember that no matter who we are or what we do, there will always be people who won't like us or will disapprove of how we go about our lives. Nobody can ever be universally accepted. There is always somebody who will say we are too smart or too dumb, too blond or too brunette, too one thing or another. Few of us genuinely believe we are completely fine, just as we are, which is such a ridiculously immense waste of internal criticism. And do we ever have such impressively tenacious inner critics! These devilish parts of ourselves are always so hard at work, constantly primed, always ready to take accurate aim and fire, forever ready to drag us down. And if we listen to their siren voices, we will only torment ourselves because, as Emmanuel Kant said, "All humanity is made with crooked timber". Nothing done by human beings can ever be "perfect".

It has helped me immensely to realize that many things in life can be absolutely wonderful, completely absent of perfection. A few years ago, as I redid my apartment instead of moving, I purchased a new light fixture to hang over my dining room table. It had a big opaque rounded glass shade nearly two feet in diameter across the bottom. After the electrician installed it, I was annoyed to realize there was a tiny bubble in the glass, a flaw, if you will. It wasn't "perfect". I called a friend, who had far more common sense than I, and she said I should think of the light fixture as "uniquely mine". This immediately tossed out my irritation that "they" had sent me a "flawed" light fixture. I thought I should keep it and enjoy it, and make no fuss, if only as an experiment in living every day with visible imperfection. And truthfully, I never even think about it anymore. Everyone who walks into my apartment and sees the lovely light fixture comments that it is very beautiful, and no one, not once ever, has noticed the "flaw". Does my impishly overactive inner critic feel compelled to point it out to people occasionally? Absolutely!

Some societies have had the good sense to value imperfection, in a systemized way. In many handmade Persian rugs and carpets, you will discover a deliberate mistake, sometimes called the Persian Flaw. Followers of Islam believe only Allah makes things perfectly, and therefore to weave a perfect rug or carpet, without flaws, would be an offence to Allah. It is interesting to consider the original deliberate mistake is usually made in the execution of the pattern of the rug and not in the dying of the wool or silk, and certainly not the quality of the weaving.

I find this very similar to flaws that occur in human interchanges, in our families, in people we know and love, or in making music. "Execution" can certainly be compared to a missed or out of tune note, or perhaps ill-chosen words said by an exhausted parent. Yet the music is still beautiful, it just has a human element to it, and the parent still speaks out of love, despite a poorly chosen phrase. Similarly, we still have the high quality of the rug weaving and dying; the rug is beautiful despite its flaw. Accepting our flaws does not mean it is OK to make a mess or play music or do our work in a sloppy way, or be disagreeable with each other. It means an acceptance that flaws are an inevitable bi-product of all that we do.

When finding ourselves in a room with a beautiful Persian rug, it can be a lot of fun to search for the "flaw". Genuine deliberate mistakes in high quality oriental rugs and carpets may even be very difficult to spot and can be as subtle as a different color used in a flower petal. Though it might take a while to find it, once you see it, it really sticks out.

In reality, with all handmade rugs and carpets, just like in making music or any performing art, or in any other human pursuit such as raising a family, mistakes creep in whether deliberate or not. When enjoying the beauty of a gorgeous rug, does this really matter? And does it really matter so terribly much if the odd mistake creeps into a very human musical performance or in a very human family?

Dr. Moshe Feldenkrais, a PhD physicist who created an innovative movement method, once approximated the vast number of cell divisions that would occur within our bodies during the course of our lifetimes. It was an astronomical number, a number so unimaginably high that I have completely failed to register anything about it in my brain. He asked us to consider whether it was realistic to think that nothing would ever go awry with any of this, in any of these individual processes, at any point in our lives? Obviously, a lifetime of perfection with such vast numbers of individual physical events and processes occurring daily, any of which might go wrong at any time, is exceedingly unlikely. Something will inevitably go wrong somewhere, sometime. Perhaps even quite often. This was confirmed many years later by molecular biologists who in fact determined a consistent error rate as cells divided, as a cell's DNA was not copied with absolute accuracy with each division cycle.

Many of us consider our remarkable computers and phones to be infallible. But think of all the things that can go wrong with them, and do go wrong, all the time. Even these awesome machines are nowhere near perfect - not even close. Does even a week pass by without something on one of your devices that needs reloading, resetting, rechecking, or updating?

In Japan, when ordinary, plain, every day pottery breaks or cracks, it is sometimes repaired with precious materials, like gold and silver, a process called Kintsugi. I love this. Can anything be more healing and comforting than to think we can mend our deepest hurts and sorrows, and, yes, our flaws and imperfections, with the most precious elements of ourselves, and come out stronger and more beautiful in the end? In truth, they don't really use gold and silver for the entire seam, but rather a lacquer process using Urushi, the lacquer from the Chinese lacquer tree. Layers of Urushi are applied, which bind the broken pieces together, and then at the end, gold or silver dust is used before a final burnishing, giving the impression that the entire mended seam is gold or silver. The process is not without its risks. The sap, called urushiol, (derived from Rhus vernicifera, the lacquer tree), has the same kind of allergy-producing oil as poison ivy. (Ha! Here, we'd just use Krazy Glue.)

There are many layers of meaning here. Among them, that something doesn't have to be perfect to be absolutely beautiful, that we become stronger in the exact places our broken places are mended, and that maybe our broken places might even become our most beautiful places. Work done to overcome a difficulty, a problem, a "crack" or "flaw", if you will, can become the most valuable part of the process, even if visible for all to see, even if this work involves risks. It can create the strongest and most precious parts of ourselves. There is a great creative opportunity here, and it is even possible we'll be profoundly grateful for all we have learned and experienced and had the opportunity to become, through the unhappiest stretches of our journey.

CHAPTER 15

Compassion in Compartments

Mass shootings have crept into our existence as commonplace events. Beginning perhaps with Columbine, the random killing of large groups of people by a crazy person with an automatic weapon has become an increasingly frequent story to lead the evening news. Sadly, there will be another one, and the next time there is another one, notice where peoples' minds go. First, everyone wants to know who the perpetrator is, and then they want to know if the perpetrator is dead, or alive, and if alive, is the perpetrator captured or hospitalized. And once they know that, there is an immediate and great interest in the shooter's family. Who are these people? How could they have raised a person who would do such awful things? What's wrong with them? Well, perhaps there is actually something wrong with us, for not showing compassion to the families of the person who pulled the trigger, the perpetrator's families. They, too, experience searing traumatic emotional pain. The parents, siblings, and spouses will themselves also face long and difficult recoveries, yet we never seem to consider them victims. We seem to compartmentalize our compassion, reserving it for the victims of the crime, but excluding the families of the perpetrators of the crime.

Who gets the credit, or blame, for how a child turns out: does this, or should this, fall on the mother, the father, or both parents? Is attaching blame to parents in these circumstances ever fair or accurate? Consider how guilty these parents must feel. Can we begin to fathom how hopelessly impotent they must regard themselves, as their efforts to raise their child have failed dismally? In the El Paso shootings of August 2019, it has been widely reported that the shooter's mother called the police the previous week as she was deeply concerned about her son's possession of an assault-type rifle.

It's not surprising her pleas for help were not answered, and perhaps this says something about where we are in this country right now. But think of how every aspect of this tragedy must feel to her. She tried to alert authorities, and they said they could do nothing as her son purchased the assault rifle legally. And another tragedy unfolded. Her son, whom without a doubt she loved dearly, has done something unfathomably horrible, and even though she was worried enough to phone the police, her concern and her attempts to avoid tragedy went nowhere. She's going to have to live with this the rest of her life.

We all have witnessed, on countless occasions, the incalculable suffering that the mentally ill cause with handguns, rifles, and automatic weapons. The horrible incidents that occur with near regularity are plastered in the news everywhere, so none of us can evade the terrifying images burned into our individual minds and our collective consciousness. They remain stuck there, etched deeper still whenever we have another incident. When we experience one of these awful events as a society, the victims are justifiably wrapped in as much compassion as the world can muster, including public outpourings of good will that raise large sums of money to cover hospital bills and other expenses. Compassion pours in from all sides, waves and waves of it, for the victims, and for the families of the victims. All of them have been thrust, unbidden, into sudden unimaginable suffering, and many of the victims, if they are fortunate enough to survive, have long painful recoveries ahead of them. Some may never fully recover, bearing the physical and emotional scars for the rest of their lives. Nobody would wish them anything less than our most profound compassion and love, in as many generous, heartfelt ways as we can express it.

Yet our treatment of the families of the perpetrators is altogether different. Imagine that you were the younger brother, or the father, or the sister of someone staring at you from the front page of the daily tabloid, handcuffed and in the company of a phalanx of police. You may have sensed your relative was troubled, but had no reason to believe that the problem could manifest itself as a mass shooting. Or maybe you recognized a serious mental issue but the treatment your family was able to obtain simply wasn't effective. This is almost cruel: for those families also suffer immensely, sentenced to a personal purgatory they will never escape. Don't we have enough compassion in our compassion bank to extend some to them? Think about what that family feels upon turning on the evening news, and learning their son or their brother unleashed an automatic weapon on a group of people at a shopping mall. When I turn my thoughts to the parents and families of the shooters, I can't begin to take in the pain they must endure.

Nobody ever seems to consider their experience. The reality, fairly or not, is that how a child turns out is often laid squarely at the feet of the parents. You will note that in all forms of media, they ask the same question: what kind of parents did the perpetrator have? The underlying question, always present, but never quite said out loud: What on earth did they do to mess up their kid so badly? This question assumes that we parents have extensive control over how our children turn out, which is arguably not a fair assumption about any offspring, but especially not when mental illness appears.

As often as we have shootings, we rarely hear about the shooter's family, save perhaps for a news program reading their written apologies. In subtle and not so subtle ways, they receive implicit blame, and there is an immediate search for clues as to what they did wrong. But for most, it is very unlikely they did anything wrong; it is very unlikely they contributed at all to whatever horror their loved one unleashed. One can assume they probably consider changing their names and their jobs, relocating, dying their hair or even plastic surgery, just to get away from all the negative attention. I can't imagine what I would do. I have to confess up front that the possibility I might find myself in their company, due to the antics of my oldest son, has been my greatest nightmare for years. And the source of countless sleepless nights.

How desperately I wish we had mental health laws that would

allow parents like them, and parents like me, to get our grown offspring into treatment. Knowing that an ill child's life, and possibly the lives of many others as well, depends on getting mental health care - and not being able to do a thing to get it - is truly a special torture. And I have boundless compassion for those whose worst fears are realized. If I knew how to reach out to them and offer my support, I would. They, along with the victims, have my sincere condolences, in equal measures.

It surely is not worth it to society to deny parents the legal power to prevent such catastrophes, when we see the possibilities of such events, often years in advance. This is one reason those of us with mentally ill children need to speak up. Society needs to realize that we need serious legal support for our ill family members, if for no other reason than to attenuate the potential of future mass shootings and future alcohol or drug related road fatalities. We need laws that will help us get our grown offspring legally treated. And yes, this means forcibly if necessary.

It is not likely that many mothers have ever given birth, and upon sight of their adorable newborn, fervently prayed that this dear little baby might become a terrorist. Most parents do their best, and whatever circumstances life throws in front of them (and who gets perfect circumstances anyway), they work around those circumstances as best they can. I would imagine very few parents ever tried to screw up a child intentionally, and I would imagine very few mothers ever dreamed of their baby becoming a mass murderer. But as a friend of mine said to me the other day, "You know Nan, crazy people come from good families".

There was a shooting in a neighboring state involving a man who shot several people to death at a medical facility. I believe at some point he had been their patient. The local paper printed irate letters from furious townspeople incensed that the man's mother and father were on vacation at the time of the shooting. Numerous members of the community offered the opinion that these parents should have been home, preventing their son (who was in his mid-thirties and did not live with them) from carrying out this dreadful deed. Exactly what were these people supposed to have done? They had tried, for years, to get their son into treatment and keep him there. Not surprisingly, they failed.

However, they committed the seemingly unpardonable offense of taking a vacation on a tropical beach. And their neighbors vilified them for doing so. How can we do such cruel things to people who have already suffered so much? NOBODY ever ponders the depth of our cruelty to them. Nobody ever considers what they must experience, the guilt, the pain, their profound sense of devastating loss. They didn't do anything, but they will never escape the horror of their son's actions.

I wrote a strongly worded letter to their local paper after these parents were treated so badly, but they never published it, in spite of verbal assurances to me on the phone that they would. I can't imagine how those poor souls continue to live in their community, with all eyes glaringly upon them. I mean, how awful. Do you think they deserve it?

I would strongly urge all of us to remember the perpetrator's families, when we feel compassion for the victims. The families are victims as well, and they deserve our most heartfelt thoughts. Dividing up our compassion, or stuffing it into convenient compartments only helps mask the incomprehensible enormity of this problem and our society's unwillingness to take truly meaningful steps to help get the afflicted into treatment, or take the necessary steps to help their families help them. The "compartments" simplify things for us "these people are good, these people are bad". But it is not that simple.

We need laws that deny the mentally ill the right to endanger others. We need laws that enable us to enforce medication if meds are called for, and laws that enable psychiatrists to hold an unbalanced individual in a safe place where they can't hurt themselves or others until they have stabilized. And we need these laws even if these actions violate civil liberties. Every single victim of a shooter would surely agree that the person who shot them, and all of society, would have been far better off with the shooter locked up someplace, undergoing treatment, rather than having the freedom to roam around and commit mayhem and murder.

Of course, we need to create new treatment centers, as there are woefully too few available beds. (The story of the government mandated closing of institutions many years ago is a long, sad story for another time.) While the whole situation is just a mess, the first thing that needs to change is our attitude towards the civil liberties afforded to those who pose an imminent danger. As a society we justifiably want to protect our civil liberties, but we have forgotten that for the mentally ill, the only liberty that has been maintained is the liberty to remain sick and crazy. This isn't fair, not to them or to the rest of us. In fact, it is cruel, and totally lacking in compassion for the living hell the mentally ill experience.

Some might say, oh well, so they are crazy, so what, most of them aren't harming anyone. Really? Let's think that through again. First, because they do not have an opportunity to live their lives in a healthy and productive state, they experience harm if they are not treated. Second, their families are harmed, because they spend years witnessing the misery of lost, misdirected and even shortened lives of people they love. And third, all of society is harmed, because the gifts that such people possess are not utilized and shared with everyone else. And fourth, all of society faces potential harm and mayhem. Isn't this worth changing?

CHAPTER 16

Shame

During the writing of this book, as I've shown bits and pieces to friends, I became aware of the impact shame has in so many of our lives. How do people generally respond to what I've written? With absolute horror, typically. When people find out what I am actually discussing, with all the inherent detail and the degree to which I am opening up, the reaction is generally shock. However, whether our stories cause strong reactions in others or not, we need to have open discussions and awareness of mental illness in our families and societies, if we are going to deal effectively with the problems that result, and if we want to find effective treatments for them.

I do not believe our attitudes about mental illness, addiction, or alcoholism will change until those of us who have lived with it talk about our experiences, and share them openly with others. I want others to find out what went on within my family and I am not concerned with how they react. For me, it's really that simple and I am done with all the pretending and covering up that can be part of our lives when we have sick family members.

Miriam-Webster Dictionary defines shame as "a painful emotion caused by consciousness of guilt, shortcoming, or impropriety, or the susceptibility to such emotion, such as 'have you no *shame?*', or a condition of humiliating disgrace, or disrepute, such as the *shame* of being arrested, or something that brings censure or reproach, or something to be regretted 'it's a *shame* you can't go', or a cause of feeling shame."

If we carefully consider each of the descriptive words in the definition of shame, many of which we've examined in this book, it becomes rather obvious that there is absolutely no reason for us to harbor the emotion of shame or embarrassment about having SMI in our families. Yet many of us do. Lots of people, like me, got used to experiencing shame about all sorts of things, because we grew up in families that were soaked in shame. Many factors contributed to this, and in my case, I believe the socially conservative communities both my parents came from was the primary cause, along with their cultural and religious heritages, a rigid combination of social forces which expected them to march forward in lock-step with commonly accepted norms of behavior.

If the overarching necessity in one's life is to appear to conform to socially accepted behaviors, then any of us might be drawn to taking all sorts of measures to force things to appear "normal". In my opinion, this is the root of enabling. Enabling includes a desperate attempt to make the actions of our loved ones with SMI fit into the patterns expected of us. This means that an alcoholic's wife will phone his office and make up an "acceptable" excuse as to why he is not able to be at work that day, or the parent of a mentally ill child will cover up his strange behavior with other excuses, rather than owning up to the situation.

I didn't begin to understand the origins of all this until my own teen years. When I was 16, my grandmother and I spent part of a summer living in the small European town from which my father's family traced its origins, and I was shocked by the power that expected norms of behavior seemed to hold over people's lives. As delightful as the town was, with its ancient stone buildings and charming hillside setting, I couldn't fathom how I would ever live an entire lifetime there, as I knew that I'd never be able to "conform". The townspeople sat in the cafes in the village square in the evenings drinking expresso and wine, nibbling on fruit and cheese, and gossiping mercilessly about the lives of their neighbors. And they especially gossiped about anyone who wasn't doing things the way everyone else thought they should. In fact, we, visitors from the US, were subjected to the same sharp tongues, often as we sat right in front of them! My grandmother had invited a friend to join us on the trip, a friend whose family had come from the same little village, and she had brought along her daughter. The daughter held an important nursing position in a large city hospital (I seem to remember she was head nurse at a major teaching hospital), but instead of gaining respect for her education and professional accomplishments, she was torn apart by the gossipers because she was over 30 and not married. I had never heard anything so cruel. In that small town, you absolutely had to conform to accepted social norms, and if you didn't, you didn't stand a chance of living peacefully or experiencing personal acceptance. Unless you kept quiet.

When we come from such a place, it is predictable that we will be afraid to tell anyone important things we feel or experience for fear of being embarrassed or feeling shamed from the judgments of others. This evolves over time into a strong habit and a way of living, so we simply do not talk about embarrassing or difficult subjects, ever, especially subjects like mental illness or alcoholism, or a variety of other loaded topics.

My family may have been one generation away from this little town in Europe, but these patterns are ancient and they run deep. In my own childhood we didn't ever discuss mental illness, alcoholism, sex, or money, to name some of the big verboten topics. As they were completely off-limits, and far too embarrassing to talk about, innumerable emotions about them were stuffed behind an inner wall, never addressed. Family secrets almost never got divulged either, though as I learned later, there were some humdingers that were kept hidden. In my family the biggest off-limit topic, by far, was money.

I mentioned in the chapters about Sam that his lack of financial success may well have contributed, along with many other factors, to his mental illness. It certainly had a profound effect on his self-worth. With so much in our modern world measured by how much we earn, how could Sam have felt otherwise? Clearly in today's world much of our self-worth depends upon the amount of money we make and the status of our jobs.

In my own family, shame around money worked the other way.

My parents both came from poor immigrant families, farmers on one side and coal miners on the other. My father had a lot of drive and ambition, with a sharp business sense, and after his own father's death (killed in a coal mine accident, on Christmas Eve, when my dad was 12), my father was determined that his family would not have to worry about surviving and having enough money. Though it cost him the rest of his childhood and his teenage years, his hard work in those years was legendary. For example, he would sleep under the truck he used to deliver coal to save time going home to his own bed, time he could spend working. I've never verified this, but family lore says that he owned the mine his father worked in by the time he was 18. In addition, he had a knack for buying up bargain real estate and making other astute investments, and so he did very well. No question about it, he was a naturally gifted businessman, besides being an unbelievably hard worker. He had very little education, and even as a child I would often be drafted into spending an evening reading legal contracts out loud to him, as he didn't read well enough to be confident he got all the details straight.

When I was growing up, we lived in a modest house, and owned nothing fancy or expensive. The paramount objective for my father was to give the appearance that we were a very middle-class family, to live in such a simple way that nothing was ever revealed that would show he was wealthy. Nobody was ever supposed to suspect the truth. We owned nothing except the basics and did not purchase things that would cause people to question our financial status. My father even had an expression, "putting on the dog", which was frequently used to tell us we were acting in such a way as to appear to be above our station in life, that is, to have money. This was presented to us as nearly a moral failing. We, his children, never had allowances and even things like bicycles were considered extravagant. I am a pianist, and grew up practicing on a beat-up old baby grand my father had repossessed from one of the fraternities at the university who couldn't pay their coal bill. How ironic was that?! My Juilliard teacher thought it was quite funny that I grew up practicing on a repossessed piano. My piano lessons were free, as my teacher, a professor at the university, recognized my talent and taught me for nothing. This was an immensely wonderful gift for me, for which I am grateful and appreciate to this day, as I would not have had lessons otherwise. And I cannot imagine having grown up without piano lessons.

I was raised in the West, but I never skied as a child because it was an expensive sport, and my father would never have spent money for something he considered so frivolous. My winter sport was ice skating on a nearby frozen pond, because I could use my aunt's old skates, with extra socks stuffed in the toes so they more or less "fit". As this was the West, many of my friends had their own horses, and I desperately wanted one of my own. In that time and place, owning a horse wasn't the huge expense it is today, and many kids had them. Regardless, this was still an unnecessary expenditure, so I just rode my friends' horses. I had won a scholarship to Juilliard, without which I might never have been able to attend, but when I would ask my father for money to live on and for school expenses, he would give me half of what I had requested. As I always worked, I made up the difference with what I earned, and I am not sure this is a bad lesson to give a young person. Nonetheless, with my own children, I am far more generous, as I do not believe deprivation is the only way one's children acquire character.

My father never gave my mother access to a checking account or any other bank account. She didn't even have a predictable household fund and would have to ask him for money for grocery shopping, each time she needed to buy food. I often saw her rummaging in my father's coat pockets for change when she needed money for something besides groceries. Little luxuries she might have enjoyed, like purchasing fresh flowers for the table, were absolutely forbidden as a waste of money. To the day, buying a lovely bouquet of flowers feels like a subversive act to me. As you might imagine, my mother knew nothing about the substantial amounts of real estate or investments my father accumulated.

I realize now that my father was extremely uncomfortable about his wealth, and very likely even actually ashamed of it, because so many of his old friends were still poor, and he himself was the product of extreme Depression-era poverty. One of his uncles was quite literally jailed as a boy for stealing some potatoes from a farmer's field and cooking them to feed himself and his friends. My mother was also a product of an impoverished life on her family's farm during the Depression. This history, coming from another time and place, is the only way to comprehend how she willingly signed their joint tax returns with papers placed across the bottom line, so she never knew how much my father actually earned. In fact, my father was known to say that any man who told his wife what he earned was a "damn fool". As a woman living in the 21st century, my mother's compliance is hard to understand, but she didn't want to rock the boat and went along with whatever my father wanted her to do. Perhaps it was understandable for a woman of her time, though to me, this seems incomprehensible today.

This situation did provide all of us with a chance to grow up understanding we had to work hard for a living, and I don't think any of us were worse off for that, except perhaps for what came later, at the very end. When my father died, we faced the sobering fact that nobody had a clue what to do with his business problems, which were numerous and complex, and had only the vaguest notion what they were, a situation that brought out the best and the worst in all of us. Solving the legal and contamination issues took years, but eventually we got it all sorted out.

In addition to cultural influences, I believe the influence of religion also played a huge role in the family's sense of shame. And I think this might have been true regardless of the religion we had been born into. It would seem to me that feeling shameful about something you did, or might like to do, is the very basis of our Western cultural religious heritage, going back all the way to the image of Eve in the Garden of Eden. Perhaps this is so for other religions as well, from the little I know about them. This is too big a topic for me to get into deeply, and for sure I'm not qualified as I'm neither a religious scholar nor a therapist. I mention it here because it seems rather obvious that the scope of our entire Western cultural heritage causes us to feel bad about doing something that others tell us is wrong, even if we don't believe it ourselves. I just keep thinking back to what it was like to live in the tiny village in Europe, and then I ponder that many other people have come from similar tiny little villages elsewhere.

In my family, our religion was Catholicism, and we had a rather typical relationship with the Church, given my parents' generation and the cultures they grew up in. Going to church was a beautiful experience for me as a young person. I loved it. I sang in the choir and played the organ, finding soloists and good singers for church services, even among my friends from other religions. The inspiration of the physical beauty of the church itself was exquisite, as was the music that filled the hushed peace and quiet, and the sense of rest and calm. To this day I have very mixed feelings about my own history with the Church, emotions that are tangled in complex ways with my lack of comprehension regarding many church teachings and policies which haven't been reexamined for centuries. Whatever my non-participation today, I was dismayed when Notre Dame in Paris nearly burned to the ground in the spring of 2019. That one incident showed me that there is still much about the Church I will always love, and writing this chapter has been most difficult for me. Even today, as determined as I am to speak openly about all the events of my life and SMI in my family, it feels somewhat uncomfortable for me to risk disapproval from those who still adhere closely to the teachings and customs of Catholicism. I realize I risk alienation by offering critical thoughts about Church teachings and how they affected us. Shame is always about fearing the disapproving judgment of others, and I can't get past this any better than anyone else until I get over being concerned about disapproval from others. Which is tough to do.

Early recollections of my family life include memories of true old-world customs. My father never set foot in a church except for weddings and funerals. My grandmother who lived with us went to Mass faithfully, every day, and was the sort of church lady intimately involved with washing altar cloths, sweeping up, and whatever church errands materialized that day. My mother never had any real interest in any formal religion, and came from a Protestant faith, so she didn't bother with any of it very much.

Still, we kids were sent to Sunday School every week and did all the expected Church related things as we grew up. I guess that happened because my parents thought it was the way a kid should grow up, or more likely, they would have been too embarrassed to explain to their friends and neighbors why their children weren't in Sunday School, or maybe my grandmother insisted. We dutifully memorized our catechism lessons, had our first communions, got confirmed, and generally adhered to established Church customs. We did what we were expected to do. My sister and I were also sent to a Catholic high school for girls, which I believe was a way to keep us away from the town's high school, and, of course, the boys that studied there. My parents wanted us to delay dating and all the issues that came with it for as long as possible.

Sunday morning after Sunday morning, we learned how to live our lives. But then you gradually begin to question what you've been taught as you grow up and as you experience life for yourself. Since there is no guidance offered about dealing with your questioning feelings, shame almost inevitably sets in. Expressing yourself honestly and being open about how you feel and what you are thinking will cause consternation at best among your parents and teachers, so you don't do it. You learn to keep your mouth shut. When you are taught one thing, and experience another, emotional walls go up somewhere in your consciousness. The walls get built to hold back massive waves of contradictory feelings and emotions that exist because of the disconnect between what you feel and what you've been taught, and once those walls are up, they are hard to notice and just become part of your internal scenery.

I believe I was attracted to music and becoming a musician primarily because all those walled-away emotions and feelings were found abundantly in the music I played, magnificently so, and I could safely express them in the context of great music, for hours a day. Thank heavens for that, as this was truly a boon to the quality of my life, and has been since childhood. And I realize that one of the reasons Sam really touched my heart was his uncanny ability to express all emotions and feelings on the cello, more fully than I ever heard with anyone else. However, I have also wondered if walling off all those emotions and feelings made me less sensitive to taking in the full breadth of other people, or an awareness of who they really were. I've often wondered if there might have been occasional hints I simply didn't recognize regarding Sam's future with SMI even many years before he was sick. With those internal walls up, I never questioned anything.

I wish my childhood religion had grown along with the times, and moved its teachings into the 21st century, but it hasn't. This means that if you cannot live your life abiding by its rules, generally you keep quiet about it. As a result, many people feel shame about what they do, and how they feel about themselves. This is not new, but with the ever-present media images, frank and open discussions about sex and homosexuality in today's culture are everywhere, especially since the emergence of the internet. As such, sinful thoughts (as defined by the Church) have not exactly diminished. But going back to my childhood, I do not remember experiencing any open, honest discussions about sexuality at any time during my association with the Catholic church. I might add that this was bad enough if you were straight and naturally inclined to marry and have children, but heaven help you if you were gay or otherwise didn't fit the norm.

Though I will leave it to others to speak with clarity about the causes of our priest pedophilia crisis, it seems obvious to me that the atmosphere of secrecy and shame produced by this lack of openness about sexuality in all its forms must have had something to do with it. This entire crisis has brought about nearly incomprehensible amounts of suffering amongst the victims, not to mention their own sense of shame induced by sexual abuse: "How could the priest have done this to me? What did I do that invited it?". The extent of the coverup, especially the unconscionable practice of transferring pedophile priests from parish to parish repeatedly, is pretty horrifying. But it also seems to me it was somewhat inevitable in a way, because none of the people involved were able, or permitted, to open up about their emotions and feelings. Perhaps had the priests themselves had the opportunity to speak openly about their feelings or their inclinations, they might have been able to get some help.

Since I grew up in this religion, I can say with certainty that Catholics, like everyone else, do pretty much what they want regardless. But often immense feelings of shame accompany what they do or want to do because they've been told so many times it's "wrong". How does that help anyone live a balanced and authentic life? And does this not, in fact, lead to unhealthy levels of self-repression and self-judgment? I will argue that it does and such levels of repression and judgment do not allow for an open and healthy dialogue. As I've said, I don't believe this is unique to Catholicism, and believe the situation would have been much the same had many other religions replaced my childhood faith. But, as we discussed before, when we grew up in families that are soaked in shame, we grow accustomed to it. This is unhealthy. Anything that contributes towards our belief that we ought to just "be quiet about it" is ultimately harmful on so many levels.

In my own childhood, the combination of culture and religion saw to it that the rules for secrecy and shame were laid down early. There were all sorts of things we never discussed and I learned to go along with it and stay quiet, never asking questions, and this was true of the adults in the family – my mother, my father, and my grandmother - as well as me and my siblings. The most dramatic example I can think of? I didn't know until I was a teenager that my father had been married at 18 in the Church and divorced, not surprisingly, a few years later. One day, the priest came to our house and informed my parents that my father's first wife had died in a car crash and so now my parents could finally get married, officially, in the Church. Seriously? These two solid citizens, parents of three children, caretakers of an aging parent in their home, owners of a successful business, active in their community, arguably even genuine pillars of their community, had been "living in sin"? The concept was ridiculous, even to my teenage self, topped only by the utter ridiculousness of the quiet little trip to the rectory so they could officially marry.

But think of this – my father felt such shame about this that he never discussed it, and the agonizing embarrassment he felt the day he explained this to me, his eldest child, was palpable. His pain is something I feel to this day when I think about it, and I can still remember the tortured expression on his face. Why was this necessary? There is nothing shameful about having an early failed marriage. Or even a later failed marriage. And also, why was it necessary to pressure my mother to convert to Catholicism at this point, before they were officially "married"? She'd been raised in a Protestant church, and while she was a deeply spiritual person, she didn't have much interest in any organized religion all her long life, and of course my parents were legally married years before by the mayor of their town. (That one didn't count, I guess.) Still, after the priest came to our house when I was a teenager with the news about the first wife and the car accident, my mother bowed under the pressure, converted, and got married all over again. They shamed her into it. It is hard to fathom why she went along with this, but I believe she was just trying to go along and get along, not rock the boat, and I doubt if anyone ever asked her how she really felt about this or what she wanted to do. I doubt she asked herself.

It occurs to me that this kind of pressure is not really that different than the shame and pressure we feel to not acknowledge or discuss mental illness and addiction/alcoholism problems in our own families. In fact, I personally didn't realize until fairly recently that my father was an alcoholic. That realization was astonishing. There is privacy, there are certain things you don't want to tell people. But certain things are healthy to discuss and we just don't discuss them because we are ashamed to discuss them. After he passed away, and after my youngest son had been in rehab, and after I began examining family patterns of drug and alcohol use, only then did I ask myself why I never thought about my father as a problem drinker. While he was never a sloppy drunk, never "acted drunk", never sounded or behaved badly in public, never had a DUI, he still drank a lot. It is incredible to me that my father's drinking never came up in our family, ever, as something that might necessitate discussion, or even just need saying out loud. And I managed not even to think about it at all for decades of my life.

Most of us are not eager to talk about the skeletons in our family closets. The subtle problem with this is that it creates the sense that our personal value will diminish if people find out the truth about these skeletons, that people won't think well of us, that we are somehow less because of these skeletons, or that they make us smaller in some fashion. And so they stay in the closet, as though ignoring them will make them go away. I knew Sam many years before I realized he had an uncle, his father's brother, who suffered from mental illness. Sam's family (though they were Jewish, not Catholic) was not that different than mine, and even though they were not religious in any way, they never discussed the uncle's mental illness, just as my family would never have discussed this either. In retrospect, I'm fairly sure Sam's maternal grandfather was also mentally ill. Though neither Sam nor I knew him as he had died many years ago, when I think about comments that were made about some things he did, I believe it extremely likely that he, too, was mentally ill. Sam's family never acknowledged this or spoke about it, but it would have been useful for Sam to know because mental illness can have a genetic component.

"Scientists have long recognized that many psychiatric disorders tend to run in families, suggesting potential genetic roots." NIH Research Matters, March 18, 2013

As far as I'm concerned, the ONLY way out of this mess, the only path to wholeness, is to TALK about our life experiences, about all our feelings and emotions, whatever they are, even if we find them embarrassing or shaming. Now I do think there are certain times and places for such discussions, and blurting out that your spouse is an alcoholic at the company Christmas party is perhaps not one of them. But it is helpful to find out other people have the same things going on with them that we do. We must directly and honestly confront the circumstances that induce our shame; there is no choice, if we want to remain healthy and sane ourselves. When we've grown up in families where certain topics are off limits, when we've been part of a culture or religions or belief systems that reject us if we don't embrace their world view, we can easily develop an attitude that we are alone and must do everything by ourselves. It can be hard to ask for help, if we are ashamed to reveal the issues for which we need help.

I had to face my feelings of embarrassment and shame all over again when I learned that Galen went on welfare. The mere idea that I could have a kid (OK, I'll say it) that I could have raised a kid who doesn't work and thinks going on welfare is a solution to his financial issues, well, this is a reality I have struggled to take in.

I am not ashamed to tell people Galen is seriously mentally ill. The general public needs to see that mental illness is a real disease. I am not ashamed to convey much of what Galen has done, because his mental illness is the driver behind everything he does. But somehow having a son who is getting public assistance is a tough one for me to swallow. We all work immensely hard in my family, as my son and daughter will attest, and we take pride in our hard work and also in our accomplishments. In addition, while we aren't a very wealthy family, we are not a poor family either, and Galen himself has some inherited funds, though they are not accessible to him directly (I've made sure of that, ever since he tried to buy the guns.) Still, welfare was designed for people who really need a helping hand and have no personal assets, and that doesn't describe Galen.

Except that I guess it does describe Galen, as he is too mentally ill to hold a job, as well as too argumentative and headstrong, and will not comply with anyone: not the agency I've engaged to help him, not the innumerable doctors and psychiatrists he's had over the years, not any of the schools, universities, or professors, and not with me in any constructive way. I guess that leaves welfare. I have much to explore here within myself, as this definitely pushes my buttons and makes me angry. But still, I recognize I have to frame the whole question of welfare differently, as I recognize I am totally comfortable with someone getting welfare as a result of physical disabilities. If I find this completely acceptable, should there really be a difference if someone can't cope with life due to a mental illness?

I also recognize that it might actually be a good thing he's on welfare. When he is given funds on a debit card, state officials will track every expenditure, so their eyes will observe what he does with every dime that passes through his hands. When I look at it this way, I don't see how this can be all that bad at all. Realizing that has helped me get past my own feelings of shame that my oldest son is on public assistance.

I believe that all of us have to monitor ourselves for the effects of all the shaming that we experience in our lives. Since many of us have endured so much shaming, and it just keeps on coming at us, there will be many such opportunities for introspection. It's important, for our own sanity and for those around us. Just being conscious of the influence of shame will help take it down within us.

CHAPTER 17

Acceptance

Like all new moms, I loved my kids deeply. And I had a mental check list of everything I wanted to teach them, all the things I felt it was my responsibility to make sure they learned or accomplished. Learn to say please and thank you, shake hands, swim, ride a bike, do laundry, cook simple meals, clean your room, sew on a button (including the boys), take care of your pets, drive, and so forth and so on, check, check, check, and check. With each mental box checked off, it was easier to feel I was gradually releasing my kids to their waiting independent futures, as well-prepared as possible.

But what happens when a particular child simply can't accomplish all the basic steps that lead to independence and maturity, or gets derailed along the way with mental illness or addiction? What do we do then? Pete Earley's excellent book "Crazy" outlines his son's lengthy struggle with mental illness, which was ultimately treated successfully, and his son went on to have a good recovery. This book also provides a sober view of the journeys of the mentally ill through our criminal justice system. Mr. Earley writes beautifully and the book is well worth anyone's attention.

"I had my son back."

That is the sentence with which Mr. Earley ends his book. Perhaps it seems odd to give away the ending, but it illustrates my point. Most people whose family members are mentally ill don't get this happy ending or anywhere close. While some people, including Mr. Earley and his son (and myself and my younger son) experience this wonderful outcome, not everyone does. Most don't, perhaps the great majority don't.

When our mentally ill loved ones accept treatment and were lucky enough to find an effective combination of helpful ingredients such as medication and therapy for their recovery, we are fortunate indeed. But other factors are needed. Persistence and a strong desire to move in a positive direction, and personal or spiritual growth experiences that many therapists believe essential are also keys to an effective recovery. Whatever the combination, if it all "works", we can count ourselves amongst the lucky few. Indeed, luck plays a prominent role. Does the right inpatient facility have an available bed, or is the right therapist back from vacation?

In the end, they did what they needed and "came back" to their families. Obviously, this is a wonderful outcome, even if it arrives most often after the whole family has been through hell with a long, miserable, expensive, drawn-out saga. I count myself blessed that I have my youngest son back, and he's happy, healthy, and thriving. We are both truly blessed, and perhaps lucky.

But…

But what about all the others, which means most of the others: the people that never get their loved ones back? What about the stories that have tragic endings, the families of people that die, after an overdose or by suicide? What about those of us who have had years and years of turmoil and crisis with our relatives, unending misery that never improves or goes anywhere? There is the heartache we suffer, watching a loved one grow steadily sicker, a worsening situation going from bad to terrible to worse. I know this painful journey, too, because I have experienced that journey with my husband and with my oldest son.

Accurate statistics seem difficult to find, but from what I can gather, and from what I have witnessed, it seems there are many people with SMI and addictions that are never successfully treated, long term. Mental illness and addictions are actual diseases, which means that like other diseases (asthma, diabetes, heart disease) sufferers will do well only as long as they stick with treatment. And that means, just like with other diseases, relapses do happen. Just like those other diseases, some people discontinue treatment altogether, and not to their benefit.

This means a great many people aren't getting better, or will probably never get better, or will even get worse, and our frustrating journey just continues with no apparent end. With each crisis, hope for a brighter future fades a bit more; eventually we feel caught in a trap, with no apparent way out. Like any animal caught in a trap, we fuss and fight and wiggle, but it only gets worse with time. Finding yourself trapped is utterly miserable and will take everything we've got to cope, to find some peace in spite of it. There is only so long that you can go on trying to get yourself out.

Ultimately you become exhausted, mentally and physically, and not only from beating your head against the walls. You recognize that in very practical terms you can't go on like this any longer. When you begin to accept that you've tried every single thing you can think of, very possibly for years on end, and that you can't find any other options, there is only one choice left - no matter how you force your over anxious mind to keep searching. That choice is acceptance. This sounds so ridiculously simple and easy to say, but truthfully it is the hardest thing I've ever had to do in my life. And yet it really helps, a lot.

Unconditional acceptance doesn't mean giving in or giving up. It just means you have opened your eyes and you have looked soberly at the truth of the situation involving your family member, more than likely with immense sadness and tears. This is all so unfair and it hurts so much! Acknowledging the depths of your pain is part of the acceptance. You keep going, and then you realize you have become very clear not only about the truth of the situation itself (you are not white-washing it in any way), but about the obvious fact that you cannot change it or influence it at all. You are especially certain you don't want to remain trapped eternally in this agonizing Bermuda Triangle of fear, worry, and pain, by attempting to influence an outcome that is beyond your influence. There is only one thing left to do, and that is acceptance.

With my oldest son Galen, I have had to surrender to the fact that I can do nothing whatsoever about the sort of life he has right now. I am powerless over his situation. It doesn't mean that I embrace his life, it just means that I accept that this is what is happening right now. For me, the key has been to accept the circumstances. It has taken me a long time to realize that surrendering to the situation is not at all the same thing as becoming defeated by it, or approving of it. Acceptance is only a practical path to live in peace.

Coming to terms with acceptance is the key to making an impossible job a bit less so. For me, as I've explored letting go of resistance, I have discovered that this letting go process also leads to an opening for some fundamental thought changes within myself, something I never expected. I had no idea this was even possible, or that it might exist. For example, I've changed my thinking about what it means to be a mother and have a mother's love for one's offspring, especially if the offspring are grown well into adulthood.

We've all heard about the stories of mothers who push their children out of the way so they are not killed by a car, or rush into a burning building to get their kids out, often endangering their own lives, and possibly at the cost of their own lives. I think this is what I always thought unconditional love was, a willingness to do whatever it took to keep my kids alive, safe, and well, even if this included self-sacrifice. I had defined mother love within myself as a love that was so intense that I would be willing to die for my child, if needed. From the earliest moments of all my children's lives on this earth, I felt that I would do whatever was needed for my kids, and I would do it in a heartbeat, without giving it a second thought, were it ever necessary. I totally got why these heroic parents acted as they did, and I was certain I would do the same if I ever needed to.

Maybe when kids are small, this all-caring attitude is understandable, as small children are so young and vulnerable. But then they grow up, and this sort of thinking outgrows its usefulness. For sheer self-preservation, it needs revision, as over-arching mother love carried on for too long comes with an enormous cost to the mother, and is not necessary for the children's development. I recognize it is harder to redefine this when one of your grown children is a psychological mess or is an addict, and this redefinition comes more naturally to those parents lucky enough to have healthy and functioning adult offspring who are well launched. But easy or otherwise, excessive mother love has to taper down. It isn't healthy for anyone.

For me, giving up the concept of self-sacrifice and responsibility for my mentally ill adult son changes how I define myself. I am still a good mother, loving and caring, but now I must take care of myself first. Failing to reorganize the dangerous all-sacrificing, all-caring mother-thinking for my life as it is today would be a big problem, if it were to continue. For me, even with a sick adult child, it blurs boundaries that should remain clear. My thinking about this needed revision and revamping for a long time.

The all-sacrificing mother-thinking is rooted in fear. When you have a crazy husband, or an addict son, or another son has attempted suicide several times, an overload of fear is certain. When your crazy son is incapable of clear thinking, demonstrated through any number of reckless actions, and lacks an ability to follow society's most basic rules, an overload of fear is certain. But it doesn't matter how afraid I am, I still don't have a bit of control over the situation, and the fear isn't changing anything, except making me miserable. Fear for my son cannot rule my actions all the time, or my attitudes and beliefs. I need my loving heart for my own life, as well as to give all my children love, accept them as they are, and deal with whatever happens to them when it happens. I can still be a loving, caring person, but the established boundaries of my own self-care have to be very firm. I cannot, under any circumstances, give myself away to others in such a way that I am hurt by the giving.

For me, the most important part of all this is that it means I won't be fretting or bleeding or losing sleep for my son any longer. This gives me more personal freedom to take care of myself and my own body. In truth, there is more to me than motherhood, and I can't center the rest of my life around being a mother to a sick son I can't help because he refuses all help, from me or anyone else.

I have also come to realize that if we continue to hold onto a need to help our ill sons and daughters, this is hard on them, as well, not just us, and it doesn't really help them in the long run. It robs them of any small amount of decision capability they might possess. Freedom for a sick adult son, to whatever extent it can exist, will only exist by my letting go and accepting.

I recognize that we feel a need to protect our children, and feel guilt when they suffer, especially if we feel we do not suffer as much as they do. The need to protect our children runs deep, based upon billions of years of evolution out of the primordial soup. When we birth a child, in our hopes and fears for our child, we mothers are fragile and vulnerable too, just like our babies, and this state continues until we realize at some point when they are grown that we don't have to have it all figured out, that we truly can let go. After all, when our kids are grown, however it has all worked out, they are launched to the best of our ability. As parents we did the best we could, even if we didn't succeed in all the ways we wanted to succeed. We need to turn all our children, sick and well, over to the Universe to live their lives the best they can.

For me, this means accepting that Galen is in a dangerous situation, that he is so seriously ill that his life is in a state of total shambles, and that he might make choices which could result in his death or the deaths of others. It also means accepting that he doesn't have a healthy relationship with me, or anyone else. But if I treat him in such a manner that he feels he cannot do anything for himself without me, this is hard on him and doesn't make a terrible situation any better. And I think this is so because it may limit his ability to make some limited progress with his situation and improve it in his own way. While it may be factually accurate that he is making awful choices, I might as well suspend judgment and accept what he does, because I can't change it anyway, and whatever is going to happen will happen regardless of what I do. It is always possible that he might learn something, however small, so it does leave the potential for positive change open.

And here's another thought – what if we don't have to be right about what they need? Their lives are, after all, their own lives, and they are free to conduct themselves however they want. As radical as it sounds, maybe it is even possible we don't really know what is best for them. If you think about it, being crazy might be the ultimate path to inner freedom. You don't have to follow any rules, or do what society expects of you, or hold yourself to any standards of behavior that are commonly accepted by most of us. It's possible that giving up our need to be right about what our kids need, or what they should do, whether they are sick or not, is the ultimate personal liberation.

There is something else to work through with acceptance, and that is accepting the inability of others, your friends and family, to face what has happened or deal with it in any way that is solidly helpful to you. They can't help it. All of us are woefully uneducated about mental illness, which also means nobody understands what to do or what to say. I'd like to give you one example of the sort of thing that happened-frequently, and made me very angry until I backed off and saw that I had to accept how my friends reacted. Not long after Sam died, I ran into a friend in the park, somebody I've known for many years. We chatted for a good long time, about her life, her family, her dog, my kids, my pets, my career, getting older, everything. She knew Sam well, for nearly as many years as I did. I hadn't heard from her since his death. Yet here we were, with plenty of time to talk, on a nice warm day, walking together in the park. She doesn't even mention his name. Finally, I ask her, point blank, do you know Sam died? Well, yes, she says. But I didn't want to bother you and thought you wouldn't want me to bring it up and to talk about it.

This is fairly mind-boggling. Here's a genuinely nice person, someone I've known two thirds of my life, who appears to actually believe that it is somehow better for me, and less bother for me, if she doesn't call me, doesn't mention Sam killed himself, doesn't ever refer to it, and won't seek me out or ask how I'm doing. Is this really what the whole world believes? Is this what we need - those of us in this unlucky club coping with surviving our family member's mental breakdowns and, in this case, suicide - to be left alone, dangling out on a branch, blowing in the wind, coping with all the turbulence by ourselves, all alone? I am completely appalled and want to start screaming at her. But I don't because she's my dear friend, and I know she just doesn't understand, she and so many others. It's not like she or they have done something wrong intentionally. People don't know any better, but when they pretend like nothing happened, it leaves me frustrated and angry.

Then she directed our conversation to Robin William's death, like it always did with everyone in those days, because Robin Williams died not long after Sam died, and I listen to her long discussion of how his death wasn't really a suicide because his disease had made changes in his brain. Seriously? How can she not see that ALL suicide victims have brains that are changed by their disease? That's why it's called mental illness, because it is a disease of the brain.

I recognize that she and other people might have been reluctant to bring up the topic of Sam because they thought they might spare me further upset about unhappy memories. And maybe that is indeed why she didn't call. But the reality was that I got almost no condolence calls, emails, or cards, and only once did a friend that I met by chance on the street head straight into the topic and say how sorry she was to hear that Sam died.

Often, after folks die, even if their families are not Jewish and sitting Shiva, friends come over, they bring food, they stay, they ask if they can walk the dog, or take out the trash, or better still, do it without asking. They are just there. They stay a long time and they come back repeatedly. But after years of mental illness, hospitalizations, bizarre behavior, embarrassing incidents, and finally a suicide, even good friends have effectively disappeared. Nobody shows up. It's too much for anybody to handle. Heck, it's too much for me to handle, but I have to because there's no one else. You have to do everything yourself. Take out Chinese substitutes for lovingly made lasagna from a neighbor. The phone is silent. This is really painful, but this experience is also very common. I have come to see that full acceptance has to include love and kindness for those who can't deal with the situation at all, or don't know how, and we all have to get let off the hook for any hurts we may have caused each other.

Instead of turning away or remaining silent, friends and family can also have the opposite reaction – they want to lecture you about what you should be doing. As we work to make this inner shift to acceptance a habit, we can't be so surprised to find friends and relatives upset with us. Whether your loved one has died, or isn't getting better, or won't accept any sort of treatment, and you are finally able to back off and find yourself at long last capable of accepting the situation as it is, certain friends and family members may stop speaking to you. And if they speak to you at all, then only to offer an opinion about what you should be doing to help. They will tell you which doctors are the best doctors, or quote something they read in the NY Times about the exact illness you describe, or they will tell you which medicines worked for their second cousin's son-in-law. They mean well.

Good friends may tell you "just forget about him" (somebody actually said that to me) as though you could possibly forget someone you birthed or someone whose life you shared for decades. Or they do the opposite and tell about treatments, already tried unsuccessfully. People lose patience with you, and even if you are inching your way forward in your life, however slowly, others don't want to be part of your journey and don't want to hear about this miserable topic anymore. Who can blame them? We're tired of it too!

I find myself wanting to shout "Basta!!!" Enough is enough! The only workable solution here is to continue to encourage myself to stop railing against the fates, and find a quiet inner acceptance of life as it is, and people as they are, and my friends and family as they are. For me anyway, as I've opened myself up to this acceptance, and given up resisting it as much as I can, and even appreciating where

I am and they are, life has become a great deal easier. And I've at long last been able to move forward with taking some steps to create the new life I would like for myself. May we all continue to move forward and it couldn't hurt to support each other as we do. And maybe let each other off the hook a little bit.

CHAPTER 18

The Future for Our Loved Ones

The future is a risky thing to contemplate. We can cook up all sorts of dire dramas that may or may not materialize, but honestly, what is the point of doing that? There is a wonderful old saying that goes something like: "I'm an old man and I've had many troubles, and most of them never happened to me." Dwelling in the future (or, for that matter, the past) is of very little help for living in the present. As many wise sages have pointed out, the only moment we ever really have is the present moment, and it is the only one we can experience and enjoy.

I want to speak about the future directly though because all of us living with someone who has SMI have one thing in common – we worry a lot. Lots and lots of worry is a fact in our lives. But here's a radical thought: worry is always about the future! By this I mean that anything rising to the level of "worry" is nearly always regarding something terrible we fear might happen at some point in the future. If we are living in the present moment, which is the only moment we ever really have, we will find there very few immediate emergencies, right here, right now. While it is true that occasionally in life, there might be a few moments where we are literally facing life or death exactly at that moment, those moments are thankfully very rare. I'm speaking about sudden and unpredictable events such as an imminent car accident, or immediate danger of a violent crime. But the worry I am speaking about is formed by constructing the feelings and drama of many such moments in our heads, in our fantasized future, about ourselves or our mentally ill loved ones. None of it is real and none of this is doing anyone any good. For most of us, for nearly all the time in the present moment, nothing terrible is happening.

Clearly, we don't know what is going to happen in the future so we can start with letting go of all the fretting and worrying, and let ourselves be: just let life be, right now, in this moment. This is not a new idea, but there is definitely an art to it. Life itself, and all that has happened to us, encourages us to let go of our agenda, and we can realize how much better things go when we come to peace with this.

Even so, there is a certain reality concerning what we are up against here. Truly, the reality of what our loved ones might face in the years to come is frightening, which takes a lot of courage for us to consider. However, this is the best possible place, and the most difficult place, to begin to practice letting go or surrender, so let's look at it anyway. We're going to need to ace this course, as surrender and a release of our iron grip of control of the present moment, are vital to our own future sanity and peace of mind.

Especially given the current mental health laws, the raw truth is that the severely mentally ill have a greater likelihood of a shortened lifespan, including a high probability of a variety of health calamities. In his excellent book on schizophrenia, Dr. Torrey states that schizophrenia patients, for example, will on average see a lifespan decrease of approximately 25 years. No mom likes to think that her child will have serious health issues besides the mental health issues they already have, but this is possible, perhaps likely.

First, there's the question about suicide. My son has already tried to commit suicide several times that I know about. There could very well have been other attempts that have not come to my attention. If this continues, what are the chances he could try again successfully, given how he is living, and the mess that he digs himself into more deeply every day? I would imagine those chances are pretty high. After all, his father succeeded.

And what about all the risky sexual behavior the mentally ill often engage in, some of which has already gotten my son into some serious trouble? Will that get him into some other dangerous situation sometime? The chances would seem pretty high. He has not really learned that it is not only dangerous, but illegal, to solicit sex from underage girls online.

Then, for my son and others, there is the enhanced possibility of total disregard for the rule of law, for obeying any simple regulation that involves someone else, or society, telling him what to do. This will be incomprehensible to most people because it is so extreme and so pervasive, and so totally off the charts. It is actually difficult to even attempt to explain how strange Galen's attitude is about this and how it affects every aspect of his life.

Think of some things we all have to do, whether we like to do them or not. File taxes. Wait in line. Pay bills on time. Obey speed limits. Show up on time for appointments. How can this attitude of "nobody is ever going to tell me what to do" not have some very negative consequences somewhere along the way? Unfortunately, he is not the only person with mental illness who thinks like this.

Then there is the whole issue of whether the mentally ill take care of themselves, even in the most basic and fundamental ways. It's pretty obvious that when you are mentally ill you might not have it together enough to make sure you eat nutritious food rather than junk food or no food at all, or even manage to take regular showers or brush your teeth. Galen has had some enormous dental bills, all caused by simple neglect. It is quite possible he will lose all his teeth in the foreseeable future due to his lack of care and refusal to see a dentist. That would be one more person telling him what to do, so he doesn't go.

I am also pretty sure that Galen has become a heavy smoker, and I believe recurrent chest infections make him a frequent visitor to the ER. Some studies show that the severely mentally ill process both nicotine and caffeine quite differently than those without mental illness, and become extremely addicted to both. Once again, I'd like to refer you to Dr. Torrey's excellent book *Surviving Schizophrenia: A Family Manual* for an excellent discussion of this in Chapter 10, "Ten Major Problems", beginning on page 239 of the Seventh Edition, and to page 443 for a list of clinical studies supporting his conclusions. Dr. Torrey also mentions other dangers in Chapter 10, not all of them discussed here (I've not gone into HIV, family planning and pregnancy, for example).

I grew up in a family that wouldn't allow people to smoke, due to my father's asthma. You couldn't smoke at all if you were a family member, and you couldn't smoke in the house if you were a friend. My father went so far as to tell his children that he'd give each of us a thousand dollars on our twenty-first birthday if we didn't smoke. When I got to twenty-one, I was so grateful I hadn't become a smoker that I refused to accept the thousand dollars. My father (who was never a smoker) had severe asthma and had worked in the coal mines when he was young so he spent a lot of time at the end of his life in the only hospital in the world at the time dedicated exclusively to respiratory issues. When you see for yourself the misery that smoking causes, at the tail end of life, which you certainly can observe in a hospital devoted to lung diseases, you become a committed non-smoker if you weren't already. I remember especially one of his hospital roommates, a fellow who had lost three quarters of his lungs, plus part of his jaw, mouth, and tongue to an aggressive cancer, and yet when wheeled outside for some fresh air, he'd smoke a cigarette through his tracheotomy hole. Of course, at that point (he died a few weeks later) I suppose it didn't matter, but the image of a cigarette stuck in a trach hole remains with me to this day.

Sam was, if possible, even more fanatical about not being around smokers than I was, putting up a NO SMOKING sign by the front door of our home which he sternly enforced, asking friends to go outside to smoke. With the two of us for parents, Galen wasn't a smoker when he lived at home.

However, I can give evidence about his ridiculously excessive consumption of caffeine. Sugar too. He would consume both by the spoonful, straight from the container. That may sound ridiculous, but more than once I discovered him with a spoon stuck in a jar of instant coffee, or instant expresso, or in a box of sugar (confectioners preferably), shoveling the whole container into his mouth as quickly as possible, heaping spoon by heaping spoon, with such intensity that he always made a huge mess.

Once, out of curiosity, I decided to quietly add up the total count of carbohydrate grams for all the sugary stuff I could see he was eating and drinking per day. This may sound unbelievable, but it was well over a thousand before I gave up and stopped counting. The biggest problem with the caffeine he consumed was that it could trigger a panic attack - which it often did. The more nervous something made him, the more coffee he'd drink, and then an inevitable panic attack would cripple him for hours.

Alcohol is also an issue for him, and Galen always wanted to drink a lot. Though it may sound strange to put it like this, we are fortunate that he could never drink as much as he'd like, as it would always make him really sick. I have often felt that, as sensitive as he was to drinking, he might have some unusually sensitive physical reaction to alcohol. This is a blessing, because if his body let him drink as much as he'd like, his diverse problems would magnify.

And then there is the issue of the friends who the mentally ill choose, and those who choose to hang out with them. The people who want to hang out with someone like Galen are often unstable themselves, or they are people who want to take advantage of him. Crimes can be committed against mentally ill people and they are often robbed or sexually assaulted. Their friends can be as unstable as they are: unsavory characters, general misfits in society, or desperate people running away from their own challenging personal situations. Over the course of a lifetime, there is a high possibility that something unpleasant or even awful will happen due to the choice of company for the mentally ill, for the addicted, and for alcoholics.

What's to be done about all this, for us, the families?

As we discussed in the last chapters, the less we worry about what the future holds for our loved ones, and the less effort we put into the futility of influencing the outcome, the better this goes for us, especially since there is actually almost nothing that we can do about it anyway. What does it mean in practice to let go? All of us have established habits and ways of doing things that have helped us succeed. We've accomplished much, and know that being good at certain kinds of controlled behavior in the world around us has led us to repeated success. We come from a place where we understand the sort of discipline and behaviors we need in our personal and professional lives.

In the process of sorting out what can be done about our loved ones, we have tried our usual trusted approaches, umpteen times probably. We have also discovered it just plain doesn't work. It just makes us tense and anxious because their situations are beyond our control. We can't force a good outcome to happen, can't go after it in our usual analytical way, and eventually we realize that the exact opposite behavior, doing nothing, seems to work best. There is no control when it comes to the mentally ill, because predictability is not possible.

I saw a wonderful quote today that applies so well to our situation. It is attributed to Martin Buber: "All journeys have secret destinations of which the traveler is unaware." Those of us on this particular journey are going somewhere we cannot see, cannot predict, and cannot know. We really don't know where we're going to end up, or where our mentally ill family members will end up. And here's another thought: by letting go, we become more fluid, more malleable, more open and receptive to wherever the situation will lead. We are also open to movement in some unpredicted direction.

There really is no choice, thankfully, as the only way out of our personal misery is to let go and give up our desire to control what happens in the lives of our loved ones. Also, it seems to me that giving up control means learning to trust life itself, the Universe, even our loved ones, or whatever else we might believe in or choose to trust. But the catch with trust is that we also have to give up wanting things to work out the way we want.

If surrendering becomes focused on what I want, then it really isn't surrendering because it is conditional, and this will bring up all sorts of fears, even from our unconscious. To trust means to surrender, and let go of all control, and also give up our agenda. We don't know how things should go. Our ideas about what should occur with our loved ones are conditioned by our experiences with them in the past. But there are lots of other possibilities for the future beyond our imaginations or abilities to predict. Trust means being open to some other outcome, not necessarily the outcome we want.

The random uncertainty of events can drive us nuts and leave us traumatized. The stress of not knowing what will happen next, the immense burden of uncertainty, is enormous. We are on edge for the next outburst, and we live in that place for years. This wears on people. It has surely worn on me. But it doesn't have to! We can learn to take care of ourselves, and the supremely good news about that is that we are always in complete control of our own self-care. And in the next chapters, we discuss a lot about self-care.

PART 4
Taking Care of Ourselves

CHAPTER 19

Taking Care of Ourselves

1. Starting to think about self-care

Up to this point, we've discussed our experiences as family members of those suffering with mental illnesses. I've shared the stories of my own family, as well as tossed out for discussion other issues we all face. However, all this discussion would be woefully incomplete if we don't deal with how we as human beings, meaning you and me, manage our daily lives while living under such tremendous stress. This stress will inescapably involve our whole selves, which includes our mental, physical and emotional selves. As Dr. Bessel van der Kolk's wonderful book title says so clearly, *"The Body Keeps the Score: Brain, Mind, and Body in the Healing of Trauma."*

I firmly believe that taking care of ourselves must be at the center of our entire discussion. What is the point of endless discussion if we can't find a way out of this mess for ourselves, such that we can still enjoy our lives no matter what our relatives do? Otherwise, we're just sitting around complaining, and who needs that beyond a point. As I'm not the only one who has had a grueling life journey with SMI in my family, others might be curious as to how I've survived all of this as well as I have, and frankly, it just seems neighborly to share at least a little with you.

One of Galen's therapists once told me that many of his colleagues liked to commiserate with their clients about the awful holes in which the clients found themselves, but that he was the sort of therapist who liked to give them a ladder so they could start to climb out of the hole. I'd like to offer others the hope that there are indeed "ladders" we can use to help us climb out of the misery of living with SMI in our families.

What exactly do I mean by self-care? Some might think I mean something like getting a haircut or similar personal care. While I would agree that most of us feel great with a fresh haircut, in our discussion here I am speaking about something deeper and more thorough. What I am referring to here is the care we take of ourselves, to the extent we can, and as fully as we can. Our family member's illnesses take a huge toll on us and can be counted on to continually challenge us in every conceivable way, physically, psychologically, and emotionally. We can find ourselves constantly on alert, and depending on the next diagnosis, this can be quite literally true, for years on end. We can also feel we are forever just waiting for the next "shoe to drop", for the next crisis, the next call from a psych ward or arresting officer. Or sometimes there are no calls at all, for weeks and months. I am not alone in having the experience of not knowing where my son is for weeks at a time, let alone knowing if he is safe. Or alive. There is danger to us in the toll these mounting crises take, especially if we haven't done some work to care for ourselves along the way. We can find ourselves floundering, even freaking out. And my take on the whole thing is this:

Whatever else is going on, under no circumstances can we afford to forget about taking care of ourselves. Our own personal health and well-being are also important, and we cannot neglect ourselves and allow our own health to decline.

When we fly on an airplane, the flight attendants always give us some simple instructions in case of an emergency. They ask us to put our own oxygen masks on as soon as the mask drops down, so we are then able to help others. If we are going to be caring for others, first we have to care for ourselves.

I am going to include in this section some small examples of my favorite self-care tools. I'd like to make it clear that this is by no means a complete list, and I'd also like to make it especially clear that I have done none of these modalities or tools real justice here. I wrestled a long time with what to include in this chapter, as I'd like to share with you many things you can do, but I am also aware that I cannot oversee what you are doing or how you might interpret my words. So I have to limit this to material everyone can do and can do safely. A lifetime of teaching has taught me to be very cautious, as misinterpretation is always possible. Language, especially when it relates to movement and sensation, is exceedingly inexact.

Think of my offerings here as the equivalent of tidbits passed around for you to sample at a social gathering. If you like them, you can always have more. My purpose in this chapter is to point the way to some possibilities for genuine, long lasting help. We can all learn to not only survive but truly thrive in our difficult situations, and these tools are great places to start. At the very least, by exploring some of them here you will know they exist.

Maybe you'd like to know something about me, too. I have come to where I am, and have learned what I'm going to share with you, in some unusual ways. I was lucky enough to be born to a mother who was a nationally known, award-winning artist. I didn't have to make any special effort to take in what she taught me, as it surrounded me all my life, so I probably got it through osmosis. I chose to become a musician rather than a visual artist, though my mother's artistic influence remains with me on profound levels, and I will share some of this with you in the next chapter. Making art is tremendously therapeutic.

All my life I've been a teacher and I have worked with musicians. When I was young, I gave piano lessons. After a potentially career-ending injury in music school I found a teacher who helped me recover my ability to play, and I wanted to pass on to others everything I learned. I gave lessons to other injured musicians, and helped them rehabilitate their playing and careers post-injury. As I found this immensely rewarding, I began exploring new methods that might help my students recover from injury and get back to performing more rapidly.

In my search, I studied a wide variety of mind/body practices.

This included Feldenkrais, QiGong, meditation, energy work, breathwork, and much more. I found had a special affinity for both Feldenrkrais and QiGong, and studied those more deeply.

Dr. Moshe Feldenkrais was a nuclear physicist with a PhD from the Sorbonne, and was the director of the Israeli Army Department of Electronics. He was an avid athlete. He was a black belt in judo and a devoted soccer player who injured his left knee in a soccer match at the age of 25. The knee injury grew worse over time, and modern knee surgery did not yet exist. Working alone and applying his knowledge of physics to calculations of body mechanics, he developed an effective rehabilitation method that was many years ahead of its time and is widely practiced today. I was so impressed with his marvelous method and its practical usefulness that I completed a four-year training in the discipline, and afterward became a certified Feldenkrais practitioner myself.

The training occupied one long weekend every month, often across holidays like President's Day, plus several longer multiple week segments per year. In addition to those hundreds of hours of study, I also worked with one of the teachers in a small weekly group for more advanced individual mentoring. Though we had reading assignments, most of our work was physical, involving our own movement lessons as well as work with others, both in class settings and individually. Toward the end of my training, I began giving Feldenkrais classes in addition to continuing my teaching practice in piano. Currently I teach Feldenkrais classes at a major New York music conservatory, for which the students receive academic credit.

Of course, while I was doing all this exploring, my husband and two of my children were falling apart, and crisis after crisis ensued. My parents were getting older and sicker, and eventually they both died. Their deaths brought about the extended family misery of the legal dramas surrounding our inheritances, complete with two ultimately successful lawsuits (one of them with the IRS), as well as the uninvited chore of remediating the environmental contamination of some of our inherited real estate. No one in my family put it there, but because it was on properties we wanted to sell, we had to clean it up. This and other unexpected details required a fair amount of our time and attention, and the dramas just kept on coming, complete with family infighting every inch of the way. It was dreadful, and it went on for years. I was close to my mother and chose to side with her, at times pitting us against my siblings, and I became the de facto family leader. These stressful events gave me the unique, trial by fire experience of testing out what worked and what didn't work, in terms of discovering what helped me stay as balanced, calm, and centered as possible as I coped with it all.

I am not a psychotherapist, nor do I have any medical training. If you have an instinct that help from a mental health professional would be good to pursue, please listen to yourself. There is nothing wrong with getting some help from capable professionals and the experience could prove worthwhile as well as interesting.

In my own life, as a result of my rather unique journey and all those many years of studying, teaching, and trying things out with my students and myself, I have become a "go-to" person to help people move through crises of various kinds. I realized that I might have some useful suggestions, based on the sort of work I have done for all these years, as well as the art play that I learned about from my mother. We will talk about "art play" in the next chapter, but I want to make some comments about art right here. Before you start getting worried and telling yourself that you can't possibly do art because you simply have no talent for it, please know that I am only talking about art used in the service of one's peace of mind. This is NOT about becoming an artist. It is about making art purely for the pleasurable and calming aspects involved in doing so. Anyone can do this.

For that matter, it's important to note that everything I will speak about, Feldenkrais, QiGong, art play, and all the other methods I employ, are meant for all people, of any age, in any physical condition. It does not matter who you are or what you need, you can derive benefit from it. Nothing I am going to suggest is just for musicians, or just for painters, or for any other group of people, and all body types can find it useful. The image-conscious age we live in makes many of us self-conscious about our bodies, so when it comes to doing things with our bodies, sadly, it is not only possible but likely we will bring self-judgment to the table. Self-judgment is not only unnecessary, but it misses the point altogether. Feeling and sensing our bodies is central to healing, and judging them is not only unhelpful, it discourages us from doing it at all.

Any consistently overwhelming amount of emotional stress and trauma will place a decided strain on our bodies, minds, and nervous systems. Of course, any one awful event in your life might have been so excruciating that it alone created a lifetime of anxiety, but even without a lone extreme event, there are daily disruptions that can disturb your equilibrium or at least your sense of inner peace and balance.

Here's the cheat sheet to all of this:

No matter how stressful the crisis of the moment is, and no matter how frequently such crises occur, if you take a moment to feel or sense something related to your body, whether it relates to movement or breathing or attention or to art creativity, then for that moment you will be out of the stress stream.

It's almost like magic. I'm not going to pretend this is an instant cure all, but for the moments you attend to something you feel or sense, you are free. I'll repeat, YOU ARE FREE. And it isn't too far a stretch to imagine that if you string together enough such moments you are going to have a better time dealing with all the stress and might even find yourself being calmer and clearer in general. It sure can't hurt!

Unlike the ongoing crises with your family, taking care of yourself in the ways I will suggest is completely within your own control. You don't have to make a massage or therapy appointment (though you may need many; I'm not knocking these at all), you don't have to go anywhere, you don't have to buy anything or spend any money, you don't have to wait, and so you aren't limited by the hours of the day. Three in the morning is fine, because you are not going to make noise or wake people up. You do not have to be anywhere special, or have any equipment ready. This will be just for you, when and where you need it, for as long as you need it, in whatever state you find yourself. How perfect is that?!

What sort of things am I talking about? How do we start? Believe it or not, it's much easier than you might think. It's nothing complicated at all. We will begin very simply and without any demands on ourselves, or any expectations, just feeling where we are right now.

Moshe Feldenkrais once said that the various movement lessons he created "are all the same lesson." How though, since they are so different? This is so because the lessons are not actually about particular movements, but rather they are about the effects those movements have on the human body, on one's nervous system. All of the movements bring us to a calmer, more organized, more coherent, and healthier place. In other words, they all lead us back to the same place. And the good news is that you don't have to do much to get to that place, as I will demonstrate shortly. Doing a tiny piece of any movement, just feeling yourself however you are, wherever you are, can help immensely. Less is definitely more.

Leave your grumpy inner critic outside or shut up in a closet (I actually call my inner critic Grumpy!). We cannot feel or do anything wrong here. There are no goals, except to sense and feel whatever you can, however you are, in this moment. We can adhere to Teddy Roosevelt's marvelous advice: "Do what you can, with what you have, wherever you are."

2. *Before we begin*

Before we start, though, there are some things to discuss. Let's remind ourselves that even though the traumas and stresses we have endured have dramatically affected us, we haven't experienced those traumas and stresses with a tension-free body, or with a nervous system or state of mind that was calm to begin with. Setting aside the family issues we are speaking about here, along with the traumas and upset that come with them, modern life is crazy and stressful all on its own. It would be hard to overstate this obvious truth.

What are the causes? There are a number of them, but many of them did not appear in our lives until relatively recent human history.

For one, consider how much time we all spend in front of a screen each day. Whether from your computer or cell phone or TV, screen time is not a neurologically neutral activity. Humanity has only dealt with this for a generation or two, and studies of many of its effects are still underway. It would seem though, the effects of screened devices on our nervous systems are anything but relaxing, for many reasons, not the least of which is the blue light disruption of our circadian rhythms. Such disruption makes a good night's sleep more difficult. And without good sleep, stressful situations are even harder to cope with. To some extent, this can be ameliorated with glasses coated to neutralize the computer's blue light. I'm wearing a pair as I write this and have found they help a lot.

And there is noise of all kinds all around us, (especially for those of us who live in cities), and not only decibel levels of actual noise, but also noise caused by political dramas that seem to have no end and no good outcomes (whatever your personal persuasions). Turn on any TV news show and you will hear human beings shouting belligerently at each other. This isn't calming for any of us.

And think of the array of awful stories or violent scenes on the evening news or plastered across the front pages of newspapers. All of this has an agitating, upsetting effect on us and none of it is conducive to letting us go in the calmer direction in which we need to go, just to be able to cope with our family's issues the best we can.

I suggest that if we want to really find peace in our bodies and selves, we might first consider turning off as much unnecessary stress as we can. You can turn off the news sometimes and stay informed in other ways, or skip it most days, only watching when you want to watch something that's important to you. The political messes will still be there and if something especially horrible or dramatic happens, you'll probably hear about it anyway, from a friend or neighbor.

Certainly, you can eschew violent language or programs wherever you can. While I will always strongly defend the right of artists to create whatever they like, you may not help yourself if you watch graphically violent movies or TV shows, or listen to music with excessively violent lyrics. As you become more in touch with what you are sensing and feeling in your body, you may find yourself making these changes automatically. And in the end, you'll be doing yourself a big favor, in terms of getting through your situation as calmly as possible, if you simply remove as much unnecessary agitation as you can, wherever you find it in your life.

Our bodies are also stressed by the continuous assault of a wide variety of synthetic compounds, most of them unheard of during all of human history, and also by elements released into nature that until the modern age of mining and dams might have never seen human contact. They are in our food, our water, the air, and have possible deleterious effects. Consider, for example, the lead contamination of the water supply in Flint, Michigan (and that is just one that we know about). As well, consider that on July 12, 1999, the BBC released a World Wide Fund for Nature (WWF) report showing that breast milk samples contained about 350 chemicals from substances in perfume, suntan lotion, and pesticides, with Dioxin levels in British infants reaching up to 42 times the levels deemed safe.

When people find themselves far from family and some of their friends, they can feel isolated, which is especially hard in the middle of the sorts of family crises we're considering. After I had kids, visiting any of their grandparents required a plane ride, which didn't happen frequently. Having our extended families and old friends far away can make our journey more difficult.

Before we begin, though, there is something else we have to mention. We are talking about self-care here. Without going into any big fuss or cooking up any more guilt we don't need (never, ever!), ask yourself if you take care of yourself in all the ways you know you should: eating a reasonable diet, getting enough sleep, maybe finding time to get to the gym or do some exercise you like. Exercise for many is a life saver. Also what about not overdoing obvious things like alcohol, caffeine and sugar. These substances swing your moods, emotions and physical sensations around more wildly than your personal situation could on its worst day.

If you aren't taking good care of yourself in these basic ways, you might choose to stop right here and spend a day or two or more implementing a gradual incorporation of whatever you know in your heart you ought to do to treat your amazing body with care and kindness. Again, forget perfection! Perfection is absolutely the enemy of everything that is helpful. Just go for some small general improvements. The smaller you make them, the more likely they'll stick.

Many of us spend far too much time over-analyzing and worrying about things. With an ill family member, worrying occupies more of our time that it should. We can become out of touch with what we are really feeling in our bodies. When we have too much stress in our lives, it may begin in our minds and emotions, with too much worry and all the rest, but it ends up in our bodies. And it stays in our bodies until we take steps to release it. It is my contention that we will only succeed in dealing with all the traumas we have if we deal with them through our amazing bodies.

As we have so much on our minds, and most of us tend to ruminate on unhappy events excessively, we can become calmer and more in touch with our bodies by following just a few things that are simple and easy to remember:

- stop for a moment,
- pay attention to your breathing,
- notice what you are experiencing physically right now
- observe any physical contact with your environment.

Please note that nothing I write or suggest is ever a substitute for professional care, if you feel you need it. If you are in doubt about whether this might benefit you, get checked out as a precaution. It can't hurt, and might help a lot.

I dearly love Feldenkrais and QiGong. But I admit that when I was at my most stressed out, getting to class and the inherent mental discipline and concentration required for the hour was more than I could handle. I learned quickly that just doing a few simple movements, parts of longer lessons I knew well, was enough to help, actually considerably more than enough. As we have said, most of the time less is definitely more! In Feldenkrais our teachers often say you can't make any movement too small and you can't go too slowly. That can be applied to getting through stress and it is how we come back to feeling what's really going on with our bodies.

Because we are all so stressed out, I am going to write these introductory sensing explorations so they are as simple and universal as possible. Feldenkrais can go into sensing and movement in great length and depth, but that's not what I'll do here. For now, let's just keep it very simple.

3. *Basic sensing and feeling, of our breath and ourselves*

Take a moment, or as long as you need, to sense what you are feeling right now. Make a mental note of how you feel, without any self-judgment. If you pay attention to how stressed or tense you feel right now, before we start, you'll be able to compare your current state with how you will feel after we've done this first section. At the end I'll remind you to look back and compare how you might be feeling then with how you feel now, before starting. By the way, this can be a very helpful and under-estimated tool for encouraging ourselves, by noting small bits of progress, and giving ourselves credit for moving forward with our situation. As I think you would agree, we can all use all the encouragement we can get.

Whatever your position at the moment, whether you are sitting or standing, or maybe even lying down, what is the first thing you notice about your body right now? Take whatever time you need to notice something, anything. It doesn't matter what you notice. There are no wrong answers and you can't do this badly. This is not a test you can fail. Just pay attention to yourself.

You might notice whether or not you feel comfortable. Do you need a sweater or a blanket or a pillow? If some discomfort is the first thing you notice, see if you can fix that by adjusting your position in some way, grabbing a pillow or blanket if needed, or finding a better chair to sit on, or a comfier place on the floor, maybe on a rug. It's harder to pay attention to your body if you are uncomfortable, so do what you can to adjust things around you.

Maybe the next thing you notice is your breathing. To make this as easy as possible, for now, just follow your breath as it comes into your body for a few minutes. Notice what happens when you inhale, what the sensations are in your nose and throat, and see if you can begin to observe some movement in your lungs and chest, and maybe even your abdomen. Do you respond to your breathing anywhere else in your body?

You might begin to notice that air comes into your lungs and fills up different places in your lungs. We have bronchial tubes on the right and the left, each funneling our breath to a different part of our lungs. After our breath goes through the bronchial tubes, it goes through progressively smaller tubes and tiny balloon-like structures called alveoli that provide a large surface area for our bloodstream to pick up oxygen from our breath as well as exhale carbon dioxide.

When I teach breath work in classes, I always enjoy asking my students to see if they can sense the total size of the area all those inner breathing surfaces would create, if they were spread out flat. As we pay attention to our breathing, sense if you can feel how large this total breathing area might be. When I ask this question in my classes, I always give my students the answer at the end of the session, which gives them plenty of time to feel what they can feel, and I'll do the same here.

Remember your upper body has a back as well as a front, so see if you sense movement in your back, that is, opposite your front side. If you don't feel anything in particular, don't worry about it, just follow your breath as you draw it in. Really pay attention. When we inhale, there is a sense of expansion, of filling up and rounding out our lungs. Without doing anything special, just notice how much of this expansion and rounding you feel. If you are holding or tensing somewhere in your chest, see if you can let that go, so more of your lungs becomes involved.

And maybe move your attention around your body, as lazily as you can, just sensing what you feel as your breath expands your lungs, and see if you can notice how this affects the rest of you.

After a few minutes, you may notice random tension somewhere you didn't expect to find it, in your shoulders maybe, or your jaw, or your eyebrows, or your arms or legs. Gently and slowly run your attention around yourself and see if there are places you can just let that excess tension go. You are stressed out enough with whatever you are going through in your life, so you don't need to drag around any extra tension that is stuck in your body. Often such tension can be released just by becoming aware of it.

Then begin to follow the breath out. With the inhale there was noticeable expansion, as the lungs filled up and rounded out, and now with the exhale there is the sense of pulling in and deflating in the lungs and feeling the air leaving the lungs. Don't do anything special. Just notice what you sense and feel. Stay with the noticing and feeling for several minutes; this can be a very calming and delicious experience; don't worry if you don't feel much or, conversely, if you feel a LOT. Anything you are experiencing is fine.

Miraculously, as your breath switches from inhale to exhale, or the other way around, if you stop breathing for a moment or two at the moment of the change, you will find yourself in a perfectly quiet moment of stillness. If you become aware of this perfect peaceful point and sink into it, you will find you might be able to stay there even while you continue to breathe and sense and feel. Considering our usual stressed out states, it can feel exquisite to stop our breathing in or out for a few moments and just dwell in this perfect quiet for a moment or two.

Just for fun, with no self-judgment whatsoever, after only these few minutes of feeling what's going on with your breathing, how would you rate your tension level compared to when you started? Have those tension levels lessened? If not, no worries, just keep going. Nothing will calm you down faster that paying attention to our breath!

Some breath experts advocate their students do paced breathing. If you are up to that, breathing five or six times per minute can be superb and there are some apps and websites that help with paced breathing. However, I would like to encourage anyone who is extremely stressed out to start very simply, without putting any pressure on yourself to succeed or "do" much of anything. Just breathe, and feel what it is like, and what is happening to you. Just pay attention to it. Don't make a big deal about it, or try to breathe extra deeply or in any unusual way. Just breathe and listen to yourself. Pay attention to what your breathing feels like. You can't do this wrong. There aren't any "rules".

Nothing is more natural than just paying attention to your breathing. It's wonderful, and attending to your breath can be lifesaving. I can personally attest to the value of paying attention to your breathing should you find yourself in a stressful situation, such as waiting for hours in a hospital for news of a loved one, or when you have had especially bad news, or anticipate receiving some bad news. At times like that, breathing is an amazing and comforting friend. I have been known to do paced breathing myself for long stretches, hours even, at especially traumatic times in my life. I swear by it.

We can pay this sort of attention to our breathing for as long as we like. There is no rush. No need to run off to do something else. Take all the time you need. Don't shortchange yourself. There is absolutely no need to hurry off to go do anything else. Eventually, though, as you are breathing, you might also begin to notice that some parts of you, depending on your position, are on the floor or on the chair and there is contact and pressure there. Notice which part of you makes contact - the bottom of your feet or your back or your buttocks. You can become aware of the pull of gravity wherever that part of you is resting solidly on a chair or the floor.

It can be a blessed relief to give ourselves up to gravity, to really let go and sink into the floor or the chair. Obviously, you can let go more fully if you are lying down, but that won't always be possible, so do what you can with your physical circumstance. Again, you can't do this wrong! Whatever you feel or don't feel is fine.

You might begin to notice the texture, temperature, or softness of the floor or chair. It can feel soft or hard, cool or warm, bumpy or smooth, or combinations of sensations. You can continue that exploration with gentle movements of your hands or feet or any other part of you.

You might also notice how your hands feel. Fingertips are especially sensitive and it can be very pleasurable to explore the sensations of touching your clothing, the floor, the chair, or your skin. Keep breathing too.

You might notice sensations in your face and head. Most of us carry tensions in our jaws or eyebrows or other parts of the face. Keep it simple, but continue to pay attention to whatever you feel. It's OK to feel whatever you feel and it is OK if you think you don't feel very much. Just keep paying attention to yourself. Self-judgment doesn't help, ever, as that brings you back to over-thinking, rather than allowing yourself to sink into the world of sensation and feeling.

Maybe these few minutes of paying attention to yourself have already shown you that our brains cannot do two things at once - you cannot be sensing and feeling your breathing or your body and also actively worry or fret about your family members, or anything else. The more time you spend just feeling whatever you are feeling in your body, the better for calming down your over-active mind. The only caveat is that you really have to do this, not just think about doing this.

Just sit or lie quietly with yourself and explore a few of these simple things: your inhale, your exhale, your contact with the floor or chair, or the sensations in your face and head, your hands, and your feet. It doesn't matter where you start, but these are easy places to start. Whatever you choose, pay attention as best you can.

If you examined how stressed or tense you felt before you began reading and following Part 2, take a moment to notice how your stress levels are now. It's possible you might feel a little bit calmer. If not, try this section again and continue sensing and feeling your breath and your contact with your environment. Just stick with it, and positive results will happen in time. Don't dump on yourself if you felt very little. After all, you've been very stressed out a long time. It might take you a bit to get past that.

And just for fun, to get back to the question I asked earlier, how large would you guess the total breathing area of your lungs is? That is, if you spread out all the little nooks and crannies, the alveoli and all the tubes, what would be the total area of your lungs that is available to take oxygen into your body? Remarkably, the total breathing area of your lungs, if everything were flattened out, is the size of a tennis court!

Did you experience your breathing as taking place over such a large area? Does your breathing feel deeper and more complete now that you do know this? And how big did you think it was before you knew the answer? The size of a sink? Or a table? Or a room? What can you learn about yourself from your guess, without any self-judgment? And can you begin to appreciate how large your lungs really are and how much they can help you get through stress?

4. Longer body scan for the whole body

In the previous section, we explored breathing, that is, sensing and feeling breath as it comes into and leaves our bodies, and also the feeling of the world under and around us. This time we'll do a scan of the feelings all over our body. Feldenkrais classes often begin with a body scan, which is similar to what we've been doing, but a bit more thorough. We are finding easy, convenient ways to get us out of our over-active worrying brains, and into feeling and sensing our bodies. If you stick with this, you will discover for yourself that you can't worry and feel your body at the same time!

Humorously, Moshe Feldenkrais once said the only really smart thing Freud ever did was make his patients lie down, as this position is generally more conducive to relaxing, sensing, and feeling. When you lie down, your body doesn't have to deal with responding to gravity, so you don't have to deal with holding yourself or your head upright, allowing you to feel and sense yourself more easily. So I would definitely recommend lying down if it is possible to do so. If getting down on the floor is troublesome, lying on a bed is fine. Still, if you can't lie down, just do whatever you are able to do. I will write this section as though you are lying down, but if you are sitting, it's fine to adapt it to your position.

To begin, take a global picture of yourself, sensing whatever you sense. Remember, we are happier when what we are doing is pleasant and feels good, and keep in mind that you cannot move your attention around yourself too softly or too slowly, and there is no way to do it badly. There is no "proper form" here and you cannot do it wrong. We are not aiming for some sort of specific achievement, only for sensing ourselves physically and noticing what we are feeling. If we have any "goal" at all, it's giving ourselves the opportunity of a break from the mental stress and physical tension caused by our situation with our families.

Begin with noticing your right foot, as it is lying on the floor, if you are lying down. Notice where the foot contacts the floor, that is, where on your heel there is pressure while it lies on the floor. Is it in the middle, or more on the side, or partway on the side? Don't change anything. Just observe yourself and notice this contact. Then sense the right foot itself, the rest of it, the toes, sole, top, all of it. Anything you might sense or feel is fine.

How far to the side is the right foot turned? My own teacher used to ask us to imagine drawing a line out from the right big toe, noticing where the line would fall if it continued on toward the wall or ceiling. The general idea is to become aware of the angle at which your foot is lying. Don't change anything. Just notice. You are fine however you are. You don't have to change anything or alter your position in any way.

Before we go on, take a moment to sense and feel if there is tension somewhere in your body you can let go. How about your jaw? Eyebrows? The other leg somewhere? Your hands? Your stomach? And are you breathing? Breathing doesn't have to be anything special, easy does it, but notice what you are doing.

If you move your attention up to your ankle, you will find a space that isn't touching the floor right behind the ankle, and if you continue up your right leg, you will find your calf is lying on the floor. Some parts of your right leg are touching the floor and some aren't, because there is another space behind the right knee that might not be on the floor. Whatever you are experiencing, notice what all this feels like. You can even notice things like the contact with the floor or your clothing or the weight and temperature of your leg on the floor.

If we move up from the right leg, we come to the right side of the pelvis and we can feel how it lies on the floor. It will touch in some places and not touch in others. It could feel like it lies flat on the floor, or it could feel bony. Keep scanning around your body to check for places you can let go and stop holding tension. And keep breathing, softly, gently, no strain, doing nothing special.

Take a moment to notice what the right leg feels like as a whole, and then begin to move your attention to your left leg and foot. Like we did before, start with noticing the contact of your left heel with the floor. Is the process of noticing what's going on with yourself becoming more familiar? This will make it easier, gradually, to sense and feel what you are doing, freeing yourself from some of the stress. Make sure you are breathing, easily and comfortably. No strain at all. When I mentioned that you might give some attention to your breathing, did something change for you? Awareness can be amazing! Sometimes we can even discover we have been holding our breath a bit, to the point where we are reminded to breathe. All of us often do that, even a lot, especially when we are stressed out, and it doesn't help us at all.

Like we did before with our right foot, draw an imaginary line from your left big toe in order to see where it would go on the wall or ceiling. But don't change a thing - it might not be the same as the other foot, but don't judge it or change it. Just notice what it is and how it is different or similar to the right foot. And keep scanning for tension you can let go.

Then begin to move your awareness upward, in order to feel where the left leg contacts the floor, and where it doesn't. Really let go and sink into the floor and allow the floor to support you. You aren't doing this to change anything, just to sense and feel yourself. And you are not in a hurry.

Feel the space behind your left knee, and the nature of the contact with the floor as you go up the left leg. It could be heavy or light, warm or cool, or whatever you feel is fine. Just observe yourself.

When you get to the left side of the pelvis, compare the weight and contact with the right side of the pelvis. They might feel more or less the same or they might be quite different. One side of your pelvis can feel "pokey" and the other flat, or one or both may not be clear to you. There is no right or wrong about what you feel, just notice how your pelvis is lying on the floor on both sides, and what it feels like on both sides.

Once you have observed your lower back, on both the right and left sides, slowly move your attention up your spine, from the sacrum at the bottom upwards. You will notice that some parts of your spine are touching the floor and some are not touching the floor. Where you are not touching the floor, at your waistline or behind your neck, it might be very hard to feel each individual vertebra, and don't worry about it if sections of your spine feel like a group of vertebrae and not individual ones. Keep scanning for extra tension that you can release.

Is your head lying in the middle, or is the pressure on the back of the head more on the right side or the left side? This can have something to do with how you see things, that is, which eye is dominant. We're not trying to change anything, just observe. There is nothing wrong with how your head is lying. We're not looking for things to fix, we're just feeling ourselves, as we are, right now.

Then look at the contact of your two shoulder blades, observing whether the right or the left is more in contact with the floor. Does one of them feel closer to the ceiling or closer to your ear? Is one of them flatter than the other?

Then feel the contact of the right arm with the floor, sensing what the hand, fingers, and forearm feel. Do you have your palm or the back of the hand on the floor, or are you standing on your hand with the pinkie side on the floor and your thumb in the air? When you have finished observing the right arm, do the same thing with the left arm.

Compare your left and right arms as they are lying on the floor, and notice that they are probably not lying there the same way, and that the elbows may not be the same. See if there is tension anywhere in your hands or arms that you can simply release, and if you can find tension anywhere else, let that go too.

Children often draw stick figures to represent humans, and it is interesting to imagine that you have five lines that you can sense in yourself. Two of the lines are your legs, another is your spine, and then there are two for your arms. Sense each line in you individually, and then see if you can sense all of them together, at the same time. Whatever way you can do this at this moment, this is the best possible way for you to do it right now. Don't change anything, just observe. And observe whether your breathing is softer, quieter, easier, after these few minutes of sensing and feeling yourself.

Now that you've spent these few minutes sensing and feeling, how are you feeling about your stress levels? It's even possible that for a brief period of time, even a few seconds, you have even forgotten you have a lot of stressful things to deal with. That's the whole idea, and I hope that happened for you. If not, it will happen if you keep at it. Just go back to the beginning and start over, and eventually it will come naturally. There is no rush. Take your time. You're going to be breathing anyway, and will feel certain body sensations anyway, so just keep going. Keep noticing what you are feeling. A sense of peace from what you are feeling will come to you in time.

How you pay attention (and what you are paying attention to) determines much about the quality of your life. It also determines whether you can live well with lots of stress. This is a marvelous tool, and I've only given you a few simple examples.

5. Troubleshooting

It often happens that we do not fully process unpleasant events we've found traumatic, and our body's reactions to such events can stall. Our journeys through our family's addiction and mental illness inevitably creates a strain in our nervous systems. So along with an openness to feeling and sensing your body comes a risk that you will step in some feelings unpredictably. Feelings that you'd rather not deal with right away. What happens then?

Clearly, if something huge gets stirred up, get some professional help. Not only because you don't have to do everything yourself, but also because a professional might shorten the time it takes for you to go through whatever you have stumbled upon. However, if you are experimenting with these simple self-care explorations at home and something huge comes up, even something unpleasant, that's actually really good news, because it means that whatever you are doing is very effective at clearing something that needs clearing. Still, you have a choice about this. If whatever you are feeling seems like too much, too soon, or just "too" something else, it's OK to back off. You are in control of this process and can do what you want to do, which includes stopping. Just keep breathing, whether you are noticing what you are feeling about your breathing or not. Just breathe.

It's not important to consider the reason this happened, as there are a range of possibilities. You might have gone too fast, you might have been sorting things out subconsciously that you are barely aware of (pay attention to your dreams, as they could give you hints), or any number or other causes. It just happened, and that's all. Just keep breathing, and if you can, maintain an awareness of your breathing.

If you decide to stop, that's OK; this may not be the right time, at least not right this very minute, to continue your sensory explorations. This isn't a question of running away, but of respecting yourself and the journey in front of you. We can take our time, go very, very slowly, and do even less than we were doing. We get to decide how much to do and how fast. Nobody else gets a vote. We may not have any control whatsoever over the craziness of our loved ones, or the state of the world or the behavior of our politicians, but we have control over this.

Gradually, by respecting our bodies and taking our time, sensing and feeling, the traumas that are stuck in our bodies and nervous systems will begin to back off, and even dissipate. Remember, physical or psychological trauma is never about a specific event, but rather about what is still stuck in you from your body's reaction to the event. Trauma may well have disrupted your ability to sense and feel, right here, right now, so take your time, be gentle and patient with yourself, and continue to breathe and sense and feel. Dr. Bessel Van Der Kolk, the author of "The Body Keeps the Score", says that trauma causes a disruption of the ability to be in the here and now. The answer to that? Just keep breathing and sensing, but without making any demands on yourself. Stay present and work slowly with these sensing practices to get yourself back into a smooth, healthy relationship with your body.

However, it is helpful to realize that when a human being has been through traumatic events, some random event can unexpectedly toss us right back into the emotional turmoil that we experienced with the trauma. Let's acknowledge up front that this can hit us when we least expect it.

I was caught by surprise myself once, when a routine dental procedure set off layers and layers of old trauma. I don't fault the dentist as I don't believe he did anything wrong, except perhaps give me a bit too much epinephrine with the anesthetic. The medication triggered a racing heartbeat and nausea, which is certainly similar to the panicky feelings caused by traumas, or at least it felt like that to me.

All of us have a lot of accumulated stress, and it has been accumulating over our entire lives, no matter how easy or challenging we have found things up to now. Throw a mentally ill family member into one's life, and the stress levels go off the charts. Most of the time I cope with life pretty well, and you may as well, but this dental experience showed me, clearly, that I haven't yet worked through all the stress rattling around in my own body.

We all have to stay open to the fact that our bodies and nervous systems have paid an exceptionally high price for all the traumas and stressful events in our lives, many of them due to the endless crisis brought about by our mentally ill relatives. We can expect that the dark shadows of some of these events will pop up from time to time, most likely when we least expect them, or are least prepared to deal with them.

In addition, we all have physical patterns of moving, or in fact not moving, which came about as we adjusted ourselves to our particular stressful situations. These patterns resulted from a response to dealing with whatever challenges we faced, and have done what they were supposed to do in terms of our day to day living. So instead of dumping on ourselves for having them, we can thank ourselves for surviving! What kind of patterns am I talking about? Patterns like tightening your chest so you don't breathe fully, or hunching your shoulders, or clenching your jaw.

As we become more in touch with ourselves and our bodies,

minds, and nervous systems calm down, we may discover these well-established patterns do not serve us well. As you work with your breathing and as you sense what you are feeling in your body, you may begin to notice the existence of some of these patterns. But you really don't have to make great efforts to change them. Just notice them. In time, with enough work, they will change on their own. For example, if you notice your breathing only takes place in your upper chest, you can explore filling more of your lungs. If you notice you habitually clench your jaw, you can gently let it go and move it, so it feels free. If you tighten and raise your shoulders, just becoming aware you are doing this may encourage them to let go and drop. And so forth.

In my experience, there is only one way to cope with all this, only one way to get back in touch with our bodies and our sense of true inner peace and quiet, and that is through giving ourselves a pause in our busy lives, and experiencing what our bodies can feel and do, through gentle movement, and through our breath, right now, in the present moment.

If we falter, because our journey is long and hard, it helps to remind ourselves of the few simple suggestions mentioned earlier in this chapter:

- pause and stop for a moment
- attend to your breathing
- notice what you are experiencing physically, right now
- observe any physical contact with your environment.
- And then do it again, and again, and just keep going.

It's all OK. You'll get through this and if you keep going, sensing and feeling, following your breath, in time you will find yourself in a calmer place.

6. Visualizing Changes

Can you imagine that there might be an easily-learned technique, one you probably already know, that will help you achieve inner peace, and achieve it easily?

This is not a fantasy, but concrete reality. Our minds are powerful beyond our ability to imagine. Famously, Henry Ford once said, "If you think you can, or you think you can't, you're right!" On every level, no action can happen physically unless the mind conceives of it first and by doing so nudges the body into executing it.

However, I'd like to suggest some caution with this concept. Our minds are helpers, but have no business trying to be controllers. Life happens as it happens, much of it without our permission or input, and we are better off if we don't get tangled up into playing manipulative mind games with a wonderful tool like visualization. I'd strongly advise any of us not to try to control anything, but to sense and feel what might be possible. There is an enormous difference.

And just what exactly is that difference? Described in the simplest way possible, we are changing the "picture" we have in our minds. We are not changing behavior. Rather than constructing an elaborate story designed to alter events, and playing it all out in our heads like a movie, complete with dialogue and a wide range of emotions, this is far simpler - we are just changing the picture we imagine. In order to be maximally effective, this process should be simple, calm, and non-verbal.

There is much benefit to cultivating quiet inner pictures, such as knowing that you will arrive safely somewhere, or getting your blood drawn for a medical test easily and painlessly, or imagining you will effortlessly get through the long list of all you have in a hectic day, and so forth. Rather than fret and worry, it feels so much better to occupy your mind with a quiet inner knowledge that all will be well.

With my own music students, I've always used a touching story, which is also true, about the effects that visualization had on the life and work of one of the great classical composers. Literally, it probably saved his life, and it helped him create some timeless and beloved music. This composer lives about a hundred years ago, and he had been in the depths of a terrible depression after being traumatized by a scathing review of the concert premiere of his first big composition. (Can any of my readers imagine how tough it is on an artist to get such an awful review? The composer's depression was so severe that it had lasted several years; his family and friends feared he was suicidal.)

In desperation, friends persuaded him to work with a psychiatrist who was employing a new therapy called autosuggestion. This doctor helped his patients sink in a state of deep relaxation via hypnosis, and then helped them visualize success by listening to repetitive positive phrases.

The daily sessions were motivational. "I heard the same hypnotic formula repeated day after day while I lay half asleep in an armchair in his study," the musician wrote. "You will begin to write your concerto," said the psychiatrist "You will work with the greatest of ease. The concerto will be of excellent quality."

The composer worked with the psychiatrist for three months, and then he wrote. "Although it may sound impossible to believe, this treatment really helped me. I began to compose at the beginning of the summer. The material grew in volume, and new musical ideas began to well up within me, many more than I needed for my concerto."

"I felt that his treatment had strengthened my nervous system to a miraculous degree. Out of gratitude I dedicated my Second Concerto to him," the composer concluded.

The composer in this story was Sergei Rachmaninoff, and the psychiatrist was Dr. Nikolai Dahl, to whom the Second Piano Concerto, one of the most beloved and popular piano concertos ever written, is dedicated. It is well worth noting that Rachmaninoff went on to have a full rich life of composing and playing, all possible though this experiment in visualization.

Rachmaninoff's experience is not unique. After the 2018 Winter Olympics, the New York Times ran a series of recorded interviews with many athletes, all of whom described in detail how they spend many hours visualizing their performances. In perhaps the most dramatic example, the gold medalist in men's figure skating had seriously reinjured his foot a few weeks before the competition, and in order for the foot to heal he could not skate at all. The only way he could practice his routines was through visualization, so he spent many hours simply imagining he was skating and mentally executing all of his leaps and spins. His gold medal performance despite his lack of practice time suggests the value of visualization.

All of these are examples of mental rehearsal, which is obviously extremely effective. There have even been scientific studies showing its effectiveness, proving that it is almost as good as actual physical practice. For those of us who have worked at physically demanding professions, like music or sports, visualization can save a lot of wear and tear on your body, and it can also prevent incorrect learning which can be a source of injury. If you can sort out an action in your mind before you actually do it, you do not have to subject your body to movement experiments that could tire it or create harmful habits. In fact some great musicians, like Glenn Gould and Mstislav Rostropovich, liked to practice first by visualizing, and then went to their instruments only when they had it all worked out mentally.

As an example of how forming mental pictures can be useful, one of my students went on a school sponsored weekend ski trip. She was from Europe and was not used to the type of ski lifts that she found on that particular slope. Every time she got off the lift at the top of the mountain she fell down, and she was fearful she would break a limb. Then she told me she remembered our discussion of visualization in class, and the next time she rode the lift up the mountain, all the way up she pictured in her mind how she would get off the lift easily and effortlessly, without falling. And she didn't fall again, not once during the entire weekend.

As I've given examples of using visualization to improve physical performance, you may wonder how it could be used effectively in your life. While this is incredibly useful for any physical skill, visualization also has a great many other uses. And it pops up in different guises across cultures and traditions. A few years ago, when I began my training with the great QiGong Master Robert Peng, I was dumbfounded when we were taught to visualize much of what we were learning and doing. I realized that this was another form, beautifully done, of work I'd been doing for a long time. It's also ancient, as QiGong has been around for 5000 years! I suppose one could say anything that has endured so long and has helped so many people for centuries is a tried and true modality for self-care.

We can visualize for many different health reasons. For our stress related purposes, you can imagine yourself stepping into a healing waterfall that washes away your stress. You can imagine writing down all the things that bother you, burning your list, and burying the ashes. If any task in front of you feels like it could be difficult, try seeing it as easily accomplished. And of course, you can invent your own.

And take a crack at using this lovely technique for your physical health too. If you break a bone, you can visualize the two sides of the break knitting back together and healing quickly. If you get an infection, you can imagine your immune system gobbling it up like characters in a video game. If you get a scrape or a burn, you can see the skin becoming healthy and smooth. If there is any part of your body that feels weak or misaligned, you can see it strong and straight. Truly, there are no limits to this, as there are no limits to your own imagination. I've always enjoyed helping my clients find the imagery that helps them, as it is a true joy to watch people use their own healing power creatively.

I urge you to give visualization a try! It's fun, free, creative, and best of all, it works! Just remember, visualization is never about control, or about forcing anything to become reality by dint of your will. It involves sitting quietly for a few moments, maybe breathing a few times to calm ourselves, and then imagine *simply changing the picture we see in our minds.* That's it. If you keep this in mind and give up wanting to control things, you might have great fun with this. What do you want in your life? Why not start by imagining it!

7. QiGong shaking

Many people have heard of the mysterious Qi, sometimes spelled Chi, but not all of us have explored it. I'd urge you to try one Qi movement, shaking, which I'll explain here, as you may find it relaxing and energizing, as well as a delightful addition to your life.

Robert Peng says in his book *The Master Key* that "Qi is the fundamental Life Force within all of us that sustains all life and permeates the Universe as well." He also notes "The Egyptian priests called the energy Ka, the Indian rishis named it Prana, the Bible's prophets referred to it as Ruah, the Greek philosophers knew it as Pneuma, the early Christians alluded to it as Spiritus, and the sages of China called it Qi." Getting in touch with one's Qi is decidedly not a waste of time. I have been very fortunate to have Master Robert Peng as my QiGong teacher; anyone who wishes to learn more can find information on his website www.robertpeng.com. There are listings of classes and events, and there are also materials for us to use, some of them free.

As I think back over all I learned in Robert's amazing QiGong classes, and all I've taught to others, I've selected one movement to share with you: shaking, which is just about my favorite. Nearly every student to whom I've taught shaking tells me later on that they use it daily. I use it daily too. And by the way, the shaking movement I am going to discuss is also one found in Feldenkrais. Moshe Feldenkrais called shaking "Oscillations", drawing straight from his physics background. This is another clear example that there are universal truths found in all cultures and times. And there are more.

In fact, all cultures, in all areas of the world, shake. People of all ages wiggle and jiggle. It can be called "shaman shaking" or labeled as the first of the Four Golden Wheels of QiGong, or called Seiki Jutsu in Japan, and it can bear other names in India or Africa, but its efficacy both for calming and energizing is amazing. Quakers shake, Shakers shake, Tibetan monks shake, African bushmen shake, and ancient tribal rituals everywhere involve shaking. All little children wiggle and jiggle too. (For more detail, see *Shaking Medicine* by Bradford Keeney.)

Human beings can find themselves involuntarily shaking after a trauma. (See Dr. Peter Levine's book *Waking the Tiger: Healing Trauma* for an example.) Shaking is a natural automatic self-healing response our body will generate after experiencing trauma. However, you can also benefit greatly doing it on purpose.

What do you do to get started? Easy! Stand up and start bouncing a little up and down. You don't have to do anything special with your arms, just let them hang loosely by your sides as if they are ropes. They can move in whatever way the shaking movement prompts them to move. No, your feet don't have to come off the floor, though the heels or the whole foot can do so for short periods of time. Mostly just jiggle up and down as though you were a little kid. Let your arms flop around freely and check that you not holding anywhere. You can even make noise with each bounce, wah, wah, wah, just as a kid would, (probably driving any listening parents crazy!). If you keep it up for a few moments, you will find your hands and arms and maybe other parts of you will be tingling when you stop. This is a direct experience of the powerful life-giving force called "Qi". It feels wonderful. You might also imagine it spreading throughout your body, anywhere you'd like it to go.

I would hope that it's obvious that this shaking should be done gently. The old saw "no pain, no gain" has no place here! If something hurts or feels uncomfortable, that is your body's way of telling you to stop. Sensation will inform you of what is going on with your physical self. If you are unable to do something I suggest here, try doing less, or even just imagining yourself doing it. Over time, with daily gentle movements, you will find your ability to move easily and well, even in a troublesome area of your body, will improve and increase.

I would like to heartily suggest that some movement activity of some sort be done every day. This cannot be overstated. You'll never survive dealing with SMI in a family without it. If you are so stressed or crunched for time that you can only do just a little, well, why not just shake for a few minutes. Movement is central to our self care.

Most of us who deal with SMI in our families accrue a lot of body tension, that's a just a fact, and you surely know it without me pointing it out. But we are also all spending a lot of time frozen in a hunched up position while we hover over our computers or stare at our phones or other devices. Face it, most of us are stiff and tight, somewhere, much of the time. There is another old saw "use it or lose it", and it is spot on. One of the remarkable things about something as simple as shaking is that all of our joints and limbs are moving or being moved gently while we shake. There is no part of us that gets left out. It keeps us "oiled", and moving freely, everywhere. This is just about the simplest and most generous gift from QiGong that I know.

But shaking does something else as well. Robert Peng once explained that this simple shaking is tremendously effective for our general health because the movements jostle our internal organs against one another in a gentle and friendly way, allowing them to give each other soft massages which mutually stimulate them, improving their abilities to function, thus keeping us healthy. When you shake, you can even imagine all your organs wiggling up and down and saying a friendly hello to their internal neighbors. We don't think much about how all those organs inside us are doing or how they relate to each other, or what they might need from us to function well. In fact, we don't think much about them at all, unless a problem with one of them begins to call our attention to it with pain or discomfort.

And as if all that isn't enough, there is something else going on too, for as Robert Peng points out, we are also giving this gentle massage to other structural parts of ourselves we rarely acknowledge - our tendons, ligaments and fascia. When do most of us ever think much about the structures that keep us all held together, without which we couldn't do anything or move anywhere? If tendons, ligaments, and fascia are not functioning well, we can feel stuck or blocked, or stiff for sure, and we can have pain, or actually develop disease in a given area. This is one way that "use it or lose it" surely applies. On many levels, shaking does a body good.

Anytime you are stressed or nervous about something, or just want to do something for fun that feels good, try a few moments of shaking and jiggling up and down. If you can, do it a few times a day. Like breathing, you can do this anywhere and you can't do it incorrectly. If you can't stand at the moment, you can shake part of yourself while sitting, gently bouncing on your chair or the edge of your bed. If you are lying down, you can push and pull your body up and down along your spine with your feet and/or hands. When you do these oscillations you are moving your whole self toward your feet and then moving toward your head, without lifting yourself up off of the bed or floor. It's not hard or complicated, and can be a lot of fun. Also, if a stressful period or even an illness has kept you from regular exercise for a week or more, and you are thinking about a gentle way to begin moving again, try shaking. You can do it as little or much as you wish, and a few minutes of shaking a few times a day gets you back into movement very gently. I recommend it highly.

8. Taking a sensory Inventory

When we are very upset, we are swirling around in our own minds, hardly aware of our bodies. But when we are gently prodded to explore our senses, in any number of ways, we are distracted from our troubling thoughts. Here are a few ways to go about exploring our senses:

The first suggestion is perhaps one of the simplest imaginable, and it can help you quickly find your way to a calmer state via what you are sensing. The concept of a sensory inventory is not my idea, as many therapists suggest this. As such, I had thought of not including it but it is so useful, and such a practical and easy thing to do if you are stressed and awake at three in the morning, that I've kept it here anyway. You can rearrange the senses and numbers of experiences any way you wish; there are no requirements.

To begin a sensory inventory, look around you and choose five things that you see. Describe them, study them, and look at them intently. Notice their shapes and colors, areas of light and shadow, any contrasts, areas that are fuzzy and areas that are clearly defined. Really look at your chosen objects and allow your attention to completely focus on what you see. (If it is dark you can do this section in your "mind's eye", as Shakespeare said.) Being in a hurry is counterproductive, and luxuriously taking care of yourself is a gift to yourself. I'd encourage you to take all the time you want.

Once you have fully explored the five things you have selected to visualize, find four things you hear. Even in a quiet home in the woods there are sounds, trees rustling, the wind rattling the windows or other house sounds, an occasional animal sound, maybe the sound of something cooking, or a fire crackling. In a city, you will have much to choose from. Really listen, and even observe if you can hear sounds coming from far away. Robert Peng often encourages us to listen like this, to sounds from far away. It is amazing how calming it can be, and how much you can hear if you listen.

Let yourself enjoy the sounds as long as you like, and then find three things you can touch. This can be as simple as touching the clothing you are wearing with your fingertips, or putting the palm of your hands on the wall you are sitting next to, or feeling the floor with your feet either in socks or barefoot. There are other aspects of touch you might explore as well, such as temperatures, textures, and other sensations. Experience as much as you can with touch on your skin.

Next find two things you can smell. Really revel in the scents of these things, whether they are pleasant or unpleasant. Maybe you smell something cooking, or the cleaner you used on the floor, or for those of us with pets, the smell of a beloved animal. You can throw the game a bit in your favor if you gather up your favorite scents for this, but whatever you choose to smell, see if you can sink your whole consciousness into the experience of smelling the two things you have chosen. When we smell something, the molecules of that odor go up into our nose to our olfactory receptors which have a neural connection to our brain. Truly, we can change our brain and its mood almost instantly with scent. Memories are often associated with smells too, but right now we want to simply revel in the act of smelling.

Last, find one thing to taste. Obviously, it would be wise to avoid possible toxins, so becoming too wildly adventurous about what you decide to taste might not be smart, but even if you stick to tasting something that is obviously food, say a raisin, really taste it and see how broad your experience can be. For those of us who are really stressed out, it is a sad fact that many of us eat without ever tasting our food.

Take a moment after all this sensing and note where your anxiety, stress, or revved up feelings are now. You've given your brain a few moments off, some minutes without any thought about your problems. Just observe how you feel. Even if you are only a tiny bit calmer, perhaps you can imagine how much better you'd feel after a period of time, if you repeat this exercise or find other ways to get away from the chatter in your head about your problems. Obviously, you can also vary the order of the senses, and the number of individual sensory experiences you find for each one.

9. A long hot bath

If we are trying to calm down, a long bath can be very soothing and calming. Why not go all the way and stay in there an hour, treating yourself to candles, music, yummy smelling essential oils, flower petals in the water, or anything else you'd find relaxing or would give you pleasure. Yes, you'll have to refresh the hot water, and you might have to make sure the candles are safe, but an hour like this is an absolute joy. Personally, I like to add salt, or baking soda, or Epsom salts or other magnesium salts to the bath water, or bath salts, or even a cup of strong tea like ginger, my favorite. Just plain hot water is fine too. Sometimes stores sell bath balls that bubble up and release scents, so you might pick up a few to have on hand at a time like this. Playing with these bubbly balls can make you feel like a kid again, and you won't be sorry you have some on hand.

10. *Don't forget your feet!*

Here's the simplest and shortest suggestion of all. Don't forget to play with your feet!

I have a tradition of asking my students to work only with their feet during the last class of the semester. I spend a few weeks gathering up tissue paper that comes with packages, brown paper bags from the grocery store, other types of packing or wrapping paper, newspaper, and in the end, I have gathered up an impressive bundle of various sizes and weights of paper.

I drag it all down to school, give everybody an assortment of paper and tell them to take their shoes off and begin ripping it up with their toes. There are no real instructions, but I encourage them to make strips at first, and then move on to smashing balls together from the torn paper, and finally to toss the balls to each other, and catch them, using only their feet. Usually there is someone who will get into this so deeply that they create an origami figure or paper airplane! In a school of music students, it isn't lost on them how neglected feet can become and more than one student has proclaimed this the best lesson of the term. There are no instructions except that you are encouraged to use both feet to tear up the paper, rather than just one. That way both sides of your brain and body can share the fun.

Clearly you can have a go at ripping paper up with your toes anytime you like. But you can experiment with doing other things with your feet. I often try to clean things with my feet, like the bathtub or the kitchen floor. (Remember to divvy up the work right and left, as your brain needs the balance of working on both sides, not only the dominant side.) I have learned to make the bed with my feet, sort of. Still, even if it is messy, it's fun and leads to giggles, which lightens things up.

Your feet carry you through the world and through your life's journey. Consider rolling a soft ball around under the soles of your feet gently, while you stand. Do this for a few moments and feel how much more alive your feet feel. Or try to walk around in unusual ways, just for fun – walk a few steps just on your heels, or just on your toes. Or massage your feet gently with a lovely lotion. Best of all, go outside and walk on the bare earth or on grass. Direct contact by your bare feet with the earth calms anybody down, and you might find it energizes you too. There is actually a whole method built on this, called Grounding, but you will get the gist of it if you just walk around outside with your bare feet on the earth. I've met people who bravely do this in the dead of winter, because they feel it helps them so much. I've tried that myself, with no harm done. The point is that any tender loving care you can give your feet will benefit you immensely. And you won't be thinking about SMI one bit while you do it.

CHAPTER 20

Awakening our Intuition Through Art and Creativity

So far, we've examined how we can care for ourselves through attention to our breath and bodies in a few simple ways. I'd like to suggest we can also do so through art and creativity, which is also a lot of fun. After all the stress we've been through why not have some fun?

My mother was a wonderful, nationally recognized artist. I have many of her artworks displayed in my home and they are a pleasure to live with. I never tire of looking at them and always find new things to see in them. In addition, they are all so lively and youthful that no one who sees them for the first time can believe they were created by an older person. Though my mother lived a long life she never became old, in mind, body, or spirit, which is something to which we can all aspire.

Mom had always intended to write her own book about intuition and creativity, but never finished it. In the process of cleaning up and sorting things out (remember Chapter 11?), I came across some notes she made for her book, written more than fifteen years before she passed away. In honor of my Mom, I'm going to share some of her delightful suggestions with you. She was always experimenting with creative ways of doing art, and used her family as eager guinea pigs. Whenever we were all together, she would ask us all to participate in her experiments with various creative art exercises, and they provided an endless source of joyful play time for all of us when my kids were growing up.

As I hope to demonstrate to you, art is an easy subject to adapt immediately to one's situation, whatever that situation. Anybody can do it at any time or place, and her ideas also have the added boon of little or no cost.

Many people feel intimidated by the notion of making art. We all have those inner critics, after all, and so we may say to ourselves: "How I wish I could paint! Artists seem to be a happy lot. But I have no talent. I can't even draw a straight line!"

While we want to discuss the idea of using art to stabilize our stormy seas, we also want to consider the possibility we will enjoy art play so much that we start to think like an artist. It was my mother's contention, and mine as well, that with some nudging and encouragement, anyone can enjoy making art a great deal and even come to think of oneself as an artist. For our purposes, for those of us having a tough time getting through difficulties in our lives, we will find that making art will reduce our stress levels merely through engaging the creative process. In fact, that's exactly what artists do notice – that is, a huge reduction in their stress levels whenever they paint, compose, write or make music. A few simple exercises will prove you do have talent for art, because everyone does. I might also point out that many aspects of our lives with SMI are not of our choice or under our control, but with art play, we have once again found something we can control. We can do these exercises exactly as we please.

Exercise 1, Sidewalk painting with water

This first exercise Mom invented is so simple, and so much fun. You should find it not only easy but interesting. Even if you are skeptical, I do urge you to try this. If my Mom were here, she would not take a refusal for an answer and would insist you take a crack at it.

Lying dormant within each of us is a marvelous quality called intuition. Though intuition itself lies unknown and unseen within us, and while it often seems elusive, it makes itself known and performs its magic by inspiration, especially creative inspiration.

My Life with Crazy

Especially when life is hard and we have to deal with tough issues, intuition is vital. Intuition knows how to do things in ways that are independent of reasoning or determination; developing our intuition sharpens our "gut" instincts and clarifies our inner knowing, which is so essential considering many of the choices we often have to make. And if you have children in your life, these exercises will be a special joy, as they are wonderful to try with people who haven't grown up yet.

Begin by breaking off a twig or a branch or hunt for a discarded stick. It should be about as long as your arm from your shoulder to your fingertips. With a rock or your heel pound the end of the stick to fray the wood, which won't be hard to do as wood lends itself to splitting. You might fray the stick end not at all or a little or a lot. Your choice. This becomes your brush. Find a container such as a small bucket that will hold the water that will be your paint. Dip your stick brush in water and mark whatever comes to mind on a dry sidewalk. Although done crudely, you might suddenly realize you are painting!

I cannot tell you how many happy hours my kids and I passed with my mother while we painted with water on sidewalks. Done in the summer, our efforts would dry almost as soon as they hit the sidewalk, while if they were done in winter, sometimes the water would freeze in interesting designs. We'd always attract a few people along the way, who'd eagerly join in the fun and traipse along with us like followers of a magical water-painting pied piper.

This simple exercise is available to all of us. It does no harm to the environment. The tools are without cost. With miles of sidewalk you have an unlimited expanse for practice. Probably you will do this when the weather is warm, and the water marks soon dry up and vanish, and so this is also an excellent antidote to those of us who want to do things "perfectly". If your painting disappears in seconds, you are freed from concern as to its quality. Nothing can teach you how to create without worry for the quality of your end product faster than painting on a sidewalk with water. If your stick is long enough you can walk along painting without stopping. You will surprise yourself, actually amaze yourself, at the beautiful swirls, drips, and lines you make.

For fun and pleasure, you might try to combine this with the body awareness we spoke of earlier. In whatever way you like, loosen your arm movement by wiggling and stretching, or even shaking, and play with how that affects the marks you are making on the sidewalk. Or try to vary the way you hold the brush, from loosely to firmly, or pay attention to the way you are walking, and how painting with the stick fits in with your gait. Try whatever comes to your mind. No one needs to tell you how to do it, or what to feel while you do it. Let your instinct and your muscles take over. Paint your way around the block. It might be fun to enlist a friend to join you in your creations. As I mentioned, I also recommend doing this with children, as they really enjoy it, and their delight is contagious. It's likely you'll all end up in giggles.

Stop for a moment and ask yourself how you are breathing. As we've spoken about becoming more conscious of your breathing, ask yourself whether you are holding your breath when you are trying to paint, and whether you need to breathe more fully. As we noted before, just becoming aware of what you are doing is exceptionally powerful. And, again, as I've said before, taking a moment to feel what is happening in our bodies gets us out of the stress cycle.

As always, your ever-eager inner critic may make its presence known, as it never seems to shut up, and it may ask you: "Why am I doing this? I feel silly marking up the sidewalk. What gain is there? Am I wasting my time?"

Explaining what you are doing to anyone is not necessary, and that includes your inner critic, or your friends, relatives, or spouse. A release from serious thought, or worry, isn't ever a waste. Instead, it is a boon for your well-being, for anyone, but especially for those of us dealing with SMI in our loved ones. Besides, you were learning how to use a brush. Your hands were busy. Your inner spirit was functioning, dreaming up endless markings. If someone questions you about your water painting on sidewalks you can reply that you are seeking a way to inner peace and happiness (guaranteed, they'll leave you alone after that). But actually, that is precisely what you are doing.

Note that when you are involved in this "doing" of painting with water on the sidewalk, you have no concern for time, and you are not involved with anything except what is going on in the present moment. Indeed, it's easy and even likely you'll lose track of time, and be surprised at how long you've been at it. You've also had no concern for cost, as this was a cost-free activity, and you didn't care whether you were typically "productive". To put it another way, you experienced the enjoyment of total freedom while doing something that is fun, a total freedom where there are no rules.

When a person paints there are truly no rules to follow. The colors, shapes, lines, and method of application result from your inner urges. Your intuition rules. This sidewalk painting demonstrates the great freedom painting can give you and it also shows that you have an ability to paint that you may have thought you lacked. Everyone can be an artist. If you can hold the stick brush in some fashion, dip it in water, and get the water onto the sidewalk, even if you simply drip it, you can create art this way.

What might happen during your excursion around the block if you were to enlist a famous artist to join you, as well as a varied assortment of other people, such as a homeless person, a successful business man, and maybe a lawyer or a politician? What would their paintings look like? Would their paintings be a lot alike or would they look different? My Mom thought they would be quite similar, and that you would not be able to tell who did which "painting". While it is true that the artist might wield his stick brush more skillfully, through a lifetime of practice, his or her painting marks would much resemble those of the other recruits. Our inside impulses are rather the same, for all human beings. It just matters how we interpret them and follow them through. Putting it another way, you can paint as well as the next person. So why not simply paint?!

If all this still seems like silliness to you, consider that there are major artists who have made names for themselves (and lots of money) doing just this sort of thing with actual paint. Jackson Pollock is the name that comes to mind. His artworks have much in common with the paintings we have done on sidewalks with water, and are created in a similar fashion.

Exercise 2, Pencil play

My Mom believed that a simple pencil is one of the greatest sources of human happiness on this earth. A pencil is not expensive, and most people have one lying around somewhere. It does need to be sharp enough to draw, so you will have to find a sharpener or knife. For paper, why not search in wastebaskets, as envelopes and backs of letters are free. If your scrap paper has a splotch or two, don't worry about it, as such flaws can be a boon to your artwork, and add interest to your endeavors.

Find a place to sit. Using some spirit and energy begin making marks on the paper. Any kind of a mark will do. The pencil marks don't have to be good, uniform, crazy, or anything special. You are not drawing. You are playing, and play is such a great antidote to the mental stress we are under. If the paper has a stain, wrinkle, or tear, it's no matter. Spend a few minutes adding marks, whatever you like. Fill the page or envelope, or maybe a few of them. Just play with the marks. After you have done this for a few minutes, note whether you feel better than when you started. Like breathing and sensing your body, playing at art takes us out of the stress stream.

It can be an interesting exercise to express how you feel about certain words through the marks you are making. To start with, perhaps pick a word that is very emotionally charged, such as "fear", for instance. Make your markings. See what you express when you make the marks this word brings out of you. You might fill an entire page, or more. You need not draw recognizable objects. The energy, direction, and feeling of your response to the word will show clearly in your marks, along with all that the word congers up emotionally within you.

Next try depicting how you feel about other words: ballet, thunder, concert, or walking. Everyone can participate in this exercise. Think of the first word that comes to your mind, and make markings expressing how you feel about it. A timid, quiet individual can draw as well as the next person, and besides, no one is judging your work. No one tells you what to do or how to do it. Your marks are yours alone. Try this exercise for at least fifteen minutes; when you discover for yourself the playful enticement of pencil marks, you'll find that time flies. You might even discover that an hour went by as you investigated word pictures. Also, by treating yourself to this form of playing you are really learning a craft. If you do this exercise with friends, after expressing several word feelings on paper you and your friends could compare and talk about your drawings.

Still, you might ask, "Was I wasting paper and time?" "What good was it?" or "What was I thinking about while I did this?"

If you were wondering about your next meal or thinking about your mortgage payment, you were not playing freely enough. The idea is to forget your burdens while you concentrate on your sketching. If we learn this tool, we have another way of mentally freeing ourselves from our troubling personal situation, and it's a tool we can use anytime, anywhere. See if you can erase all thought, except for mentally dealing with expressive ideas of mark variations. Banish serious thoughts during this exercise. With your hands busy drawing and your mind in an intuitive state, you are achieving peace, a sense of calm, and even happiness. With what you've been going through, that is definitely an achievement and not a waste of your time!

The markings you made are unique, which is another interesting aspect of this exercise. Your marks carry your own distinctive personality, your own playfulness. Whether you are only after inner peace, or strive to create art you can exhibit, your marks are yours alone, and you have the rights to your exclusive product. You own the copyright, with which you can experiment however you want.

Exercise 3, Mom's three step drawing process

For another pencil exercise, begin by drawing a rectangle, freehand or with a ruler. Inside the base of the rectangle draw a horizontal line, parallel to the base of the rectangle. Your eye can judge if the two lines, your line, and the rectangle base, are exactly parallel. By now your hand, pencil, and eye are working together. You probably can draw approximate parallel lines at the first try, even if you do this freehand.

Next place a vertical line inside the rectangle. Draw the line parallel to the rectangle edge, perpendicular to the base. If your first try is not right repeat the line until it is parallel.

Next draw a bump on one of the rectangle edges and try to duplicate the bump you created on your inner line. Do it in this way:

First step: follow the shape of the bump with your eye.

Second step: trace it in the air with the pencil.

Third step: draw the bump on the inner line.

This is a three-step way of drawing that allows you to draw anything at all. Use your eye, then trace with your hand, and finally draw with your pencil. Some practice time with three-step drawing will convince you that you really can draw anything.

As you gain drawing skill you will become aware that this sort of pencil play is always readily available. You own it and can use it to express yourself throughout your lifetime. The quality of pleasure in your life will be enhanced considerably, along with your inner peace and quiet.

Exercise 4, Drawing an Object

As another exercise in drawing, choose a familiar object as your model. It might well be a worn glove, shoe, or household object. Don't choose something like a baseball, because we all know that shape without looking at it. We need to find a model that requires our close attention so that we can determine by eye, and by following certain steps, the directions, shapes, and lengths of lines present in that object. To repeat, here are the steps to follow:

Step 1. Just observe. Let your vision wander over the object finding its edges. Follow, with your eye, every edge you see. Take care to be sure you find and cover all the edges.

Step 2. Without actually touching the object, but working freely in the air with your finger or pencil, trace all edges again. Though it might be tempting to take your pencil and paper and actually draw, until all aspects of the object are clear to you, continue to work in the air.

Step 3. When the object is familiar to you, with your pencil and paper draw all the edges, skipping none. When you stop drawing and inspect your work you should be quite pleased with the result.

If you'd like to make a second try, let's do this again, but first turn the now familiar object in another position or move your own drawing position. This will produce an entirely different set of edges for practice.

The more drawing you do, the better your skill becomes. Practice does make perfect. Most essentially, you should be noticing that you are in a happy state and time passes swiftly. For those of us in stressful situations, this carefree, happy time is priceless!

Here's a drawing hint that can be a tremendous help, as it will help you easily zero in on one line that goes in an unusual direction. When you observe a line or edge leaning in an unusual direction place your pencil along that edge. Follow with your eye along that edge, then follow this direction with your pencil. Test out this helpful drawing hint on roof lines which seem to be shooting off in peculiar directions due to the perspective or the appearance that they are receding. The roof will not look "right" until the edges are placed in the correct slanted position. For convenience, curved lines could be broken down in a series of straight lines. Afterward the corners could be smoothed off.

A few minutes per day spent drawing would improve your ability as well as your spirits. The happy calm you experience while busily drawing spreads outward, in a manner similar to the spreading ripples when a stone drops in water. Who among us who has lived with SMI couldn't use an ongoing source of peace and happiness in our lives?

Exercise 5, Mental drawing

One can also find pleasure in mental drawing, where we don't even need to have a pencil or scrap of paper. While observing an object, you can trace the edges of everything you see, keeping an eye out for directions, forms, spaces, and so forth. When conversing with someone, mentally check the facial features. Be observant at all times of edges, light and dark areas, and shapes. Ordinary life presents a new dimension for enjoyment, at any moment, wherever you are. Mental drawing is a new way of looking. It arouses curiosity, invigorates, and satisfies. It also calms your mind, because you cannot simultaneously fret and worry, and draw mentally. Could anything be more essential to us than finding a way to calm our minds, and keep them free from worry and fear?

If you plan well and carry a small pad and pencil, you can record the images you see. Every time we spent a few days with my mother, she'd give each of us a small pad and pencil, and each time, we'd fill them up as we drew. Sometimes I still find these little notebooks, tucked here and there around the house. It is always magical to look at them and remember those happy times.

Every drawing you create increases your artistic ability along with your inner peace and happiness. It could also be said you increased in your skill for drawing, as you are surely getting better at it. Some of the finest art produced in the history of the world were pencil drawings. Rembrandt comes to mind. Artists made drawings to prepare for major works such as oil paintings. In many cases, at least in my opinion, the lovely drawings were more beautiful than the final product. Drawings reflect a personal, intimate sprit of the artist and they display a magical beautiful quality.

As we are talking about taking care of ourselves in this chapter, surely making some simple art play is a lovely and delightful way to find some inner peace. It's easy, it's fun, it's free, and quite simply, it works. When my Mom was still alive, we did an awful lot of this, and had a tremendous amount of fun doing it. In retrospect, I wish we'd done even more.

EPILOGUE

As we go through our journeys with our ill and addicted family members, it can help to realize that we can't really know, with certainty, whether the nerve-wracking things that happen to us or to them are positive or negative events. Sometimes, often, things aren't what they seem.

For example, I think about one of Galen's experiences with the police. Though much about this was awful, it led me to meet a wonderful policeman who became central to helping my son. I am blessed to have met him and it is not lost on me that I would never have met him otherwise. There are other experiences as well that at first blush seemed comprehensively negative at the time, but turned out positively. Maybe the point is that it is best if we give up our need to be so darn sure about things, because in truth we are never going to have a perfect view of all aspects of any situation.

I keep thinking about an old once-upon-a-time Zen tale you may have heard. Though this story appears in many books, I'll offer a recap, in case you aren't familiar with it.

The story concerns an old farmer who had been raising crops for many years. He worked his land with one horse, and his son helped him. One day this old farmer's horse ran away, and the neighbors all said this was a great misfortune.

The farmer replied, "maybe yes, maybe no".

The next day, the horse returned, and he brought several wild horses with him. The neighbors agreed this was wonderful news and such good fortune.

The farmer replied, "maybe yes, maybe no".

Then the farmer's son tried to ride one of the wild horses, and he was thrown off and broke his leg. Now the neighbors wailed about the farmer's misfortune.

The farmer replied, "maybe yes, maybe no".

The army came through the area, drafting all the able-bodied young men. Because the farmer's son had a broken leg, he was not conscripted. The neighbors offered congratulations for the farmer's good fortune.

And the farmer replied, "maybe yes, maybe no".

And so forth and so on. Though the tale continues, its point is clear. In truth, we really don't know whether the events in our lives, or in the lives of our loved ones, are good or bad. They just are. They are just events that happened to us. Maybe it would help to borrow this old farmer's answer "maybe yes, maybe no" when confronted with our own judgment when the next tough situation with our ill loved ones comes along. At the very least we might choose to adapt a more flexible and curious attitude of "I wonder what's going to happen next?" instead of the dread many of us live with, as we wait for the next dramatic event to show up.

But, we don't know what will happen next. We never do and never will. As Tom Hanks said at the end of the movie Cast Away, "The sun always comes up the next day, and you never know what the wind is going to blow in." All we have is the experience of our own personal journey, lived in each moment, and with so many unknowns in our lives, we always seem to have a question mark hanging over us. Living with a question mark is actually OK. In some ways, it's a wonderful relief to realize we don't have to know everything.

I wish us all well as we cope as successfully as possible with mental illness in our families, and as we live through all the inherent drama that results. I know and trust that we can thrive as we all move forward. Let's be patient with each other, and with ourselves. We're going at our own pace. We're doing the best we can. That's good enough. Actually, it is plenty.

ADDENDA

Mental Illness Statistics

Having read my book, you might still feel that my family's problems with mental illness, or even perhaps your family's problems, are unique, rare or unusual. This is not true. By any metric, mental illness is a staggering problem. Listed below is a description of its scope, as conveyed by statistics from 2018 that are listed on the website of the National Alliance on Mental Health, or NAMI:

Prevalence of mental illness:

- 1 in 5 (19.1%) of U.S. adults experience mental illness each year (47.6 million people)
- 1 in 25 U.S. adults experience serious mental illness each year (11.4 million people)
- 1 in 6 youth aged 6-17 experience a mental health disorder each year (7.7 million people)
- 50% of all lifetime mental illness begins by age 14 and 75% by age 24
- 3.7% of U.S. adults experienced a co-occurring substance abuse disorder and mental illness (9.2 million people)
- Suicide is the 2nd leading cause of death among people aged 10-34.

Prevalence of mental illness among U. S. adults by demographic group:

- Non-Hispanic Asian: 14.7%
- Non-Hispanic white: 20.4%
- Non-Hispanic Black or African-American: 16.2%
- Non-Hispanic American Indian or Alaska Native: 22.1%

- Non-Hispanic mixed/multiracial: 26.8%
- Hispanic or Latino: 16.9%
- LGBTQ: 37.4%.

Annual prevalence by condition:

- Major depressive episode: 7.2% (17.7 million people)
- Schizophrenia: <1% (estimated 1.5 million people)
- Bipolar disorder: 2.8% (estimated 7 million people)
- Anxiety disorders: 19.1% (estimated 48 million people)
- Post-traumatic stress disorder: 3.6% (estimated 9 million people)
- Obsessive compulsive disorder: 1.2% (estimated 3 million people)
- Borderline personality disorder: 1.4% (estimated 3.5million people).

Annual treatment rates for mental illness:

- U.S. adults with mental illness: 43.3%
- U.S. adults with a serious mental illness: 64.1%
- U.S. youth aged 6-17: 50.6%
- The average delay between onset of mental illness symptoms and treatment is 11 years.

Annual treatment rates by demographic group:

- U.S. adult males with any mental illness: 39.4%
- Females: 48.6%
- LGBTQ: 48.5%
- Non-Hispanic Asian: 24.9%
- Non-Hispanic white: 49.1%
- Non-Hispanic Black or African-American: 30.6%

- Non-Hispanic mixed/multiracial: 31.8%
- Hispanic or Latino: 32.9%

Insurance coverage:

- 11.3% of U.S. adults with mental illness had no insurance coverage and 13.4% of U.S. adults with serious mental illness had no insurance coverage.

Medical issues:

- 60% of U.S. counties do not have a single practicing psychiatrist.
- People with depression have a 40% higher risk of developing cardiovascular and metabolic diseases than the general population, and people with serious mental illness are nearly twice as likely to develop these conditions.
- 19.3% of U.S. adults with mental illness (9.2 million individuals) also experienced a substance use disorder.

Social issues:

- The rate of unemployment is higher among U.S. adults who have mental illness (5.8%) compared to those who do not (3.6%).
- High school students with significant symptoms of depression are more than twice as likely to drop out of school compared to their peers.
- In our families, at least 8.4 million people in the U.S. provide care to an adult with a mental or emotional health issue, and caregivers of adults with mental or emotional health issues spend an average of 32 hours per week providing unpaid care.
- In our communities, mental illness and substance use disorders are involved in 1 out of every 8 Emergency

Department visits by a U.S. adult (an estimated 12 million visits), and mood disorders are the most common cause of hospitalization for all people in the U.S, under age 45 (excluding hospitalizations related to pregnancy and birth).

Economic issues and homelessness:

- In the U.S. economy, serious mental illness causes lost earnings of $193.2 billion each year.
- 20.1% of homeless people have a serious mental health condition.
- 37% of incarcerated adults in state and federal prison systems have a diagnosed mental illness.
- 70.4% of youth in the juvenile justice system have a diagnosed mental illness.
- 41% of Veteran's Health Administration patients have a diagnosed mental illness or substance use disorder.
- Depression and anxiety disorders cost the global economy one trillion in lost productivity each year and is the leading cause of disability worldwide.

Suicide:

- Suicide is the 2nd leading cause of death among people aged 1-34, and the 10th leading cause of death in the U.S.
- The overall suicide rate in the US has increased by 31% since 2001.
- 46% of people who die by suicide had a diagnosed mental health condition.
- 90 % of people who die by suicide had shown symptoms of a mental health conditions according to interviews with family, friends, and medical professions.
- LGBTQ youth are four times more likely to attempt suicide than straight youth.

- 75% of people who die by suicide are male.
- Transgender adults are nearly 12 times more likely to attempt suicide than the general population.
- 4.3% of all adults have annual serious thoughts of suicide.
- 11% of young adults aged 18-25 have such thoughts, as do 17.2% of high school students, and 47.7% of LBGTQ high school students.

Those are the facts. How incomprehensibly sad that each of these numbers represents literally millions of suffering people! While it is true we might not be able to change the prevalence of mental illness, anyone who has looked at this book might realize that we haven't even begun to consider the changes we might make so that the lives of the mentally ill and their families and friends are easier and more bearable. It is my fervent hope that we recognize the gravity of our current situation and implement positive change. And there is no time like now to begin doing so.

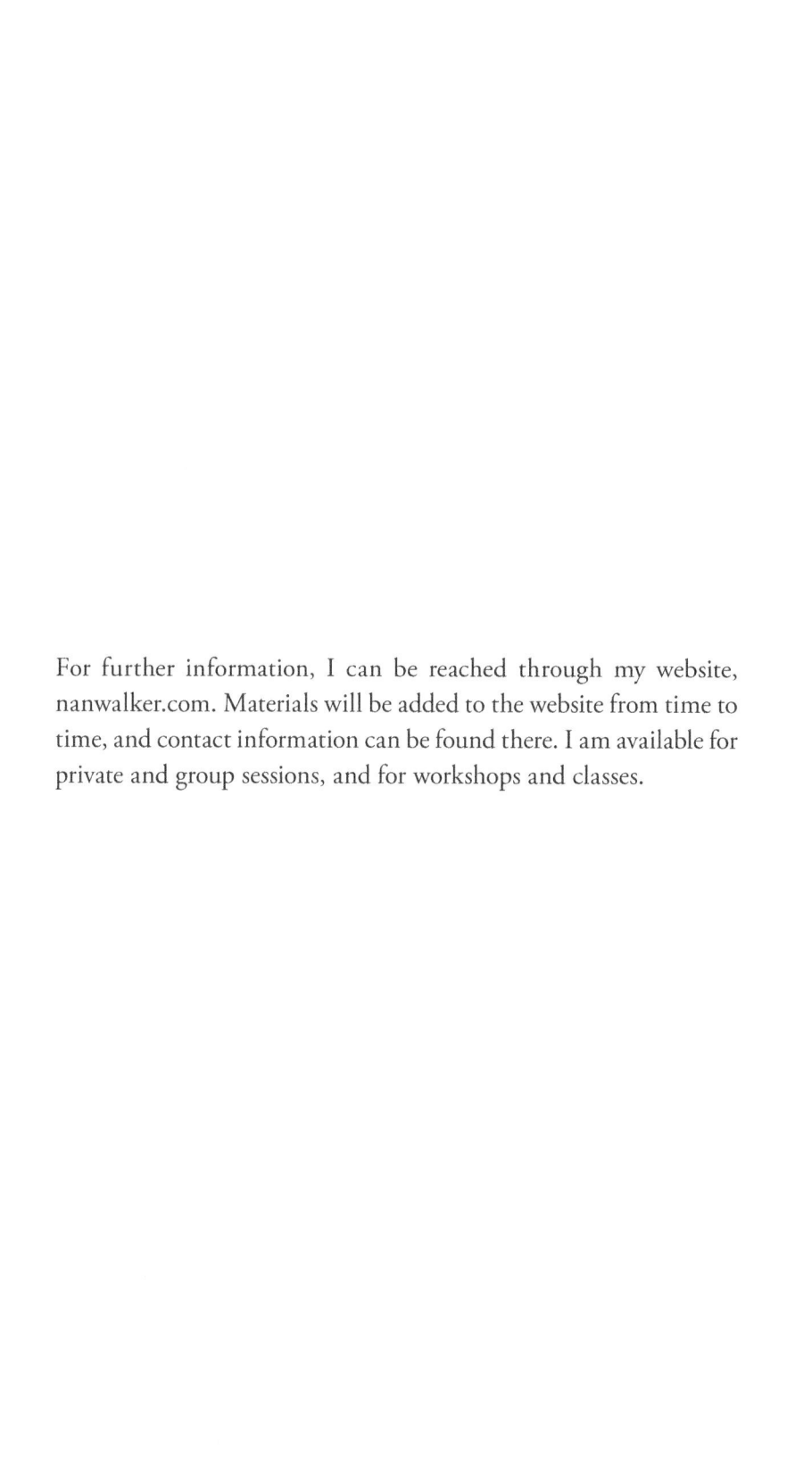

For further information, I can be reached through my website, nanwalker.com. Materials will be added to the website from time to time, and contact information can be found there. I am available for private and group sessions, and for workshops and classes.

window edge
← left side
flushair unit   window

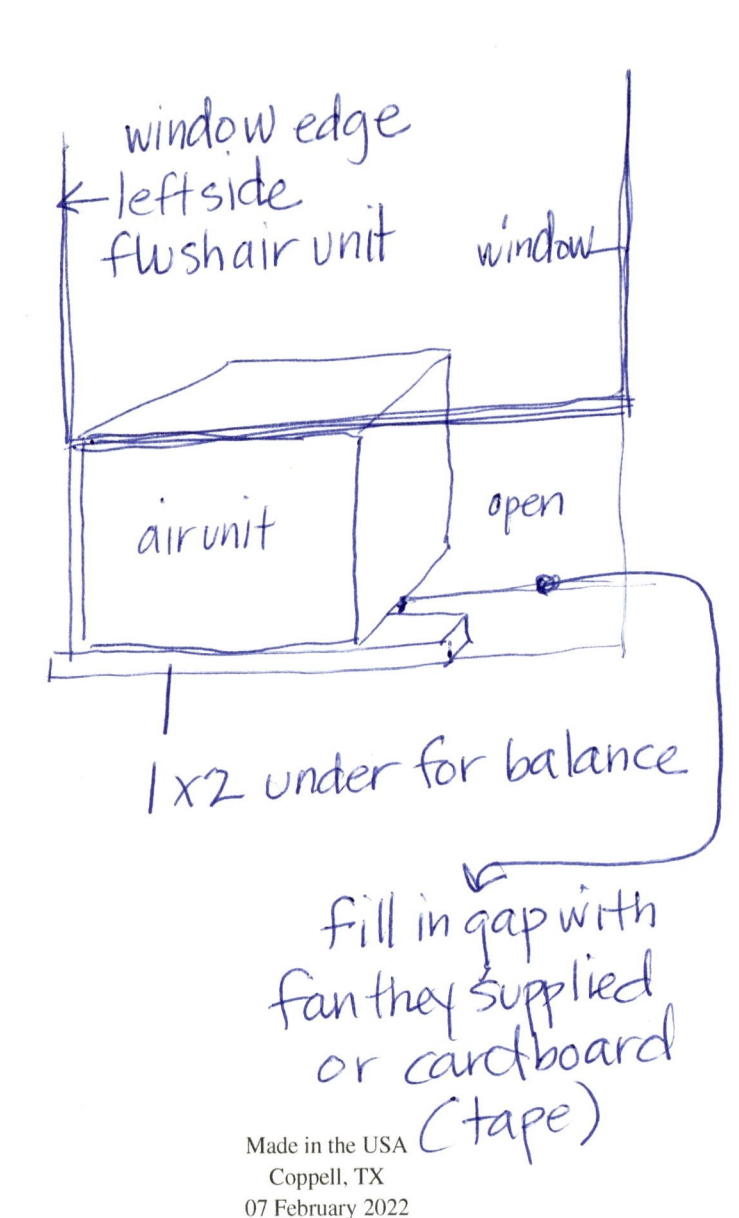

air unit   open

1x2 under for balance

fill in gap with fan they supplied or cardboard (tape)